# Tennis Shorts

# Tennis Shorts

## GREAT WRITING ON TENNIS AND LIFE

**Edited by**

## Adam Sexton

**CITADEL PRESS**
Kensington Publishing Corp.
www.kensingtonbooks.com

CITADEL PRESS BOOKS are published by

Kensington Publishing Corp.
850 Third Avenue
New York, NY 10022

For my parents

*First Amb.* Thus then, in few.
Your highness, lately sending into France,
Did claim some certain dukedoms, in the right
Of your great predecessor, King Edward the Third.
In answer of which claim, the prince our master
Says that you savour too much of your youth,
And bids you be advis'd there's nought in France
That can be with a nimble galliard won;
You cannot revel into dukedoms there.
He therefore sends you, meeter for your spirit,
This tun of treasure; and, in lieu of this,
Desires you let the dukedoms that you claim
Hear no more of you. This the Dauphin speaks.
*K. Hen.* What treasure, uncle?
*Exe.* Tennis-balls, my liege.
　　　　　　　　—William Shakespeare, *King Henry V*


Tennis, anyone?
　　　　　—Humphrey Bogart's only line in his first play

# CONTENTS

## Part V. (Sudden) Death

# ACKNOWLEDGMENTS

Thanks, first of all, to the indefatigable Janet Rosen, without whom this book would still be an idea that gnaws at me while I watch tennis on TV. Thanks to Sheree Bykofsky. Thanks also to my editor at Citadel, Margaret Wolf.

Thanks to those authors whose fiction is included in *Love Stories*, especially the ones who wrote or adapted short stories and novel chapters explicitly for this collection: Jenny Belle, Emmy Chang, Phil Edwards, Lee Harrington, Tara McCarthy, Dalia Rabinovitch, Caroline Rabinovitch, Liana Scalettar, and Sarah Totton. Rand Richards Cooper and Marcy Dermansky provided stories that have never before appeared between the covers of a book; thanks to them, too. In fact, thanks to all those who submitted material. I enjoyed reading every submission and apologize for not including them all.

Thanks to Wally Levis, whose enthusiasm for the initial idea was crucial to the book's creation. Thanks to Jocelyn Cox for alerting me to the existence of three of the stories within—you deserve a finder's fee! (Oh, well.) And thank you, Karen Moulding, for your invaluable comments on my own writing, especially generous considering your (baffling) indifference to tennis. Thanks to Amy Bloom and the delightful Patty Volk for their interest.

Thanks to Elizabeth Tippens for her support and friendship—talk about a finder's fee. David Richan, thank you once again for your sage legal advice and limitless generosity when I really needed it. Very belated thanks to tennis-lover Holcomb Noble, who went to bat for me (forgive the mixed metaphor) not once but twice; I will always remember your interest in my career, such as it was.

For interest, support, *and* friendship, thanks to Stefan Fatsis. Thanks, as always, to Paul Chrystie, with whom I watched the U.S. Open Men's Final in 1980 (Connors-McEnroe, I believe) and '89 (Lendl-Edberg, snooze . . .). Also Wimbledon in 1984, the setting of the following unforgettable exchange between commentators Bud Collins and Dick Enberg (topic: headphones on the net judge).

COLLINS: He's not listening to Mike Jackson, I'll tell you that.
ENBERG: He's not listening to Dave Bowie, either.

Thanks to Windridge counselors Jan and Soper. *Merci beaucoup,* Lucie Legault!

Thanks to James Sexton, for always indulging my need to consult the *O.E.D.* while viewing televised sports.

My parents, Mark and Marie Sexton, stood at the net, tossing endless balls from buckets, boxes, and bags at their feet; later, they patiently stood by while I threw tantrums—racquets, even. My apologies, my gratitude, and of course my love.

Finally, thanks to my wife, Kira Niederland Sexton: The Girl with the Sunflowers at the U.S. Open. You are the heroine of my favorite love story.

# INTRODUCTION

All sports are storylike. Every athletic contest is populated by at least two characters, a protagonist (the player or team you're rooting for) and an antagonist (the other guys). Sports offer conflict, of course, as well as a clear if not always indisputable resolution; at the end of the day, unless you're watching a game postponed by rain, or the Tour de France, somebody will have won, lost. Like a proper story, all sporting events—even cricket—have a beginning, middle, and end. That's one of the reasons we like them so much. Life is mainly shapeless. Sports and stories are anything but.

To judge by the number of great writers who have adopted it as their subject, tennis might be the most storylike sport of all. Grand Slam champions, if you will (Martin Amis, Margaret Atwood, Vladimir Nabokov, Paul Theroux, and John Updike among them), have written short stories about tennis or included pivotal on-court scenes in their novels—and a number of these pieces have been collected here in *Love Stories*. Same goes for cult favorites like Ellen Gilchrist, Anne Lamott, and David Foster Wallace. There are even tennis mysteries out there, by the likes of Harlan Coben and Stuart Woods, though the cause-and-effect coherence of the well-wrought mystery novel discouraged inclusion of excerpts from them in this book.

Tennis shows up in the movies, as well, from *The Philadelphia Story* and *Sabrina* to *Blow-Up* and *Shoot the Moon*; from Neil Simon's *California Suite* to *The Royal Tenenbaums* by Wes Anderson and Owen Wilson. Defying stereotype (tennis is for upper-crustaceans) there's even a tennis-oriented episode of *The Sopranos*. Carmela Soprano's substitute tennis instructor, Birgit, takes an interest in Adriana while FBI agents staked out near the court take an interest in both of them. (Okay, their panties.) Meanwhile, across town, the Bureau races to install a surveillance device in Tony's basement before the lesson ends and Carmela pilots her SUV homeward to uncover the operation. Sex and class, crime and punishment converge among the straight white lines of the country-club court—and the dramatic tension is all but unbearable.

Oh—the Simpsons play tennis, too.

I've organized the stories in the pages that follow into five groups: Junior Tennis, Women's Tennis, Men's Tennis, a section I call Mixed/Doubles, and finally, (Sudden) Death.

Thus, a tale of five tennis courts:

### 1. Junior Tennis: *Courts 1-?, Breezy Hill Tennis Camp, Northern Vermont*

Tennis is a sport in which male, female, and "mixed" couples compete at every level of play, so is it any surprise that almost all tennis stories involve (sorry) *love?* Tennis is sexy—Bjorn Borg sexy, Anna Kournikova sexy. For proof, see especially "Bunny Fever" by Caroline Rabinovitch and "Adults at Home" by Marcy Dermansky, herein.

The summer after I graduated from junior high, my parents drove me from the New York metropolitan area to Breezy Hill Tennis Camp (not its real name): seven or eight hours, total. The illustrated leaflet had made Breezy Hill, in the shadow of Vermont's Mt. Mansfield, look like a country club for kids. As brochures do, however, the Breezy Hill brochure obscured reality, prettified it. The camp's facilities were ... *scruffy*, to put it euphemistically. Chickenwire had been staple-gunned to raw wooden posts, forming the fences that divided one backcourt from another. (How much could chain-link cost?) The clay for the courts themselves came from the crumbling banks of a broad, brown creek at the rear of the Breezy Hill grounds. The campers bunked in a two-story Quonset hut (girls upstairs, boys downstairs), the common room of which contained a Ping-Pong table, a black-and-white TV, and two leather club chairs spilling stuffing. The carpet there (orange, natch) stank of mildew. My parents took a long look at the ramshackle, jury-rigged campus, and nearly drove me home.

They didn't drive me home. (I'm not sure why, although a nonrefundable deposit may have been involved.) And so I spent the summer hiking up ski trails, swimming under waterfalls, drinking the richest, sweetest milk I have ever tasted, traversing sinuous mountain roads in the bed of a Toyota pickup, screening ancient movies at the Jeffersonville Cinema, roller-skating in a converted barn one rainy afternoon, and watching the tall ships on the rec-room television come Fourth of July. It appeared to be snowing back in New York City.

There was tennis instruction, too—four or five hours' worth each day, as promised in the otherwise less-than-forthcoming camp literature. My fellow Breezy Hillers and I learned proper form, then strategy. We learned how to run Suicides and how to play Breezy Hill Mini-Tennis. How to roll and sweep a clay court. We played round-robins and competed against one another in challenge matches that determined our places on the camp ladder.

After my parents left for Westchester, a kid named Greg Zaff, younger than I and considerably smaller, invited me to hit some balls. During the first few minutes I spent on the court with him, he hit those balls so hard and with such vicious topspin that I thought there was something wrong with the balls, or the court, or his racquet. Or me.

It didn't matter. Tennis was not the point of Breezy Hill Tennis Camp. Not to me, at least. The point of Breezy Hill Tennis Camp was

Girls.

Girls.

Girls.

The girls slept directly over the boys' heads—inches away, if you occupied a top bunk. This fact made regular "raids" via the fire escape at the back of the building a foregone conclusion. (What we were "raiding" *for* was never quite clear to me, and still isn't.) The girls received their instruction from female counselors on courts immediately adjacent to those where the boys' lessons took place, resulting in a deafening amount of intercourt sexual static. We never played tennis *with* each other, however, not even mixed doubles. The camp director posted Their ladder near his office, right beside Ours. Separate, but Equal. Sort of.

We did play volleyball with the girls—games during which the teen hormonal tension was breathtakingly palpable, viscous as the maple syrup on the tables in the camp dining room. (Ever since those Breezy Hill volleyball games, I've found the word "rotate" impossibly erotic.) We ate together at mealtimes, and hiked and swam together, went to the movies together and roller-skated together. And yet the precise thing we'd ostensibly come to camp for, to learn and play tennis, we did separately. It was like going to school with girls, but splitting up for history, math, science, and English. It was gym times ten. It was strange, a tease. It was delicious.

And then there were the dances: three a week, *three*. Two on the weekend and one midweek to tide us over. On a hi-fi set up inside a closet off the common room, two junior counselors played the same songs, dance after dance after dance: Beatles chestnuts, and the up-tempo numbers from *The Eagles' Greatest Hits*. Steely Dan's "Reeling in the Years," with its false ending midway through; every time I hear it, I remember a girl named Amy with a blond Dorothy Hamill haircut walking away then, never to return. I can still see the back of Amy's tawny neck. The Slow Songs: "Dream On" by Aerosmith and of course "Stairway to" goddamn "Heaven." Did anyone actually dance during "Stairway to Heaven"? Well, yeah: a girl named Ellen who blow-dried her tumbling auburn hair into fabulous Farrah-esque wings each day, and the nerdy guy named Pete, I think, with whom she inexplicably Went Out. Maybe another couple. The rest of us lurked at the edges of the darkened rec room, watching, wanting, wishing, and (me) whining inside, resolving to do better at the next dance—which, after all, lay only a couple of days away, tops.

Even Lucie Legault, everybody's favorite Canadienne camper, stood on the sidelines. In an irony not atypical of adolescence, Lucie was too colossally charming for boys to approach with confidence. Way too charming for me, at least. And *cute*—she had a Hamill 'do, also. A counselor named Bob Underhill had been nicknamed Undies. Lucie decided I looked like Bob, and so took to calling me "Leetle Hunties." Though flattered to be noticed, I wondered if she was mocking me. (What did she mean *Leetle* Hunties?) I never asked her to dance.

I submit that tennis is the most *adolescent* of American sports. Baseball's for boys (and girls now, too)—thus T-ball and trading cards and the nostalgia that drenches the game, all but drowning it. Football is redolent of college in the Midwest (or in Pasadena on New Year's Day); similarly, everyone knows that no basketball game thrills more, *means* more, than those played during March Madness. As far as I can tell, *only* college students compete at sports like crew and water polo. Pot-smoking slackers and Tiger Woods notwithstanding, golf's for old people.

But tennis is played, and played darn well, by teenagers. Most of the greats broke through well before age twenty; some (Tracy Austin; Martina Hingis?) never maintained their dominance past twenty-one. Maybe it's because the game mimics the teen experience: Thrills beckon, but they're strictly limited—all those boundaries! And, yes, at least once every game both players think "love."

It makes sense that the most famous teenager in American literature plays tennis. (Lolita is way better-known than Holden Caulfield, who probably found the game "phony.") *Infinite Jest*, David Foster Wallace's hypnotic doorstop of a novel, takes place mainly at a tennis academy. "Pubertas Agonistes" by Jonathan Ames all but equates tennis and the onset of adolescence. And you will not find a finer description of cheating in sports than the one excerpted here from *Crooked Little Heart*, a junior-tennis novel by Anne Lamott.

I ended my second and final Breezy Hill summer at thirty-one out of thirty-two on the boys' ladder. (Number thirty-two broke his racquet arm on the first day of camp. I'm not kidding.) The counselor who filled out the report card sent to my parents afterward struggled for positive things to say about my game.

It didn't matter. Tennis camp was about Girls. And Lucie Legault asked me, Leetle Hunties, to the final banquet.

## 2. Women's Tennis: *Galerìe du Jeu de Paume, Paris, France*

Aside from "Home, James," is there a remark more dripping with snobbery than "Tennis, anyone?" ("Fore!" doesn't even come close.) It is therefore fascinating that so many of the big American names of the past decade in pro tennis by no means resonate with country-club overtones: Capriati, Sampras, and Agassi are all the children of immigrants. Venus and Serena Williams first punished the ball on the municipal courts of the city that rappers call The C-P-T: Compton, California. It's a whole new ballgame out there—as *Love Stories* selections by Tara McCarthy, Philip K. Edwards, and Jennifer Belle illustrate. Certainly this anthology acknowledges tradition, as leaving out Nabokov and Updike would be the literary equivalent of a double fault. But *Love Stories* stresses the contemporary. As a result, it is flashy and boisterous and . . . well, *loud* at times. Think Goran Ivanisovich (Bad Goran, not Good Goran), his fist a post-passingshot piston. Think night matches at the U.S. Open.

And yet, the country club in my hometown didn't drop its "restrictions" (no Jews) until well into the seventies. My family didn't belong anyway, and had no plans to join.

My parents played tennis on public courts. On the high school courts in the village of Pelham, New York. (There were two of them, green inside the baselines and red everywhere else.) On the gouged asphalt at Parkway Field in neighboring Pelham Manor, and, during summers, on the come-one come-all courts that dotted the elbow of Cape Cod like oblong freckles of gray and green.

They often argued after playing tennis—during the match, for all I know—or else they stopped speaking altogether. I think my mother wanted to win more than my father, who greatly prefers a lengthy rally (even one he eventually loses) to putting the ball away for a point. The last time I hit with my mother, I sprained my ankle trying to return a masterfully placed backhand. The pain was indescribable.

She grew up on the Wrong Side of the Tracks in posh Fairfield, Connecticut. For her, tennis was something you took up and studied so you wouldn't stand out by virtue of not knowing about it—like how to behave at the symphony (don't clap between movements), and what, precisely, to do with a finger bowl. As boys, my brothers and I attended Young People's Concerts at Philharmonic Hall. Saturday nights we ate by candlelight in the family dining room. I now listen passionately to classical music, and my brothers are both foodies.

We also went to museums that no one else knew existed (South Street Seaport before it was a mall, Thomas Edison's house in New Jersey), and obscure galleries in the museums everyone did know (the musical instruments collection at the Met); since coming of age, my siblings and I have traveled to distant cities to visit the art and architecture there. The Galeríe du Jeu de Paume in Paris, for instance. In May of 1983, as Frenchman Yannick Noah was plowing through the draw at nearby Roland Garros, I was plowing through the masterworks of Cézanne, Degas, Manet, Seurat, and Van Gogh. Jean jacket, backpack, running shoes, *Let's Go France!*: Yes, I was a college junior. With a single, disastrous semester of elementary French under my skinny belt (it went with my skinny ties), I didn't realize that *jeu de paume* meant "game of the hand"—and had no clue that this, in turn, meant tennis. In 1862, Napoleon III installed a court for Royal Tennis (ancestor of the modern game) in a former orangery on the grounds of the Jardin des Tuileries. By 1909, the building had mutated into an informal picture gallery, and in 1947 the Louvre moved its Impressionist paintings there to take advantage of the space's excess of natural light. (In 1986 they moved on, to the Musée d'Orsay; now the Jeu de Paume exhibits contemporary art.)

My brothers and I take enormous pleasure in tennis, music, food, and museums, and we owe that pleasure to my mother. It wasn't about pleasure for her, though. I seldom heard her utter the word "fun" in connection with culture, with tennis. These were things you learned, and cheerfully, whether you wanted to or not.

Briefly we did, in fact, belong to a country club. On the Rye coast a half hour from home, Coveleigh offered lawn bowling, a saltwater swimming pool, and a courtside grill famous for its "black-and-blue" hamburgers *à la* 21 in the City. It was here that a gang of longtime members' kids called insults through the chain-link fence while my older brother played a match against one of their own. He was not in with, but outside of, the in-crowd—exactly what my mother dreaded most. We only belonged (while never really *belonging*) for two years or so. Then it was back to the municipal courts of Pelham and coastal Massachusetts.

### 3. Men's Tennis: *The Grandstand, West Side Tennis Club, Forest Hills, New York*

I saw Rod Laver, the greatest male tennis player of all time give or take Big Bill Tilden, play . . . *someone* at the Forest Hills Grandstand court on a September afternoon in the mid-1970s. It was my first professional tennis match—I was twelve or so—and one of his last.

"Look at his *form*," my mother whispered, all but swooning, when Laver in whites tossed the ball (white, too, back then) *waaaaay* in front of the smeared white baseline, falling through it toward the net to do his serve-and-volley thing. I recall this as having transpired in the shade, for which we gave silent thanks; it was Mad-Dogs-and-Englishmen hot that day. Before the match was done, I got sick from the heat anyway. But under the stands—and quietly, quietly. My mother had taught me spectator etiquette while we crossed the Bronx-Whitestone Bridge:

No talking. (This excluded whispering about Rod Laver's *form*, apparently.)

Applause was okay, but only at point's end.

And nobody booed; you *whistled* to protest a bad line call. No, not with teeth and fingers. Through O-puckered lips, like Disney dwarfs with a job to do.

A Good Boy, I didn't boo at athletic events anyway, or catcall or jeer or cry "Kill the ump!" Booing evinced Poor Sportsmanship. Whistling didn't, it seemed. So I whistled, too—whistled in concert with the man beside me, his wrists obscured by matching sweatcuffs of plush terry.

That's right. Some fans sported tennis togs, like ice skates to a hockey game. Short shorts on the men and snugly cut white shirts and even the occasional polo of yellow or baby-blue; it was the dawning of the age of the solid-color top. (Sponsors' badges lay far in the future, with steroids and electronic let-sensors.) These fans sat ready to fill in at a moment's notice, should Laver or his opponent expire due to the beastly weather. Some even carried racquets.

That dorky Australian bucket-hat was everywhere, like Tab in pink cans and the scent of Sea & Ski. (Where have all the Aussie hats gone?) Also ubiquitous: funny-looking but effective cardboard sun-visors you assembled yourself according to the directions printed on the visor itself. These were distributed free by Mr. Peanut, who attended the Open annually and must have been delirious much of the time due to the blazing heat inside his curvaceous carapace, beneath his top-hat, under his spats.

Was it the first day of that year's U.S. Open? I remember matches occurring on nearly every one of the still-grass courts. You could walk around the grounds, my mother explained—shuffle along the grid of gravel allées formed by the W.S.T.C.'s dozens of courts, free to watch any match anywhere. We split up, post-Laver. My mother scoped out Ken Rosewall, another great from Down Under past his prime and another favorite of hers.

I watched Roscoe Tanner and Vijay Amritraj—how many remember those names now?—through a tarp-hole, on the toes of my blue Puma Clydes. I, too, had come in the clothes I wore to play tennis, circa eighth grade: the Pumas and a New York Knicks T-shirt and cutoff Levi's, front pockets exposed by the shorts' hand-hacked hems. Concentration proved elusive. The multitude of simultaneous matches brought out the latent ADD sufferer in me. So did the aroma of cheap white wine and overpriced hot dogs in the cool gloaming behind and beneath the stadium seats, which I can still smell in my mind's nose. Hear, too—it was loud back there. Briefly, I was riveted by the plaques lined up along the sweating concrete walls, to which had been bolted the names of all the U.S.L.T.A. titleists ever. (The L stood for Lawn.) Men's champions began in 1881 with R. D. SEARS, whoever he was. Did RENÉ LACOSTE have anything to do with Alligator Shirts? (Yes. Only it's properly a crocodile, the *nom de tenis* of Tilden's archrival, that grins and flips its tail for Izod. For more on tennis and rivalry, read the excerpt I've included here from Martin Amis's *The Information*.) There was JACK KRAMER, like the racquet. I was surprised to see ROBERT L. RIGGS on the winners' tablet, unaware that he'd been a genuine champion once and not merely the obnoxious huckster who challenged Margaret Court (and won) and Billy Jean King (and lost). Around '67, the tags appeared less tarnished and the names grew thoroughly, rather than sporadically, recognizable: JOHN NEWCOMBE, STAN SMITH, ROSEWALL, and LAVER himself. Oh, and ARTHUR ASHE.

The guard was changing in the wake of the sixties, and soon the guardhouse would change as well. The U.S. Open left leafy Forest Hills in 1977; now, of course, it happens on hard courts (DecoTurf II, to be precise) in proletarian Flushing Meadows–Corona Park a couple of miles to the north. The United States Tennis Center lies at the end of New York's Number 7 subway line, sometimes called the Bengali Express after the Indians who live along the route. (It could just as easily be nicknamed for the Koreans, Colombians, Chinese, Mexicans, Greeks, or Ecuadorans who also inhabit Northern Queens.) You can still buy a grounds pass that grants access to all early-round matches. Correction: all of them *except* those in Arthur Ashe Stadium. Considering the sport's baseline-white aura, the fact that both the biggest arena at the United States Tennis Center *and* the arena next door (Louis Armstrong Stadium) are named for black men is a racial irony worthy of Theroux's "The Tennis Court," which leads off the Men's Tennis section of this book. Actually, even with a special ticket in hand, the plague of lower-tier "corporate boxes" limits anyone unaffiliated with a white-shoe law firm or Madison Avenue ad agency to the top half of the stands at Ashe Stadium. (*Plus ça change . . .*)

Though time and the U.S.T.A. have passed it by, championship tennis lives on at Forest Hills via VHS and DVD. It is there, in *The Royal Tenenbaums*, where racqueteer Richie "Baumer" Tenebaum implodes on-court vs. "Sanjay Gandhi" (a Vijay Amritraj reference?)—a scene excerpted in Part III of *Love Stories*. As if unable to put that traumatic day behind him, Richie spends most of the movie in a Bjorn Borg headband, his camel-hair suit worn over a vintage Fila shirt.

If you rent the movie (and you should), or see it on TV sometime, look closely at the shot in which Royal and his warmup-suited grand-sons race go-carts through a sort of arcade, morning sun slanting past the concrete pillars behind them. They're beneath the seats at the Stadium in Forest Hills. I wonder if it still smells like hot dogs there.

## 4. Mixed/Doubles: *Public Courts, Parkway Field, Pelham Manor, New York*

> *Your outstanding record in the field and even on the courts com-pels us to invite you to enter the Pelham Husband and Wife Doubles Championship.*
>
> *Play will begin promptly at 12:30 P.M., October 2nd at Parkway Field and the tennis should get under way about the same time. Dress is always optional but it ought to be white if you do.*
>
> *The tournament committee has arranged to provide food, alcohol, pacifiers, and Divorce Court for the seeded, seceded, conceited, receded, and families of the deceased after the matches. . . .*
>
> *Each couple must bring an unopened can of new tennis balls.*

Our next-to-next-door neighbors, Hoc and Clue Noble, dug tennis even more than did Mum and Dad. When I remember Hoc—pro-nounced "Hoke," short for Holcomb—I see a late-sixties model Plymouth convertible, its top down, cruising past our house toward a court somewhere. He had pulled an old crewneck of Shetland wool over his rumpled whites and tossed a wooden racquet in its press and a couple of cans of balls on the backseat. In lower Westchester at the turn of the 1970s it didn't get much more glamorous than that.

His wife, Clue (*née* Carolyn Louise Uto), an interior decorator with exquisite taste and a surplus of energy, was Martha Stewart before Martha Stewart was Martha Stewart. Except Clue was nice, spilling over with Italian warmth and the best kind of charisma: the weird kind. For instance, Clue Noble laughed backwards, somehow sucking sound in through her nose rather than expelling it, via her mouth. Not *ha-ha-ha*, but *Mnuhhhh!* (Pant, pant.) *Mnuhhhh!* (Pant.) Seeing that, hearing it, made you want to laugh, too. To make Mrs. Noble laugh more, and harder. Her portrait in oil, in which she looked like a Neapolitan princess as depicted by Willem DeKooning, hung on their living-room wall just past Hoc's family's Civil War drum—and directly above two baby grand pianos, interlocked like yin and yang so Clue and Hoc could play duets. The Nobles owned a series of German shepherds named for minor Greek deities: Andromeda, Kardia, Echo, and others. Their house smelled like Chanel No. 5.

The Tennis Party was probably the Nobles' baby. Or maybe Clue and my mother dreamed it up. In any case, the idea was this: a highly informal mixed-doubles tournament at the cracked and pitted public courts in Pelham Manor, followed by drinks and cheese and crackers at our house and dinner, something simple (read "cheap"), at the Nobles'. Hoc would oversee the competition, the winners of which would snag a bottle of champagne, nothing fancy. My father would mix the cocktails afterward. My mother and Clue, being women, were to cook and serve the meal. My guess is that the original draw, around 1969 or so, included no more than eight married couples in it, counting the hosts and hostesses.

By the last time they threw one a decade later, the annual Tennis Party (or Pelham Cup Invitational, as Hoc's Selectric-typed and photocopied invitations dubbed the tournament with mock grandiosity) was an Event. Not eight mixed-set teams, but *thirty-two* competed. As a result, my father needed to obtain special permission, an all-day reservation, from the rec department at Town Hall—which the rec department duly granted. Why not? The Tennis Party had become a kind of municipal carnival. Everyone I knew was aware of it, certainly. As of roughly 1974, couples were asking to be invited. Some invited themselves, even.

History's partly responsible. Since the first Tennis Party, tennis had boomed. Of course it had. Soccer had boomed, even jogging. (Golf hadn't boomed yet.) One turning point: its late-sixties transformation from an "amateur" game paid for under the table, to an unapologetically professional sport. Another was the King-Riggs match, held on a weeknight but the focus nonetheless of spirited, Super Bowl–like celebrations all over the country. Racquets of steel and plastic, and the general demise of whites helped, too. Maybe even the heavily hyped romance between Chris Evert and Jimmy Connors, who knows? One result: the Pelham Country Club was de-restricted. Another was that in the mid- to late-seventies, all the town's public tennis courts were resurfaced.

The final few Tennis Parties were Gatsbyesque in scale. Cheeverian, at least. Under the slanting afternoon sun of early autumn, sixty-four players ranging in ability from first-timers to Hoc himself battled it out—jovially, for the most part—on the newly glowing green hard courts. Ball cans of cheap tin and pricey metal racquet rims flashed in the October light. Kids stole Fantas and Cokes from an ice-filled laundry tub, and, jacked up on sugar and caffeine, ran the bases on the adjacent ballfield or got lost in the woods by the burned-down Boy Scout cabin where my father had camped as a boy. Bill Muller shook and shook and shook a can of black-cherry soda, then patiently dribbled it soccer-style around the quarter-mile running track; he tossed the can in the air a few times, and finally ripped off its poptop in an ejaculation of sticky foam. Everything smelled spice-rackishly of autumn. Katydids clamored in the untrimmed grass around courts' edge and babies cried for their tennis-playing mothers and "Ad-in!" and "Thirty-love!" rang out above the ker-*thwok*, ker-*thwok* of sustained rallies and Mrs. Noble laughed backwards.

At night, the Pelham Cup Invitational having been concluded (or nearly so—sometimes the finals and a semi- or two took place the next afternoon), parked cars lined both sides of our street and cigarette smoke curled upstairs from the living room, the dining room. From the kitchen, where my father cracked open aluminum ice trays with a yank on that handbreaklike lever and Mr. Schultz squatted before the open fridge, seeking a Schmidt's. (He was the only regular beer drinker in the bunch—hard to imagine during the current microbrewery era.) Couples in navy blazers and party dresses, sunburnt or merely flushed from exercise and the excitement of it all, munched on whatever hors d'oeuvre Clue and my mother had experimented with that year. I recall only a dreadful tomato aspic in clear plastic cups. Somebody, usually a woman, plopped into my parents' canvas butterfly chair, and soon empty glasses and full ashtrays and abandoned cups of tomato aspic obscured the coffeetable, a slab of polished marble on four legs of polished wood.

If you stood near an open window, you could taste the new fall air.

After an hour or so, sixty-four Tennis Partiers burbled down the front-porch steps and streamed past the Perrys' house like a babbling brook of *vin blanc* and sun-bleached hair; to the Nobles'. There, something concocted by Julia Child or Pierre Franey was ladled over white rice at the Ping-Pong table buffet (a giant, inflatable ball-can twirled on a string overhead), and the partying began in earnest. Loading our dishwasher two houses away, I had no trouble hearing the shrieks and guffaws—the punchlines, even, of bellowed jokes, though I never heard the jokes themselves. Cutlery on crockery, and the splash of glass dropped onto the floor of the Nobles' screen porch. Not to mention the songs around the piano(s) that commenced immediately and concluded long after midnight. (My parents belong to the last generation that sings songs around a piano.) The party officially ended each year when Hoc and my mother serenaded the rest with "Rubber Duckie" from *The Sesame Street Songbook*. At that point, the last of the revelers drove or walked home, dog tired, to rub on Ben-Gay and sleep off their hangovers. (For tennis court as suburban marriage metaphor, be sure to look John Updike's majestic "Separating," the single best tennis story I know of, though the game is never actually played therein.)

The Nobles have long since divorced. Clue still lives in the house down the street from my parents, only my parents don't live there anymore. Sometimes I wonder if the Tennis Parties ended because couples were coming apart in the latter half of the domestically turbulent seventies, rendering spousal doubles tournaments impractical if not impossible. Husbands left wives, mainly: One lifelong friend of mine and her little brother learned from a note on the fridge that Daddy wouldn't be living with them anymore. My lovely, bespectacled Sunday school teacher and the soft-spoken superintendent of schools ran off together shortly after I'd left town for college. Another friend's parents separated, then reunited when his mother's breast cancer, in remission for a while, returned for good. At least that's the way I remember it.

People have partied at their country clubs since country clubs began, with formal celebrations (dinner dances and the like) following tennis and golf tournaments, and drinks after a couple sets or eighteen holes—or no sets, no holes, at all. The tennis tournament as social ritual continues to thrive within corporate culture; I once attended a law firm's annual round-robin tournament at the U.S. Tennis Center, in the shadow of Ashe Stadium. (I was a waiter.)

But I like to think that the Tennis Parties embodied a certain place and, especially, a particular time. Personal fitness was a novelty then, though it soon would become a duty. Women's participation in sports was thought to inhabit a continuum that ran through Title IX to the E.R.A.; Gloria Steinem and Billy Jean King were considered, in some sense, interchangeable. (Can you imagine someone including the words "feminism" and "Kournikova" in the same sentence?) Even the public-courts aspect of the Tennis Party bore social weight on its warmup-suited back: a post-sixties go at egalitarianism, touching in retrospect, that conveniently overlooked the need to be invited to attend, not to mention the relative exclusivity of Pelham in the first place. Still, there's just no way that this event, at least as originally conceived, could have lasted through the Greedy Eighties, much less to the present day. Where would people park their SUVs?

Other questions: Is it significant that the tennis courts nearest Pelham High School, the green-and-red ones, were torn down recently and replaced by a field for kiddie soccer? (The Parkway Field courts remain, to my knowledge.) And how, exactly, *do* you tear down a tennis court?

One couple at a time, apparently.

Now and then I sit in my Park Slope apartment, in my parents' butterfly chair. I look at their marble coffee table, and I wonder if my wife and I should throw a Tennis Party of our own. Kira and I have lots of friends, but many are in single-sex relationships or no relationship at all. Do they even play tennis? Where, exactly, would we reserve a sufficient number of courts on which to hold a tournament—the Brooklyn Parade Ground, across Prospect Park from our home? Then I remember that my serve is pathetic (thus that number thirty-one tennis-camp ranking), and that Kira has never taken a lesson.

We watch tennis on TV. I make up whimsical nicknames for the players, and my wife comes and goes, collaging at her art desk or cooking something or walking our dog and stopping in now and again to ask about J. Cap (Jennifer Capriatti) or Andy Boy (Andre Agassi).

"How's Lady Vee doing?"

"She's about to win."

"The set?"

"The match."

I keep meaning to take some lessons, maybe teach Kira how to hit a two-handed backhand, but I never do.

## 5. (Sudden) Death: *Tennis Court, The Grove, Harrow School, Harrow-on-the-Hill, England*

Tennis courts are indices of our decay. Tennis is a game for teenagers, but it's one you can play in middle age, too—*old* age, even. George Blanda notwithstanding, you can't play football—real football, tackle football—when you're forty.

And you can't play tennis as well, then, as when you were eighteen. (Ask John McEnroe. Ask me.) You can't react as quickly at the net, through chi-chi designer spectacles, as you could glasses-less, 'neath the brim of a ridiculous Aussie hat. You don't dive for balls anymore. You're not as brave—as foolhardy—as you once were. Things change, and tennis courts make that dramatically evident.

So many of the tennis courts I've known are twilit in my memory:

—The court in Weekapaug, Rhode Island, where I squinted into the tangerine sunset, screwing up the courage to kiss my first real girlfriend.

—Arthur Ashe Stadium at the start of a nighttime match, the sky above New York still purple while Serena Williams lugs a multi-racket shoulderbag through the players' entrance and onto floodlit Center Court, to the ecstatic cheers of her fans.

—Long Meadow in Prospect Park, past which I jog in the early evenings year-round; at the turn of the twentieth century, three hundred lawn-tennis courts there were insufficient to sate the public's appetite for the faddish new sport. Now it's just grass.

—A private court by the house on Squam Lake in New Hampshire, where I lived and worked as an S.A.T. tutor one summer—it was simply too hot to play during midday—and the grass courts at the club in Southampton, New York, the next summer, where I didn't play though my tutees did; I ran past these, too, longingly.

And a tennis court at Harrow, in England: the ancient "public" boys' academy, Eton's archrival, attended by Lord Byron and Winston Churchill. They still wear black at Harrow—black neckties, black top hats and tails on Sundays—as a sign of mourning . . . for Queen Victoria. A high school student of my English-teaching grandmother had grown up to marry a Harrow housemaster and invited my family to stay in their home, The Grove, while Melisa and Geoffrey and their four daughters vacationed in the Cotswolds one summer.

I don't recall whether the court was surfaced in asphalt, clay, dirt, or what. (It wasn't grass; I've never hit on grass, I regret to say.) I do know that my mother and my brothers and I, punch-drunk with jetlag, tried to play doubles there late one evening. Very late. It was September. It was London (far to the north of most of the U.S., latitudinally). It was way past 9:00 P.M., and we didn't need lights. (Lucky for us, since of course there were none. This was Harrow.) Stinging nettles lined the edges of the court, so foraging after a mis-hit ball left welts on one's forearms and legs. And everything was so grayly indistinct, past sunset, that it was hard to be sure if a serve was good or not, if a shot was in or out. The ancient net sagged badly, as ancient things will. Aside from the sounds we made, tennis sounds, and the chirping of nighttime birds, all was quiet.

School—Harrow itself, where my older brother would be studying for a year, and my high school back home in the States—would resume in less than a week, at which time summer would conclude informally. It would end for real a couple of weeks later. You could play tennis in winter, in a big shed or a plastic bubble, but even if the weather turned mild, you couldn't play outside after November or so in New York; any groundskeeper with his head on straight took the nets down during autumn, rolled them up and stored them somewhere. (Thus the net purchased by a tennis buddy of my father's, and squirreled in the trunk of his car for guerilla-style wintertime play.) In any case, you couldn't play outside after dinner much longer. Not like this.

Finally it was too dim to see not just the lines, but the tennis ball itself. We reached into the nettles one last time, gathered up the balls and screwed on our racquet presses, and walked back to the house in the dark.

# Part I

# Junior Tennis

*I'd grown up inside vectors, lines, and lines athwart lines, grids . . .*
—David Foster Wallace
*A Supposedly Fun Thing I'll Never Do Again*

*In this story, novelist/memoirist Jonathan Ames trains his gaze on the crossroads where childhood and maturity, desire and fear intersect—and finds competitive tennis there. He also considers multiple meanings of the word* balls.

# Pubertas Agonistes

## Jonathan Ames

I started puberty very late. I was nearly sixteen. And for complicated reasons this late arrival of my puberty caused me to stop playing competitive tennis. But before my puberty problems, I had trouble with my lower back and with my left testicle.

The back was the first thing to go—in the third grade, at an introductory Cub Scout picnic. I had gone to this picnic against my better judgment. I must have heard some rumors about the Cub Scouts and I was afraid that I would have to build things at the picnic and use tools, and I already knew by the third grade that I wasn't mechanically inclined. I put up as much resistance as an eight-year-old could—there may have been some tears—but my father insisted that we go. And as it turned out there were no tools at the picnic, only game-playing. I started having a pleasant tennis ball catch with another boy, and after several tosses the ball sailed over my head. I went to retrieve it, and though I thought I was all right, I must have still been nervous about joining the Cub Scouts, because when I bent over to pick up the ball, I experienced terrible spasms in my lower back. It was crippling, the muscles clenched like fingers into fists, and I folded up and fell to the ground. My father had to carry me out of the picnic past all the other boys and their fathers. I remember him laying me in the backseat of the car.

This was upsetting for my dad: He was a former Boy Scout. He had hoped that I would become an Eagle Scout one day, a goal he had been unable to achieve himself because he couldn't really swim and one of the Eagle Scout tasks has to do with treading water for many hours in an icy lake in your blue uniform, or something like that. My father could doggy-paddle, but he couldn't risk putting his head underwater because of a Depression-era mastoid operation in his ear that had left a large hole. So, like my father, I never became an Eagle Scout. I never even went back to the minor leagues of the Boy Scouts—the Cub Scouts. That picnic ended my scouting career.

A few days after the picnic, and after several more episodes of

painful, constricting back spasms, my mother took me to an orthope-
dist, who had unusually hairy fingers and a stern manner. He tapped
me all over and massaged me roughly with his unattractive digits, seeking a diagnosis. I'm not sure he came up with one, but he prescribed
that I wear a corset, saying that my back needed to be held in, and the
way he said it made me feel as if I was being punished for some weakness of my character, rather than just a weakness in my lower back. And
what an unusual, outdated prescription—how many other boys, I wonder, in 1972, were advised by physicians to be corseted?

So my mother, thinking that you always obey doctors, took me to a
hospital pharmacy that had prosthetic devices and other gadgets—special toilet seats, harnesses, organ trusses—and I was fitted and meas-
ured for my corset by a small, bald pharmacist who used the same kind
of measuring tape as a tailor.

My corset was white with silver buckles and had metal rods to keep
my back from dissembling. I wore it for a year and was deeply humiliated. Only once did that corset give me any pleasure. I was with all the
children on my street watching a Ping-Pong game in the garage of a
neighbor. One of the players, an older boy, had perceived that I had in-
terfered with one of his shots (this was untrue—he was losing badly and
wanted someone to blame), and he started chasing me. I raced up my
neighbor's driveway and across their lawn. I was wearing a heavy sweatshirt to cover the bulk of my corset, so my pursuer didn't know about
my condition. He was right behind me, but even with the corset, I was
able to scoot quickly. The other kids came running, too. The enraged
boy was fat and had white-blond hair. He still held his paddle. He
was going to try and smack me with it. He ran well despite his weight.
Like in a dream, where you can't run, my legs did begin to feel heavy,
and I felt the nausea that comes before the inevitable submission to
a beating.

So when he caught up to me at the end of my neighbor's lawn, he
hit me as hard as he could with his Ping-Pong paddle right in my lower
back. It was going to be the first of several blows, but I didn't feel a thing
and I heard a snapping of wood and I turned around just in time to see
the circular part of the paddle fly in the air like a Frisbee and then land
at the feet of the other children, our audience. The blond boy had un-
wittingly smashed his little racquet against my hidden metal rods, my secret armor, and it had severed the disclike head, which in a strange act
of physics had ricocheted dramatically upward and, as I said, come
down to earth at the feet of our amazed peers. So my attacker stood there
holding the handle of his decapitated paddle, and he was stunned, defeated. Everyone laughed at him. It was a moment of triumph.

But that was the only victory my corset gave me, and in the middle of this time of wearing my corrective garment, I had another problem: My left testicle ascended and wouldn't come down. I was taken to another doctor and he told my mother that this wasn't uncommon in young boys and was usually a temporary condition. So luckily for me, he didn't recommend some kind of organ truss to pull the testicle down, which would have complemented my white waist-cincher, but the doctor did say that if my testicle didn't return home by the time I started puberty, then surgery might be necessary. And I was mature enough to know that surgery in the area of one's penis was not a desired event.

I'm not sure why my testicle went into hiding, but, like my back problem, I think it was fear-related: I found the third grade to be very stressful academically. There was an enormous quota of dittoes to be filled out each day, and three days a week, in the afternoons, I was starting to go to Hebrew school; so this overload of education had me quite nervous. My mother, a schoolteacher herself, expected me to be a perfect student, and I was terribly afraid that I couldn't be. In fact, I pleaded with her to let me drop out of everything (it was all too difficult; for the first few weeks of third grade I cried every night and pounded my feet into my bed), but she wouldn't let me quit—how could she?—and I started learning then that we spend most of our lives doing what we don't want to do. And so like a scared soldier in a bunker whose testicles are known to elevate during heavy shelling (to protect them, and then they descend during peacetime, which accounts for postwar baby booms), my testicle elevated during this fearful period of my life. Why only one went up, and not two, is a mild flaw in my theory, but let me press on.

So I was missing a testicle and wearing a corset. I was eight years old.

Then my health, on its own, improved. By the time I was nine and a half, all my problems cleared up. The testicle ended its strike and returned to work and the corset was banished to my underwear drawer, where it stayed for several years, a terrible sight, a terrible reminder.

I began to play a lot of sports, and I excelled at soccer and tennis. I was quite happy for almost two years. I had nothing to worry about. But then when I was eleven something unexpected occurred: My best friend started puberty. I saw him naked when we were changing to go swimming. I was shocked. His enlarged penis and thatch of public hair looked vulgar to my eyes, and yet I wanted the same thing to happen to me. I didn't say anything to him about his hairy penis; I pretended not to have noticed, but I was secretly hurt that he hadn't mentioned his transformation. It seemed like the kind of thing that a best friend should confide in you about. So I didn't really enjoy our afternoon swim, the whole thing had me feeling conflicted, and that evening, looking for parental counsel, I asked my mother when I would get hair and have a big penis.

"One day," she said, "some fluid, not urine, will come out of your penis. At night. And after that happens you'll get pubic hair and your penis will get bigger."

Some fluid. *Not urine.* This was very mysterious. I thought it must be a once-in-a-lifetime secretion that marked one's passage into adulthood, something akin to a caterpillar transforming into a butterfly, which was the scientific equivalent I came up with—back then one was always seeing in school slow-motion films of such metamorphoses. So I was naive and unusually innocent; I never figured out until well after the fact that my mother had been referring to a wet dream.

Thus, I waited for this unknown, unnamed fluid for the next four and a half years, while all the girls and boys around me began to change and grow. As a result, I developed an acute awareness and fascination for that surest and most visible sign of puberty—armpit hair. I was always noting with sad jealousy the armpit hairs of my peers in the gym locker room; and I was forever inspecting my own armpits in the mirror at home. I'd shine a flashlight on them, hoping to spot the most meager follicle. But my pits were barren; no hairs flourished. Then one time on the school bus, in the spring of sixth grade, I saw a *girl's* lovely blond armpit hairs when she grabbed hold of the pole near the driver. I was mesmerized, enchanted. My little penis turned immediately to stone. This girl was becoming a woman before my eyes—*she had hair!* Beautiful, gold-blond armpit hair. It was glorious. I desired her and I envied her and I never forgot her. Fourteen years later, while visiting the Greek island of Santorini, I saw an attractive German woman's blond armpit hair and I was transported back in time—like Proust with his Madeleine—to that vision of blond armpit hair on the school bus, and my reaction in Greece, all those years later, was exactly the same: I was enchanted and my penis turned to stone.

One summer during my teenage years, when I was waiting for my Godotish puberty, I went away to a Jewish Camp in Upstate New York. I was in the Levi division (Levi was the name of one of the original Hebrew tribes before it became a pair of jeans) of newly christened teenagers, and to my horror I discovered that I was the only boy who still had a small, undeveloped penis and no pubic hair! So I had to hide myself the whole summer. I would quickly change my clothes with my back to my tentmates, and I only showered early in the morning when no one else was around. It was nerve-racking. But one person did see my naked form—the head counselor of Levi, who was the best-looking counselor in the whole camp with his curly blond hair and perfect physique, and who decided one night that he should assist me in putting calamine lotion on my body for a very bad case of poison ivy I had contracted. To do this, he took me up to the shower room when no one was there. He had me strip down to my underwear and he began to coat me with the pink lotion. Then he inquired as to whether or not I had the rash in my groin area. I admitted that I did, so he knelt in front of me and began to pull down my underwear. I was extremely embarrassed and before my secret, tiny penis was revealed, I made an apology—I whispered, "I'm very small."

I wasn't worried about being sexually abused; it was the 1970s and sexual abuse hadn't been invented yet. I was simply concerned about someone finding out that I hadn't started puberty. So down came my underwear and the counselor put the lotion on my small penis, and he said, "Don't worry, you have plenty of time." This was very sweet and kind of him, though I felt a little funny when he quickly pulled up my underwear when he heard the door to the shower room open up. I intuited that what had occurred was perhaps not proper. And sure enough, this very nice, handsome counselor left the camp several years later under ominous circumstances. I still do wonder what became of him. For me, my encounter with him was actually quite tender. Before the judge, if I was ever called, I would say, "He was very reassuring."

And that counselor was right. I did have plenty of time. I turned fourteen, then fifteen, but still no armpit hair or fluid. I was starting to lose my mind over this. Then in the spring of my freshman year of high school, this puberty situation got really out of control when I made the tennis team. It was late March when I was selected for the squad—it was an honor to have been chosen as a freshman—and because it was still cold out, our practices were held at an indoor racquet club before school started. At the end of the first practice, our coach, who was short and dark and bore a slight resemblance to my father, announced that every day after we were done playing we were to go for a jog around the parking lot and then come in and shower. Showering was mandatory, he said, because we couldn't go to school smelling of sweat. "It's not healthy," he explained.

I didn't know how I was going to escape exposure and humiliation. I hadn't been seen naked for years, except by the understanding counselor at camp. I was practically of normal height for my age, but that was the only normal thing about me. My lack of puberty was my most guarded secret. I regretted having tried out for the team. I hadn't considered the showering. There had been no showering during try-outs, and in the fall when I was on the freshman soccer team, none of us had showered.

I thought my only chance, after we finished that first practice, was to be the fastest runner. So when we took off for our jog, I dashed ahead of the pack, raced around the lot, sped into the locker room, stripped down to my underwear, and headed for the showers. But before I could get anywhere, some of the other boys, who had also run fast, began to straggle in. It was impossible to go through with it. The shower area didn't have private booths; it was just a large tiled room with spigots coming out of the walls.

I sat down on the bench and began to dress. I watched enviously as the other boys marched around carefree with their large penises. They took towels out of the towel bin and didn't even bother to put them around their waists. Each boy's penis and surrounding pubic hair seemed to be as distinctive as his face and hairdo. Some of the boys were eighteen years old—they were practically men. It was unfair. I was a cherub compared to them. My penis was indistinguishable from that of a five-year-old's. I could still do the trick of pushing it in so that it disappeared momentarily, went to Connecticut or someplace and then came back to me in New Jersey.

So that first day, I didn't shower. I got dressed and headed out of the locker room just as the coach was coming in. He looked at me accusingly and said, "Showered already?" I lied immediately. "Yes, Coach," I said, and he let it pass, though I knew he was suspicious.

I was nerve-racked for the next twenty-four hours, and at the end of the second practice, I again sprinted ahead of everyone in our tour of the parking lot, running even faster than the day before, and my teammates all thought I was trying to be the coach's pet. But I was running for my life. A sophomore on the team tried to keep up with me, the bastard, but I left him behind. I made it to the locker room and had about a minute to take a shower. I got down to my underwear but could go no further. I was too afraid. Then a few of my teammates came in. I tried to summon the courage to reveal myself, but I couldn't. So I sat on the bench and got dressed and I felt surrounded by the hairy penises of my teammates; it was dizzying, things felt out of focus, all those penises, it was like being in Hitchcock's *The Birds*.

I staggered out to the lobby to wait for a ride to school from one of the hairy seniors. As I stood there the coach came up to me. He looked at my hair and said, "You didn't shower, did you?" It was incredible; it was only the second day of practice and he was already homing in on the most vulnerable aspect of my life.

"I don't want to get a wet head," I said. "I have a little cold, and if I go out with a wet head, it might get worse. I washed a little in the sink." I was always being warned by my great-aunt Pearl, who often stayed with my family, about the dangers of a wet head, that a wet head could lead to serious illness.

"All right," the coach said, "but tomorrow you better shower."

Why did he care? Why couldn't he leave me alone? The next day after practice I just sat on the locker-room bench in my underwear, my barrier to humiliation, and I was practically catatonic with indecision. Should I just do it? Let them see me and laugh at me? Then the coach came and stood before me. He was nude. A towel was draped over his shoulder. His penis looked like a purple old man hiding in a black marsh. It looked like a poisonous mushroom, a chanterelle from hell. It looked like my father's penis. My father's penis, which I was always seeing in the bathroom and I would try not to look at it, but it would look at me no matter where I was, like the Mona Lisa.

But the coach, despite his unattractive penis, wasn't a bad man and he had an inkling of the problem I was having. He may have even thought he was helping me, as my coach, to conquer something. He probably figured I was only suffering from shyness. If he had known how small I was, he might have left me alone.

"So you're going to take a shower," he said cheerfully, yet forcefully, trying to manipulate me. "There's nothing to be worried about. It's healthy to take a shower after exercising. But you better hurry up, you're running late."

He walked off to the tiled room, sure that I would follow him. I regarded his unbecoming lower-back hair, and then dressed as fast as I could and escaped out to the lobby to the pay phone. I called my mother in a panic to come save me. I was almost crying. I said, "Mom, come get me right away. Please!" Luckily, she hadn't left early to go teach at her high school, and I begged her to meet me at the gas station, which was down the street from the tennis club. I didn't want the coach to find me.

When she pulled up in her car, I felt tremendous love for her. We were very close back then and always had been. I was an immature boy, not just physically, and my mother had encouraged this. Behind my father's back she had continued buying me G.I. Joe dolls, though by the time I was fifteen I would only play with them in my closet so that my father couldn't see me. I would have them hold on to the hangers with their special gripping hands, and when I wasn't playing with them, I just liked seeing them hiding in the closet when I would get dressed in the morning. I felt less alone and I must have identified with them—they were masculine but had no genitals.

So my father didn't know about the G.I. Joes, but he was quite aware of my close relationship with my mother. Long before I knew what it meant, he often called me Oedipus. He would summon me to the dinner table by shouting, "Oedipus! Oedipus!" He also said it whenever he saw my mother giving me a kiss. And when that would happen, my sister, three years older than me, would join my father in calling me Oedipus, and she would also make a heart shape with her hands.

My father's other frequent nickname for me was Dick Tracy because of my large, bent nose. My penis was small but my nose was big. So there was a certain parallel to my father's nicknames for me: Oedipus and Dick Tracy—two mystery-solvers.

And my father was right. It was all very Oedipal. For years my mother and I had played this game where she would ask, "Who loves you?" It became a game because she asked me so often. I'd answer by naming one of my grandparents or my father or my sister. Then she'd ask again, "Who loves you?" And the more relatives or friends of the family that I could think of, the more suspenseful it became. But then finally I'd always submit and shout, "You do!" And this shout not only affirmed that she loved me, but that I was crazy about her. And when I was with my mother in that car, being saved from my tennis coach and my teammates, I loved her very much. I told her what was going on.

"The other boys won't notice," she said.

"They'll notice! I'm the only one who hasn't started puberty. They'll kill me!"

My mother wanted me to talk to my father, but I wouldn't do that. I hadn't let him see me naked for a long time. I must have sensed intuitively the other side of the Oedipal dynamic—that if my father knew I wasn't a threat, i.e., a mature male, he could easily do away with me. He was a member of the NRA.

So I wanted to quit the tennis team immediately, but my mother wouldn't let me. Still, she was sweet to me; she reassured me that someday soon I would develop. You have plenty of time, she said. I had heard it before, but I was running out of time—I needed to start puberty by the next practice.

It didn't happen. The next day, the coach was going from court to court observing us. I was on line for a backhand drill and he stood next to me and said in a snide way, "Think you'll shower today?" I didn't say anything to him. I was too embarrassed, and he walked away from me. And then a few minutes later during a volley drill, as I made my approach to the net, I fainted. I remember seeing the net cord and rotating my hand for the proper grip on the racquet, and then there was the cement of the court rising up to slap me, but there was also the feeling of relief, of going to sleep. I'm sure the coach, for a moment, saw an opening as I lay passed out. "Let's strip down Ames and see what he's got!"

But he restrained himself and my mother was called and I was taken to a doctor. I had mononucleosis. I had never kissed a girl, I was still in love with my G.I. Joes, and yet I had come down with the kissing disease. I must have picked it up from a water fountain or an improperly washed utensil in the cafeteria, or a wet head had done the trick. In any event, it was the best thing that could have happened to me—I missed the rest of the tennis season, and I never played competitively again.

That summer, a few months removed from my trauma on the tennis team, I began to experiment instinctively with masturbation. I still hadn't started puberty, but each night I strummed myself for a few minutes before falling asleep. I found it soothing, and I say *strum,* because I've never been one to jerk on my penis, unlike most men, who employ that rapid up-and-down yanking, which when I've witnessed other men masturbating—I've always found to be somewhat violent and unattractive.

Anyway, one night as I strummed in the motion and rhythm peculiar to me, my penis seemed larger than it ever had been before, and then a dribble of clear substance came out with a noticeably pleasurable feeling. I had heard about orgasms by this time, but it was only at that moment that I made the connection between "coming" and the fluid I had been waiting so long for (which I had just about given up on). I immediately went running to my mother.

My father was out of town, which he often was as a salesman, and my sister had already left home, on her long journey to becoming a psychiatrist, having sensed early on, I imagine, what was going on in the old Oedipal household. So it was around ten o'clock at night and I sprinted down the hall to my parents' bedroom completely nude. I burst in upon my mother, who was propped up in bed reading. I shouted at her with joy, "Mom, it's happened! The fluid came out! I think I'm starting puberty! My penis seems bigger!"

I got onto the bed next to her. She didn't say a thing to me. She kept on reading her book, she wouldn't look at me, but I could see that she was smiling. I figured that she was happy for me. I knew that I was happy. In fact, I was delirious, which seems to be the only explanation for my unusual behavior. In my delirious, exuberant state it felt perfectly natural to share this with my mother, who looked beautiful and kind sitting there. Her long blond hair, normally fastened in a bun, was loose and lay over her shoulders. I felt like snuggling next to her. In my mind, she had been waiting four and a half years with me for my pubescence, ever since I first asked her when I would change. She had been my sole confidante. She was the only person who knew my secret about how tiny I was, and she was the only one who knew what I had gone through on the tennis team.

And as I lay beside her on the bed, I admired my penis. I felt like all my problems were over. I decided to masturbate again. I wanted to show her how I could do it. "Watch, Mom," I said. "It gets big." I wanted to impress her. She was still smiling, but still not looking at me, which I thought was strange—she was always attentive to my accomplishments. And then when I touched myself, she said, "Maybe you should do that in your room."

She didn't say it with disgust or anger, her tone was gentle, but suddenly I felt shame. I knew then that it wasn't normal to show your mother your first official erection. I slid off her bed and I ran to her bedroom door, cupping my penis in my hands, holding myself like Adam, guilty with knowledge. I scurried down the hall, wondering if she might tell my father. I was embarrassed, but I also wanted to try masturbating again. I had started puberty! My troubles were over. New ones were beginning, but I didn't know it yet. I opened the door to my room. I was leaving my mother behind, and she may have sensed this, felt the umbilical-Oedipal cord snapping, and she tried to bring me back. She played our game, but it was too late. She'd had her chance. She called out, "Who loves you?"

*Anne Lamott's* Crooked Little Heart *uses junior tennis as a lens through which to observe an entire northern California community. Thus the novel tells the story of not only Girls 14-and-Under champion Rosie Ferguson, but that of her doubles partner, Simone; their coach, Peter Billings; Rosie's mother, Elizabeth; and stepfather, James; and Elizabeth's friends and lovers present and past. This excerpt stands out for its bravery, its precision, and its accuracy in exploring the psychology of two phenomena familiar to players and fans of all competitive sports: choking and cheating.*

# From *Crooked Little Heart*

## Anne Lamott

Rosie was seeded fourth, which meant she had been expected to get to the semifinals, and this was the round she was playing. Her opponent was an eleven-year-old named Marisa DeMay who'd won her quarterfinal round by default—the second seed had come down with leg cramps during the match. Rosie had been relieved just to get to the round she was expected to make, but now she was dismayed to discover that this unseeded girl, who'd gotten into the semis on a fluke, was actually very good. Rosie was so anxious about losing—even before they'd started keeping score—that it threw her game off. She and Marisa were playing long hard rallies, and Rosie had just barely won the first set, seven-five. Mrs. DeMay was doing needlepoint on the sidelines (an eyeglass case with a picture of teddy bears) and rarely looked up. Rosie was spooked. Her usual strategy and strength were consistency and infinite patience. Other players—Simone, for instance—lacked the patience for endless rallies and would try to put the ball away out of sheer boredom, but Rosie could wait all day for an opening if she had to. She didn't care. She just wouldn't miss until, like a break in the weather, a corridor opened down which she could discharge a lethal ground stroke.

But today, against tiny little Marisa, she was in trouble. It was like playing Thumbelina, except that Thumbelina hit as hard as a boy. On top of it all, she bounced around a lot and made an annoying squeaky noise. Rosie, a foot taller, two years older, was unnerved. She wanted the trophy so badly she could taste it, the trophy she'd get for playing in the finals, and here was this runt on the other side, chasing down every shot like a crazy little Chihuahua. She thought of her mother in bed the other day, depressed and overwhelmed.

She began patting in her second serves, like the old people did at the club—"Hey, nice serve, Ruth Ann," Peter would have said—and

13

chanting to herself in an incantory way, "Head down, head down, one two three one two three." Tiny Marisa flitted around the court making squeaky sounds of effort, a little cat toy that just wouldn't miss.

Both of them held serve until four all, and fear beat inside Rosie. She could hardly manage a forehand, while little Squeak-jump on the other side batted the ball from side to side. Rosie served a puffball forehand at thirty all, and Marisa put it away down the line. Adrenaline flooded Rosie like a sudden fever. Her hands were shaking; one more point and Marisa would break serve, be ahead five to four, zipping along on a roll, with her irritating mother stitching away, maybe humming, Rosie began to fixate on Marisa's mother and whether she was in fact humming or not. She was about to serve, but stopped and tilted her head toward Mrs. DeMay, straining to hear.

"What?" said Marisa.

"Nothing," said Rosie.

It was hard to catch her breath. She served a deep loopy backhand that miraculously dropped in, and Squeak-jump lobbed it back, and Rosie pushed back a forehand that barely landed over the net, and Marisa tapped it back, and they rallied for this critical point like that—dinking, pushing, patting endlessly, until Marisa hit a ball near the baseline. And it was not solidly on the line, but it was definitely in, touching half an inch of white. It was the most basic rule of tennis sportsmanship that you always gave your opponent the benefit of any doubt. If her ball was so close you honestly couldn't say for sure whether it was in or out, you played it as in. This ball was definitely, though barely, in, and time became thick and vacuumy and so silent that it was almost noise, and Rosie turned as if to hit this backhand, saw that Mrs. DeMay was reaching for something she'd dropped, and without really thinking about it, Rosie caught the ball on her racket and called it out.

Nonchalantly, heart pounding, she whacked the ball over the net to a stunned Marisa and walked to the forehand court.

"That wasn't out," said Marisa. "That hit the line."

"No," said Rosie innocently. "It was just barely out."

Marisa looked over at her mother. Her mother looked up kindly at Rosie.

"It was out," Rosie explained.

"I saw it. I looked at it," said Marisa. Rosie shrugged sympathetically.

"Why don't we take it over?" she offered.

"But that was my game!"

"Look, I'm sorry." Rosie walked to the alley and pointed with her racket to a spot just outside the line, a spot where a part of her was now convinced the ball had landed. "It was right here. But you can take two if you want."

Marisa looked with despair at her mother, who shrugged and held up her hands.

"Sorry," said Rosie. "Want to take two?"

After a moment of fidgeting, Marisa walked to the baseline to receive the serve. Rosie felt strangely calm, even cold, calculating: after she tossed the ball, she suddenly glanced away, as if distracted, and Marisa was thrown off by the sudden movement. She hit Rosie's easy serve into the net, and began to fall apart. She was fighting back more tears, while Rosie stood there waiting nicely, almost encouragingly. Then she nonchalantly aced her. On the next point, at ad-in, she once again glanced away after the toss, which so startled and distracted Marisa that she hit the ball over the fence.

"Four-five," said Rosie. A strange maturity filled her, and excitement. She felt terribly sorry for Marisa: when they changed over, Marisa was staring at the ground, so teary as to sound asthmatic. Rosie broke her serve for the match in four crisp points.

The mother made everything okay, gathering up her embroidery as she gushed over both of them: what a wonderful match, she said, and they'd both played so well, and to Marisa, wouldn't her father be proud that she had gotten so many games off a seeded player? She had cold cans of orange soda in an ice chest she kept in the trunk of her car, and Marisa began to cheer up, standing by the car, and Rosie looked at her proudly, for getting so many games off a seed, and then Mrs. DeMay leaned forward to tug at a loose button at the neck of Rosie's shirt, and it came off in her hands, as if she had just produced a coin from behind Rosie's ear.

"It was just about to drop off," Mrs. DeMay said. Rosie reached for it apologetically. "You sit down," she instructed Rosie. "I am going to sew that right back on."

"Oh, no," said Rosie, reaching again for the button, which Mrs. DeMay had already dropped into the pocket of her sundress. Rosie watched with disbelief as Mrs. DeMay began threading an embroidery needle with white thread. Give me the fucking button, Rosie wanted to cry. This could not be happening. Marisa was sitting in the dirt, taking off a shoe and sock to check for blisters, and Rosie looked around for help and, seeing none, saw herself smashing nice Mrs. DeMay over the head with her racket. As if in a dream, Mrs. DeMay led her to a chair beside the court and had her sit down, while she stood bending over Rosie, holding Rosie's shirt out by the collar, with hands that smelled of soap and lotion, hands that moved close to her and then away, close and away, as Rosie sat there hardly breathing, her head level with Mrs. DeMay's stomach, smelling a faint womanly underwear smell and connected by a long white thread to the mother of the girl she had cheated.

The cold clamminess of the fog soothed her. It covered everything, erased the world, the colors and shapes. Sitting in the back seat on the way back to the club, Mrs. DeMay and Marisa bubbling away in the front, Rosie saw in her mind the Walt Disney paintbrush that magically washes color into the world and felt now the relief of its opposite, the fog. In the fog, ships hit icebergs and sink. She liked the mystery, the shroud. It meant you got to wear jackets at night, blankets when you slept. It surrounded her now with silence, a silence she didn't hear anywhere else, and she realized how profoundly, in this car with two other people, she was alone.

*Like tennis itself, Caroline Rabinovitch's mesmerizing short story is "about" class. (Interestingly, its title character is downwardly mobile— which only adds to her allure, at least as far as the story's narrator is concerned.) Death—and death by murder, at that—visits this tale, too. Mainly, though, "Bunny Fever" is about sex.*

# Bunny Fever

## Caroline Rabinovitch

I'm the tallest guy at the party. Naturally, petite girls flock to me, chickadees and sparrows, but tonight those little birds stay away. I can guess who it is they're scared of: the tallest girl at the party, a long-limbed athletic type wearing cutoffs and cowboy boots. From across the lawn, I see her kick her legs out, walking like a man. I watch her throw her head back to laugh or drink from a beer. She catches my eye, puts her hand on her hip, and turns away.

Half an hour later I'm filling a glass with water in the kitchen when she walks out of the bathroom and right up to me. She is carelessly beautiful, with the subtle slouch that tall girls have, and she is bronze all over, the kind of tan that only a hazel-eyed blond can achieve. Her hair is pale amber, long and fine; her eyes are the color of her hair boiled down to molasses. Dark circles under her eyes anchor them, increasing their beauty by contrast.

She stands in front of me, grinning. Her lips are level with my neck—she's that tall. I return her stare until my fingers go numb. I realize I'm holding my breath. Her grin is not all smile; a sneer lurks inside it.

She sighs and shifts. Finally I see that she's holding an unlit cigarette cocked between two fingers, and with the same grin, she says, "Got a light, big man?" Her voice is boyishly low and raspy.

"No," I say, "I don't drink and I don't smoke."

"I didn't think so," she says, "you look like a big tame preppy pussycat."

She works a book of matches out of her back pocket and lights the cigarette, arching her neck and aiming twin streams of smoke at the ceiling. Her neck is tanned and smooth, without the filigree of pale lines that hides in taut skin.

"Having fun in this shithole town?" she asks.

"Seems all right," I say cautiously. I gesture to the party's host with my chin. "I know Chip from Duke. He talked me into spending the summer up here, said I could get a job at the country club."

"Which one?"

"Oh. Lakeside?"

"Huh. Doing what?"

"Teaching tennis."

She rolls her eyes. "I can't stand tennis."

She's wearing a flimsy tank top, which skims the healthy terrain of her breasts. On her chest is tattooed an image of storm clouds pierced by a sword. The sword is the size of my pinky.

"And you—what do you do?" I ask her.

"What do I *do*? I'm still in high school!"

I try to reconcile my memories of high school with the blond gazelle before me. "Well, you could work," I say, "or volunteer. Or maybe you're studying. I don't know."

"Man, I don't have to work." She tells me her father's last name. "And as for that other crap, I don't care. I really don't care."

We are silent for a moment. I watch her take a sip of beer. The can is sweating and drops of condensation slip through the crotch between her thumb and finger and roll down her wrist.

"Yeah, Alice tried to make me take lessons. She had some fantasy of us winning the mother-daughter tournament, maybe double-dating the father-son champs. *I* think she thought it would resurrect her modeling career. But I said no way, man! You're not getting me into that fucking skort, into those white sneakers. I mean, white sneakers? I'm not putting a fucking headband in my hair! So—grounded by Alice at the age of thirteen. It wasn't the first time, either. But it was the first time I stood up for my rights." She's holding her cigarette like a pointer and jabbing it towards my chest.

I say, "I'm sure you'd be a natural. You've got the perfect nose."

She laughs. "The perfect nose? For tennis?"

Her nose is long and sturdy, with a slight flare. A strong nose. The nostrils are not too broad, not too delicate, and evenly spaced. A straight shot to her lungs for those oxygen-rich breaths.

She's pushing the hair off her face with one hand, her left hand, as if to clarify these delightful matters between us. "You make me sound like a racehorse."

I put my glass of water on the counter. "No. Not a racehorse, a racing dog. A greyhound."

A look of mock insult is on her face—her eyebrows pinched together, her lips in an oval. She slaps me. "Bad tennis man!"

Is this what it's like to be drunk? The heat from her palm thumps in time with my heart, and resounds in my neck, my wrists, my ankles. My entire body tries to catch hold of the imprint of her touch, even as it fades away.

"But you're really more of a gazelle," I tell her, "with that hard, pointed hoof."

This time she skips the theatrics and goes right for the slap. The sting of this blow revives the ebbing warmth of the first; my cheek feels swollen and hot, and pulls up the corner of my lip.

I grab her hand. My fist fits around her wrist like a cuff. "What's your name, boxer?" I ask, feeling my face twist into a gigantic smile.

"Guess," she says. "No, we'll be here all night. It's Bunny. Everyone calls me Bunny."

Bunny puts her hand on my leg as I drive, a five-pointed sail on the smooth expanse of my thigh. Her fingertips feel like magnets; if she lifts her hand, my thigh will follow, helpless, light as a bottle cap.

"Does your body ever feel crazy, Bunny?" I ask.

"I feel pretty crazy right now." She's sprawled next to me, a beer in a green coozy between her legs.

"Really?" I look at her profile. Her hair is whipping and flapping in the wind, obscuring her face but for the tip of her nose. A lock of hair is caught in the stubble of my upper lip; ticklish, but let it remain. "You feel like you're not yourself? Like you need a workout?"

"I'm supposed to be on meds, but I don't take them. They make me feel boring. I have to sleep way too much."

"Meds? Medication?"

"Yeah." She drinks from her beer. "I was on the basketball team, but I had to quit."

"Oh." I am relieved. "A sports injury."

"No. I punched a girl in the tit." Her voice is hoarser than ever, roughened by beer, cigarettes, wind. "I guess you could say my fist felt crazy."

"What happened? Did she check you? Were you defending yourself?"

"It wasn't like that," Bunny says. "She was on my team." She gives my thigh a squeeze. "Here it is."

Bunny opens the door while the car is still moving, scissoring her legs out and trotting up the sidewalk to the 7-Eleven. A small man in a business suit comes out of the store, carrying a pint of ice cream caught in a translucent bag. He turns to watch Bunny pass, transfixed by the blur of tattoo, the flashing gazelle legs, her long, wind-snarled hair. I beep the horn, gently. His head swivels, his eyes meet mine, he hesitates, and I mouth the words "Scram, psycho." His forehead wrinkles in confusion. He puts the ice cream under his arm like a football and gets in his car.

My legs and arms feel crazy. I press my thumb hard into the meat of each muscle, trying to relieve the pressure. It's no good. I won't feel at ease until I have a real workout, until my head is pounding and my vision's gone white, until my heart is thumping and my lungs are gasping for breath. If I miss too many days, my body acts funny. I'll drop things, forget how to walk down stairs.

I hear Bunny before I see her; she's at the door of the 7-Eleven, cushioned by male laughter, laughing herself, and yelling "Later, dudes!" over her shoulder. She's eschewed the bag. She swings the six-pack by its plastic yoke and hops into the car.

"Guess what I got."

The word *condom* bumps in my mind like a moth drawn to light.

Bunny puts her hand down the front of her shorts, and pulls out bright yellow packets of cheap trucker's speed. She leans back and cackles.

"You bought that?" I ask. The moth of a thought withdraws.

She grins. "Nope."

"They gave it to you?" I complete the U-turn and we're back on the road.

"Guess again." Her feet are on the dashboard, tapping the windshield. "Five finger discount," she says. "We'll share them."

"I don't know."

"Oh, come on. Please."

Bunny opens a beer. The sound scrapes along my muscles. Empty yellow packets are fluttering in the car, settling, and fluttering again. Bunny grabs one from her lap and flings it out the window impatiently. She shakes her cupped palm to make a neat pile of the tiny white pills, then claps it to her mouth. She takes a slug of beer. "Ahh."

"I'm going to show you something," she says.

Her body is pressed close to mine, her thigh along my thigh, her hip next to my hip. She slides her arm behind my back. Bunny. I am driving. Her hands are hot and dry on my face. She turns me slightly, and somehow my face is below hers. Her face is very close to mine, and her throat—I can see, for a split second before her lips meet mine, the ridged tunnel of her windpipe pressing against her skin from the strained angle.

Her tongue slips in my mouth, soft, slick, sour with beer; I want her to choke me; I want to crush her face against my teeth. The skin all over my body feels plucked and numb, but my face, where she touched me in anger, or a semblance of anger, feels warm. Oh, Bunny. Something is on her tongue. Pills. She pushes them toward my throat. They are bitter and dissolving, our saliva is bitter with pills. She pulls away.

We are going four miles an hour. Bunny laughs and wipes her mouth.

"Oh my God!" she screams. "I just got the best idea."

"What?" Speech, and the accelerator, and mirrors, and Bunny's hand, resting there again, seem like faint, boxy puzzles.

"I'm taking you to the club. Have you been there yet? You probably had your interview at what's-her-name's bungalow. She actually calls it a bungalow! We can go swimming, and get into the snack bar. I know how to work the fryer, they made me work there for two weeks last year. And paddleboats. Damn, I should have gotten more beer."

She snuggles next to me. The glowing hives of suburban houses wink by in the distance. The yellow lines ticking by my left wheel are re-assuring, and as I squeeze the steering wheel—it's covered with a kind of soft-wicker wrapper—I realize I feel like I'm holding a tennis rac-quet. That's reassuring, too, but it feels wrong. A racquet that's gone all curved and useless, without a start or an ending, a racquet which can-not smash or slice.

Bunny is singing softly, in a low-throated buzz I can hardly hear.

"Preppy cat, tom cat, tennis man who?"

I answer, the night air soft in my mouth, watching the blurry cones of light spilling from the headlamps alive with startled insects. "Bunny cat, bunny rabbit, hip hop, you."

We've driven past the gatehouse, with its striped, reflective gate as spindly as an arm bone. I'm still saying, "Bunny, I think this is a bad idea. I just got hired. Let's go someplace else."

But she is hunching forward towards the glass, directing me down a side path. "This is where the employees park. They're not allowed to use the front gate." There is no gate here, just a folding chair pulled against a tree and flattened soda cans in a pile by the road. The dark spots under her eyes have picked up the molasses color of her irises. Her cheekbones, too, are hollowed by mahogany shadows. We roll slowly, headlights off, through crunching gravel, to a parking lot sur-rounded by tall pines on all sides. Several golf carts, sagging, or with ripped upholstery, are lined up by a cinderblock building. I park away from them, aligning my car on its long side, so it's less visible from the road. A cicada screeches violently nearby.

My limbs feel bunchy and erratic. I wonder when I will feel the speed, when I will surrender to the fervent mechanics of my body.

"Alice would have loved you," Bunny says.

"Is she—"

"Dead? No. Not really. I mean, she would have loved you, at the time that she was fucking with me. With the lessons and everything. I was a tomboy, and she didn't like it."

"Is it really so bad to learn a new sport?"

We're walking on a dirt path, going slightly downhill. To the left, the lake glitters in the slender wedges between tree trunks, and farther ahead are the fried-egg shapes and clipped smoothness of the golf course.

She stops me by grabbing my arm and pushing it back. "It wasn't just the lessons. It was everything. The makeup. The clothing. She wanted me to fucking *curtsy* whenever a man was around." Her eyes hang on mine; I feel she wants me to make a leap that her words don't specify. She looks at me like she's trying to get something from me. I can see exactly where her wrinkles will be ten, twenty, thirty years from now—little pinches at the corners of her eyes from pulling, pulling something invisible from people.

I kiss her, but this is the wrong thing. She pulls away, annoyed, tugs a strap back up her shoulder.

"If you don't fucking get it," she says, "then just leave me and get out of here. I've spent the night outside, by myself, plenty of times and it's fine."

I apologize, but for what? We walk on in silence.

"Bunny, what's your real name?" I ask. I am uncomfortably aware of the hearty casualness of my voice.

"I can't tell you." She pauses. "Oh, all right. It's Bernadette. Isn't it horrible? That's my aunt's name, but it suits her because her hair is really curly. I can legally change it in ten months."

"Change it to what?"

"I don't know. There'd be no point in changing it if I still lived here. But if I move—" She corrects herself. "When I move, I'll buy one of those baby books, get drunk, and stick my finger in the middle of a page."

At the mention of Bunny moving, my heart seizes nervously. Suddenly I am aware of it pressing into my chest. I touch a finger to my throat, find my pulse leaping there. "Where, move to where?" I say.

"Same deal."

I miss her point. She chugs her beer, then in a woozy-faced pantomime circles a finger above her palm. Oh. She throws her head back and laughs.

"Hey, up there are your instruments of torture," she says, pointing.

The tennis courts are set on a little hill, probably man-made, and edged with tangled vines. At the entrance to the courts, "Lakeside" is spelled in a rectangle of white gravel with bunches of wilted red flowers.

I stop. "If you play with me, Bunny, I'll prove to you that it can be fun."

She keeps walking. "No way, dude."

I press my knees to the ground. "Please."

She doesn't look back. Her snug cutoffs blend into the shadows, and all I see of her is the blond hair gleaming in the moonlight, and her long gazelle's legs, from her hips to where they disappear in her boots.

"Come on, big cat," she calls.

While I'm down here, I pull my leg back into a sprinter's starting-line stretch. My calf burns with a miniature fire. On your mark, get set . . . Somewhere a twig snaps and falls from the sky. Go.

I'm off.

Bunny's doing dolphin dives in the pool. Each time, her tank top creeps up her back a little bit more. The bare swatch of golden torso, with its hidden nuggets of vertebrae, is the source of all gazelle within her, the arched, leaping center to her nimble limbs. The bottom of the shirt is frayed, and through bleach-burned holes I spy secret flesh, bronze coins revealed for a flash as her dive pulls the waterlogged fabric tight against her skin. After a while, she floats on her back, looking incredibly long.

We are in the kiddy pool. The heavily chlorinated water reaches to my knee. Poolside tables and chairs in the shapes of toadstools hunch mysteriously in the moonlight. Sculptures of woodland creatures—a bird, a gopher, a mouse—are mounted on springs in a semicircle, overlooking this midget world. A pair of tiny flip-flops on the deck awaits its master's return.

"Isn't it kind of weird to be here," I say, "in the kiddy pool? It would be worse than getting caught anywhere else; it would be weird."

"Weirder things have happened here."

"What do you mean?"

She turns and wriggles through the water silently, then crouches down in front of me so that only her head, her finely shaped head with her nose flaring slightly from exertion, is above the water. "Years ago, there was a lifeguard who got off more on drowning kids than saving them. That's why besides Lakeside, there's Evergreen. Parents were like, we can't *enjoy* this fucking place now. That's why those little tables, those animals—" She lifts a dripping arm and points to the mushrooms. "They tore out the pool and rebuilt it from scratch. Made it look magical and cozy. Then all the kids had to see a shrink." She dips underwater, resurfaces. "That summer sucked because I'd just learned how to dive and they didn't let kids dive in the grown-up pool."

"When did this happen?" The wind is lifting a chill from my body.

"Ten years ago? I knew the guy, too, the lifeguard. He was my first crush." She stands up, her wet skin shining in the moonlight. Her shirt is clinging to her breasts, and the pale threads fringing the bottoms of her cutoffs are plastered to her thighs at jagged intervals. Water drips down the sword tattooed on her chest. "He looks a little like you. Same sandy hair, same build. Not as tall, not as serious. You know those crushes little girls get. I guess he reminded me of my dad, somehow."

I don't like this. "Wait. You knew him when you were a girl?"

"He was nice to me. Nothing really happened."

"Nothing really happened?"

"Well not to me! They said he drowned two kids, but I wasn't friends with them."

"And he looks like me." Suddenly my evening with Bunny feels distasteful; suddenly I am aware of how ridiculous it is that we are here, late at night, in the children's pool of the country club at which I've just gained employment.

"Well, he *did* look like you. I don't know about now. I guess he's still in jail." Her voice breaks a little in indignation. "God, I never even think about this guy! I only told you to spook you out."

She turns and goes to the steps. She takes them one at a time, although she could easily span all four in one stride. I like the way even her butt looks grumpy, hitching to the left and hitching to the right as she climbs.

I hear the click of a lighter. I think about leaving, about my solitary walk on the path through the woods, about my car lurking under the line of trees and of the relief I'll feel when I see it.

Bunny sits cross-legged beside me and taps me on the shoulder.

"What's the matter, Preppy Man? Did I hurt your feelings?" Her voice is raspy and teasing.

I want to get up but the echo of her fingertips on my shoulder holds me in place. "Why are we here, anyway?" I ask her. I focus on the divot of her upper lip, where there is an imperfection, a chicken-pox scar or a blemish.

"Don't you want to hang out with me?" she says, pouting.

"So that's what you like about me, that I look like a killer, like a pervert?"

"Whoa. Pervert?"

"Yes. Pervert. As in someone who drowns a kid." I stare at the pool. My feet feel soggy and wrinkled.

Bunny exhales loudly, and her cigarette plops in the water, twirling on the surface a few feet away from me.

"I'm not the only one who liked him," she says. "Everyone did. He said I was a good swimmer. He said I looked like I could swim around the whole world."

My heart is racing, but I feel tired. "Tell me," I say slowly, "tell me you're not one of those rich girls who only likes assholes."

She stiffens. "Fuck you," she growls.

I risk a glimpse of her. From this close, if I look at her shoulder, her face is blurry, and I can see, in the hunch of her back and in the tips of her ears parting wet strands of hair, the ghost of the eight-year-old girl within her. I look in her eyes and I see a minuscule motion in the arrogant stillness of her head. Her pupil puckers. In the depth of her eyes, dripping with shadows, I watch the striated, golden-flecked brown of her irises contract.

She has never looked so majestic, so long and lean, with her slender tan legs folded up under her, white teeth gleaming between parted lips, residual smoke still trailing from her nostrils. Childish anger looks good on her; it puts a fierceness in her jaw, a gazelle's elegance in her neck. I'm not ready to give up—to give her up. I can't relinquish the postcard images that have been blinking in my brain all night: Bunny and I laughing and stumbling down the hill hand-in-hand, tennis racquets slung like rifles over our shoulders, sweat glistening on our golden skin. Bunny careering through the woods in a golf cart while I clutch the seat, game but terrified. Bunny accosting me on the court, jealous of the flirtatious older woman who needs help with her backhand.

Bunny, I will do whatever you want, I will twist the facts the way my guts are twisted now, I will shove my own bitter pills down your throat. The summer lies ahead—hot, languid, long—and I prefer to settle these matters at the start of it.

I smile. I know what to do. My heart is giddy, fluttering from the anticipation of her skin on mine. My mouth is dry—I could drink all the water in the pool.

"Bunny." I think of children crossing their fingers when they tell a lie. Is the thought of it enough? "You are worse than a racehorse, worse than a dog. You are dirt. You are a worm. You are this stupid fucking country club."

For a moment, shock and disgust distort her face. And then, as if powered by its own desire to drive those words back into my mouth, her fist, a flesh-colored glow, collides with my face. It pushes me over, and I use that motion to help hoist myself out of the pool. The pain feels strangely neutralized on a chemical level by the volume of adrenaline in my blood. My face feels warm, and there is a slight throb, like a purring, in my jaw.

Bunny is rubbing her hand and looking at me uncertainly. I walk to a toadstool and sit down. Water drips from my calves and pools around my feet. My body feels serene and cool, my flesh feels smooth and tight. My face ticks with a pleasant warmth.

Bunny is staring at me. She's neither running away, nor preparing to strike. Her chin juts up, her chest heaves. I shift my buttocks on the stool and pat the space next to me.

"It's all right, Bunny rabbit," I say. "Is that what you wanted, are you okay?" I try to keep my voice calm and soothing.

Her bare feet are slightly apart, and she's poised lightly; she tosses her hair, wet and moonlit and now of indeterminate hue. She's holding one fist in the other under her breasts, like a bodybuilder preparing for a front-lat spread.

I watch her stand. I wait. I have a sense of all my body's organs humming away happily, happily constrained in the factory of my body.

Again she tosses her hair. She rubs her fist. The notion that the same pain stretches invisibly, across twenty feet of space, knitting her fist to my jaw, makes my body hum patiently.

When she finally moves towards me, I feel a surge of joy so fragile, looming and complete that I must close my eyes to breathe. A blueprint shape of her body, a trick of the moon, hovers beside her, then jumps as I look away. But Bunny is no trick of moonlight and shadow. She walks towards me slowly, like a gazelle stepping gingerly through the forest, a million-dollar smile growing on her face.

The joy swells in me. I rise, take a half-step back on dizzy feet. I am aroused. Bunny, I have you now. Right here inside this country club, with the moon drawing jittery oblongs on the surface of the pool, and with the same pin-stroke shapes forming tentatively on the wet muscle of my heart.

I will have you by the pool. I will press your velvet lips to my neck. I will have you in the cabana, while your mother suntans on the grass. In the locker room, on the golf course at night. Nearly capsizing a paddle-boat. Bunny, you are a tall gazelle, but oh I am much taller. My thigh could feed a battalion of starving men. My hide could dress the floor of your mansion. My sneakers are boats in which to skirt the volcano. One day, my name shall be inked on your tattoo. People will ask, are you twins? Brother and sister? Lord and lady? They will shield their eyes from us as if from the sun. They will say, there go the giants.

*Once a ranked player on the junior tennis circuit, David Foster Wallace has written some of the best nonfiction on the game for magazines like* Tennis, Harper's, *and* Esquire. *"Year of Glad" is the first chapter of his magnum opus,* Infinite Jest: *a footnoted, thousand-pages-plus novel of international intrigue, substance-abuse recovery . . . and junior tennis. Here, readers become acquainted with the book's main character, Hal Incandenza—and with the damage, to put it mildly, that an adolescence spent at his family's ferociously competitive tennis academy has wrought upon Hal's psyche.*

# Year of Glad

## David Foster Wallace

I am seated in an office, surrounded by heads and bodies. My posture is consciously congruent to the shape of my hard chair. This is a cold room in University Administration, wood-walled, Remington-hung, double-windowed against the November heat, insulated from Administrative sounds by the reception area outside, at which Uncle Charles, Mr. deLint and I were lately received.

I am in here.

Three faces have resolved into place above summer-weight sportcoats and half-Windsors across a polished pine conference table shiny with the spidered light of an Arizona noon. These are three Deans—of Admissions, Academic Affairs, Athletic Affairs. I do not know which face belongs to whom.

I believe I appear neutral, maybe even pleasant, though I've been coached to err on the side of neutrality and not attempt what would feel to me like a pleasant expression or smile.

I have committed to crossing my legs I hope carefully, ankle on knee, hands together in the lap of my slacks. My fingers are mated into a mirrored series of what manifests, to me, as the letter X. The interview room's other personnel include: the University's Director of Composition, its varsity tennis coach, and Academy prorector Mr. A. deLint. C.T. is beside me; the others sit, stand and stand, respectively, at the periphery of my focus. The tennis coach jingles pocket-change. There is something vaguely digestive about the room's odor. The high-traction sole of my complimentary Nike sneaker runs parallel to the wobbling loafer of my mother's half-brother, here in his capacity as Headmaster, sitting in the chair to what I hope is my immediate right, also facing Deans.

The Dean at left, a lean yellowish man whose fixed smile neverthe-

less has the impermanent quality of something stamped into uncoopera-
tive material, is a personality-type I've come lately to appreciate, the type
who delays need of any response from me by relating my side of the
story for me, to me. Passed a packet of computer-sheets by the shaggy
lion of a Dean at center, he is speaking more or less to these pages, smiling down.

'You are Harold Incandenza, eighteen, date of secondary-school
graduation approximately one month from now, attending the Enfield
Tennis Academy, Enfield, Massachusetts, a boarding school, where you
reside.' His reading glasses are rectangular, court-shaped, the sidelines
at top and bottom. 'You are, according to Coach White and Dean [un-
intelligible], a regionally, nationally, and continentally ranked junior
tennis player, a potential O.N.A.N.C.A.A. athlete of substantial promise,
recruited by Coach White via correspondence with Dr. Tavis here com-
mencing . . . February of this year.' The top page is removed and
brought around neatly to the bottom of the sheaf, at intervals. 'You
have been in residence at the Enfield Tennis Academy since age seven.'

I am debating whether to risk scratching the right side of my jaw,
where there is a wen.

'Coach White informs our offices that he holds the Enfield Tennis
Academy's program and achievements in high regard, that the
University of Arizona tennis squad has profited from the prior matricu-
lation of several former E.T.A. alumni, one of whom was one Mr.
Aubrey F. deLint, who appears also to be with you here today. Coach
White and his staff have given us—'

The yellow administrator's usage is on the whole undistinguished,
though I have to admit he's made himself understood. The Director of
Composition seems to have more than the normal number of eyebrows.
The Dean at right is looking at my face a bit strangely.

Uncle Charles is saying that though he can anticipate that the
Deans might be predisposed to weigh what he avers as coming from his
possible appearance as a kind of cheerleader for E.T.A., he can assure
the assembled Deans that all this is true, and that the Academy has
presently in residence no fewer than a third of the continent's top thirty
juniors, in age brackets all across the board, and that I here, who go by
'Hal,' usually, am 'right up there among the very cream.' Right and center Deans smile professionally; the heads of deLint and the coach in-
cline as the Dean at left clears his throat:

'—belief that you could well make, even as a freshman, a real con-
tribution to this University's varsity tennis program. We are pleased,' he
either says or reads, removing a page, 'that a competition of some
major sort here has brought you down and given us the chance to sit

down and chat together about your application and potential recruit-
ment and matriculation and scholarship.'

'I've been asked to add that Hal here is seeded third, Boys' 18-and-
Under singles, in the prestigious WhataBurger Southwest Junior
Invitational out at the Randolph Tennis Center—' says what I infer is
Athletic Affairs, his cocked head showing a freckled scalp.

'Out at Randolph Park, near the outstanding El Con Marriott,' C.T.
inserts, 'a venue the whole contingent's been vocal about finding absolutely top-hole thus far, which—'

'Just so, Chuck, and that according to Chuck here Hal has already
justified his seed, he's reached the semifinals as of this morning's apparently impressive win, and that he'll be playing out at the Center
again tomorrow, against the winner of a quarterfinal game tonight, and
so will be playing tomorrow at I believe scheduled for 0830—'

'Try to get under way before the godawful heat out there. Though
of course a dry heat.'

'—and has apparently already qualified for this winter's Continental
Indoors, up in Edmonton, Kirk tells me—' cocking further to look up
and left at the varsity coach, whose smile's teeth are radiant against a
violent sunburn—'Which is something indeed.' He smiles, looking at
me, 'Did we get all that right Hal.'

C.T. has crossed his arms casually; their triceps' flesh is webbed with
mottle in the air-conditioned sunlight. 'You sure did. Bill.' He smiles.
The two halves of his mustache never quite match. 'And let me say if I
may that Hal's excited, excited to be invited for the third year running to
the Invitational again, to be back here in a community he has real affection for, to visit with your alumni and coaching staff, to have already
justified his high seed in this week's not unstiff competition, to as they
say still be in it without the fat woman in the Viking hat having sung, so
to speak, but of course most of all to have a chance to meet you gentlemen and have a look at the facilities here. Everything here is absolutely
top-slot, from what he's seen.'

There is a silence. DeLint shifts his back against the room's pan-
elling and recenters his weight. My uncle beams and straightens a
straight watchband. 62.5% of the room's faces are directed my way,
pleasantly expectant. My chest bumps like a dryer with shoes in it. I
compose what I project will be seen as a smile. I turn this way and that,
slightly, sort of directing the expression to everyone in the room.

There is a new silence. The yellow Dean's eyebrows go circumflex.
The two other Deans look to the Director of Composition. The tennis
coach has moved to stand at the broad window, feeling at the back of
his crewcut. Uncle Charles strokes the forearm above his watch. Sharp

curved palmshadows move slightly over the pine table's shine, the one head's shadow a black moon.

'Is Hal all right, Chuck?' Athletic Affairs asks. 'Hal just seemed to . . . well, grimace. Is he in pain? Are you in pain, son?'

'Hal's right as rain,' smiles my uncle, soothing the air with a casual hand. 'Just a bit of a let's call it maybe a facial tic, slightly, at all the adrenaline of being here on your impressive campus, justifying his seed so far without dropping a set, receiving that official written offer of not only waivers but a living allowance from Coach White here, on Pac 10 letterhead, being ready in all probability to sign a National Letter of Intent right here and now this very day, he's indicated to me.' C.T. looks to me, his look horribly mild. I do the safe thing, relaxing every muscle in my face, emptying out all expression. I stare carefully into the Kekuléan knot of the middle Dean's necktie.

My silent response to the expectant silence begins to affect the air of the room, the bits of dust and sportcoat-lint stirred around by the AC's vents dancing jaggedly in the slanted plane of windowlight, the air over the table like the sparkling space just above a fresh-poured seltzer. The coach, in a slight accent neither British nor Australian, is telling C.T. that the whole application-interface process, while usually just a pleasant formality, is probably best accentuated by letting the applicant speak up for himself. Right and center Deans have inclined together in soft conference, forming a kind of teepee of skin and hair. I presume it's probably *facilitate* that the tennis coach mistook for *accentuate*, though *accelerate,* while clunkier than *facilitate,* is from a phonetic per-spective more sensible, as a mistake. The Dean with the flat yellow face has leaned forward, his lips drawn back from his teeth in what I see as concern. His hands come together on the conference table's surface. His own fingers look like they mate as my own four-X series dissolves and I hold tight to the sides of my chair.

We need candidly to chat re potential problems with my applica-tion, they and I, he is beginning to say. He makes a reference to candor and its value.

'The issues my office faces with the application materials on file from you, Hal, involve some test scores.' He glances down at a colorful sheet of standardized scores in the trench his arms have made. 'The Admissions staff is looking at standardized test scores from you that are, as I'm sure you know and can explain, are, shall we say . . . subnormal.' I'm to explain.

It's clear that this really pretty sincere yellow Dean at left is Admissions. And surely the little aviarian figure at right is Athletics, then, because the facial creases of the shaggy middle Dean are now pursed in a kind of distanced affront, an I'm-eating-something-that-makes-me-really-appreciate-the-presence-of-whatever-I'm-drinking-along-with-it look that spells professionally Academic reservations. An uncomplicated loyalty to standards, then, at center. My uncle looks to Athletics as if puzzled. He shifts slightly in his chair.

The incongruity between Admission's hand- and face-color is almost wild. '—verbal scores that are just quite a bit closer to zero than we're comfortable with, as against a secondary-school transcript from the institution where both your mother and her brother are administrators—' reading directly out of the sheaf inside his arms' ellipse— 'that this past year, yes, has fallen off a bit, but by the word I mean "fallen off" to outstanding from three previous years of frankly incredible.'

'Off the charts.'

'Most institutions do not even *have* grades of A with multiple pluses after it,' says the Director of Composition, his expression impossible to interpret.

'This kind of . . . how shall I put it . . . incongruity,' Admissions says, his expression frank and concerned, 'I've got to tell you sends up a red flag of potential concern during the admissions process.'

'We thus invite you to explain the appearance of incongruity if not outright shenanigans.' Students has a tiny piping voice that's absurd coming out of a face this big.

'Surely by *incredible* you meant very very very impressive, as opposed to literally quote "incredible," surely,' says C.T., seeming to watch the coach at the window massaging the back of his neck. The huge window gives out on nothing more than dazzling sunlight and cracked earth with heat-shimmers over it.

'Then there is before us the matter of not the required two but *nine* separate application essays, some of which of nearly monograph-length, each without exception being—' different sheet—'the adjective various evaluators used was quote "stellar"—'

Dir. of Comp.: 'I made in my assessment deliberate use of *lapidary* and *effete*.'

'—but in areas and with titles, I'm sure you recall quite well, Hal: "Neoclassical Assumptions in Contemporary Prescriptive Grammar," "The Implications of Post-Fourier Transformations for a Holographically Mimetic Cinema," "The Emergence of Heroic Stasis in Broadcast Entertainment"—'

' "Montague Grammar and the Semantics of Physical Modality"?'

' "A Man Who Began to Suspect He Was Made of Glass"?'

' "Tertiary Symbolism in Justinian Erotica"?' .

Now showing broad expanses of recessed gum. 'Suffice to say that there's some frank and candid concern about the recipient of these unfortunate test scores, though perhaps explainable test scores, being these essays' sole individual author.'

'I'm not sure Hal's sure just what's being implied here,' my uncle says. The Dean at center is fingering his lapels as he interprets distasteful computed data.

'What the University is saying here is that from a strictly academic point of view there are admissions problems that Hal needs to try to help us iron out. A matriculant's first role at the University is and must be as a student. We couldn't admit a student we have reason to suspect can't cut the mustard, no matter how much of an asset he might be on the field.'

'Dean Sawyer means the court, of course, Chuck,' Athletic Affairs says, head severely cocked so he's including the White person behind him in the address somehow. 'Not to mention O.N.A.N.C.A.A. regulations and investigators always snuffling around for some sort of whiff of the smell of impropriety.'

The varsity tennis coach looks at his own watch.

'Assuming these board scores are accurate reflectors of true capacity in this case,' Academic Affairs says, his high voice serious and sotto, still looking at the file before him as if it were a plate of something bad, 'I'll tell you right now my opinion is it wouldn't be fair. It wouldn't be fair to the other applicants. Wouldn't be fair to the University community.' He looks at me. 'And it'd be especially unfair to Hal himself. Admitting a boy we see as simply an athletic asset would amount to just using that boy. We're under myriad scrutiny to make sure we're not using anybody. Your board results, son, indicate that we could be accused of using you.'

Uncle Charles is asking Coach White to ask the Dean of Athletic Affairs whether the weather over scores would be as heavy if I were say, a revenue-raising football prodigy. The familiar panic at feeling misperceived is rising, and my chest bumps and thuds. I expend energy on remaining utterly silent in my chair, empty, my eyes two great pale zeros. People have promised to get me through this.

Uncle C.T., though, has the punched look of the cornered. His voice takes on an odd timbre when he's cornered, as if he were shouting as he receded. 'Hal's grades at E.T.A., which is I should stress an Academy, not simply a camp or factory, accredited by both the Commonwealth of Massachusetts and the North American Sports Academy Association, it's focused on the total needs of the player and student, founded by a towering intellectual figure whom I hardly need name, here, and based by him on the rigorous Oxbridge Quadrivium-Trivium curricular model, a school fully staffed and equipped, by a fully certified staff, should show that my nephew here can cut just about any Pac 10 mustard that needs cutting, and that—'

DeLint is moving toward the tennis coach, who is shaking his head.

'—would be able to see a distinct flavor of minor-sport prejudice about this whole thing,' C.T. says, crossing and recrossing his legs as I listen, composed and staring.

The room's carbonated silence is now hostile. 'I think it's time to let the actual applicant himself speak out on his own behalf,' Academic Affairs says very quietly. 'This seems somehow impossible with you here, sir.'

Athletics smiles tiredly under a hand that massages the bridge of his nose. 'Maybe you'd excuse us for a moment and wait outside, Chuck.'

'Coach White could accompany Mr. Tavis and his associate out to reception,' the yellow Dean says, smiling into my unfocused eyes.

'—led to believe this had all been ironed out in advance, from the—' C.T. is saying as he and deLint are shown to the door. The tennis coach extends a hypertrophied arm. Athletics says, 'We're all friends and colleagues here.'

This is not working out. It strikes me that EXIT signs would look to a native speaker of Latin like red-lit signs that say HE LEAVES. I would yield to the urge to bolt for the door ahead of them if I could know that bolting for the door is what the men in this room would see. DeLint is murmuring something to the tennis coach. Sounds of keyboards, phone consoles as the door is briefly opened, then firmly shut. I am alone among administrative heads.

'—offense intended to anyone,' Athletic Affairs is saying, his sportcoat tan and his necktie insigniated in tiny print—'beyond just physical abilities out there in play, which believe me we respect, *want,* believe me.'

'—question about it we wouldn't be so anxious to chat with you directly, see?'

'—that we've known in processing several prior applications through Coach White's office that the Enfield School is operated, however impressively, by close relations of first your brother, who I can still remember the way White's predecessor Maury Klamkin wooed that kid, so that grades' objectivity can be all too easily called into question—'

'By whomsoever's calling—N.A.A.U.P., ill-willed Pac 10 programs, O.N.A. N.C.A.A.—'

The essays are old ones, yes, but they are mine; *de moi.* But they are, yes, old, not quite on the application's instructed subject of Most Meaningful Educational Experience Ever. If I'd done you one from the last year, it would look to you like some sort of infant's random stabs on a keyboard, and to you, who use *whomsoever* as a subject. And in this new smaller company, the Director of Composition seems abruptly to have actuated, emerged as both the Alpha of the pack here and way more effeminate than he'd seemed at first, standing hip-shot with a hand on his waist, walking with a roll to his shoulders, jingling change as he pulls up his pants as he slides into the chair still warm from C.T.'s bottom, crossing his legs in a way that inclines him well into my personal space, so that I can see multiple eyebrow-tics and capillary webs in the oysters below his eyes and smell fabric-softener and the remains of a breath-mint turned sour.

'. . . a bright, solid, but very shy boy, we know about your being very shy, Kirk White's told us what your athletically built if rather stand-offish younger instructor told him,' the Director says softly, cupping what I feel to be a hand over my sportcoat's biceps (surely not), 'who simply needs to swallow hard and trust and tell his side of the story to these gentlemen who bear no maliciousness none at all but are doing our jobs and trying to look out for everyone's interests at the same time.'

I can picture deLint and White sitting with their elbows on their knees in the defecatory posture of all athletes at rest, deLint staring at his huge thumbs, while C.T. in the reception area paces in a tight ellipse, speaking into his portable phone. I have been coached for this like a Don before a RICO hearing. A neutral and affectless silence. The sort of all-defensive game Schtitt used to have me play: the best defense: let everything bounce off you; do nothing. I'd tell you all you want and more, if the sounds I made could be what you hear.

Athletics with his head out from under his wing: '—to avoid admission procedures that could be seen as primarily athletics-oriented. It could be a mess, son.'

'Bill means the appearance, not necessarily the real true facts of the matter, which you alone can fill in,' says the Director of Composition.

'—the appearance of the high athletic ranking, the subnormal scores, the over-academic essays, the incredible grades vortexing out of what could be seen as a nepotistic situation.'

The yellow Dean has leaned so far forward that his tie is going to have a horizontal dent from the table-edge, his face sallow and kindly and no-shit-whatever:

'Look here, Mr. Incadenza, Hal, please just explain to me why we couldn't be accused of using you, son. Why nobody could come and say to us, why, look here, University of Arizona, here you are using a boy for just his body, a boy so shy and withdrawn he won't speak up for himself, a jock with doctored marks and a store-bought application.'

The Brewster's-Angle light of the tabletop appears as a rose flush behind my closed lids. I cannot make myself understood. 'I am not just a jock,' I say slowly. Distinctly. 'My transcript for the last year might have been dickied a bit, maybe, but that was to get me over a rough spot. The grades prior to that are *de moi*.' My eyes are closed; the room is silent. 'I cannot make myself understood, now.' I am speaking slowly and distinctly. 'Call it something I ate.'

It's funny what you don't recall. Our first home, in the suburb of Weston, which I barely remember—my eldest brother Orin says he can remember being in the home's backyard with our mother and in the early spring, helping the Moms till some sort of garden out of the cold yard. March or early April. The garden's area was a rough rectangle laid out with Popsicle sticks and twine. Orin was removing rocks and hard clods from the Moms's path as she worked the rented Rototiller, a wheelbarrow-shaped, gas-driven thing that roared and snorted and bucked and he remembers seemed to propel the Moms rather than vice versa, the Moms very tall and having to stoop painfully to hold on, her feet leaving drunken prints in the tilled earth. He remembers that in the middle of the tilling I came tear-assing out the door and into the backyard wearing some sort of fuzzy red Pooh-wear, crying, holding out something he said was really unpleasant-looking in my upturned palm. He says I was around five and crying and was vividly red in the cold spring air. I was saying something over and over; he couldn't make it out until our mother saw me and shut down the tiller, ears ringing, and came over to see what I was holding out. This turned out to have been a large patch of mold—Orin posits from some dark corner of the Weston home's basement, which was warm from the furnace and flooded every spring. The patch itself he describes as horrific: darkly green, glossy, vaguely hirsute, speckled with parasitic fungal points of yellow, orange, red. Worse, they could see that the patch looked oddly incomplete, gnawed-on; and some of the nauseous stuff was smeared around my open mouth. 'I ate this,' was what I was saying. I held the patch out to the Moms, who had her contacts out for the dirty work, and at first, bending way down, saw only her crying child, hand out, proffering; and in that most maternal of reflexes she, who feared and loathed more than anything spoilage and filth, reached to take whatever her baby held out—as in how many used heavy Kleenex, spit-back candies, wads of chewed-out gum in how many theaters, airports, backseats, tournament lounges? O. stood there, he says, hefting a cold clod, playing with the Velcro on his puffy coat, watching as the Moms, bent way down to me, hand reaching, her lowering face with its presbyopic squint, suddenly stopped, froze, beginning to I.D. what it was I held out, countenancing evidence of oral contact with same. He remembers her face as past describing. Her outstretched hand, still Rototrembling, hung in the air before mine.

'I ate this,' I said.

'Pardon me?'

O. says he can only remember (sic) saying something caustic as he limboed a crick out of his back. He says he must have felt a terrible impending anxiety. The Moms refused ever even to go into the damp basement. I had stopped crying, he remembers, and simply stood there, the size and shape of a hydrant, in red PJ's with attached feet, holding out the mold, seriously, like the report of some kind of audit.

O. says his memory diverges at this point, probably as a result of anxiety. In his first memory, the Moms's path around the yard is a broad circle of hysteria:

'*God!*' she calls out.

'Help! My son ate this!' she yells in Orin's second and more fleshed-out recollection, yelling it over and over, holding the speckled patch aloft in a pincer of fingers, running around and around the garden's rectangle while O. gaped at his first real sight of adult hysteria. Suburban neighbors' heads appeared in windows and over the fences, looking. O. remembers me tripping over the garden's laid-out twine, getting up dirty, crying, trying to follow.

'God! Help! My son ate this! Help!' she kept yelling, running a tight pattern just inside the square of string; and my brother Orin remembers noting how even in hysterical trauma her flight-lines were plumb, her footprints Native-American-straight, her turns, inside the ideogram of string, crisp and martial, crying 'My son ate this! Help!' and lapping me twice before the memory recedes.

'My application's not bought,' I am telling them, calling into the darkness of the red cave that opens out before closed eyes. 'I am not just a boy who plays tennis. I have an intricate history. Experiences and feelings. I'm complex.

'I *read*,' I say. 'I study and read. I bet I've read everything you've read. Don't think I haven't. I consume libraries. I wear out spines and ROM-drives. I do things like get in a taxi and say, "The library, and step on it." My instincts concerning syntax and mechanics are better than your own, I can tell, with due respect.

'But it transcends the mechanics. I'm not a machine. I feel and believe. I have opinions. Some of them are interesting. I could, if you'd let me, talk and talk. Let's talk about anything. I believe the influence of Kierkegaard on Camus is underestimated. I believe Dennis Gabor may very well have been the Antichrist. I believe Hobbes is just Rousseau in a dark mirror. I believe, with Hegel, that transcendence is absorption. I could interface you guys right under the table,' I say, 'I'm not just a creātus, manufactured, conditioned, bred for a function.'

I open my eyes. 'Please don't think I don't care.'

I look out. Directed my way is horror. I rise from the chair. I see jowls sagging, eyebrows high on trembling foreheads, cheeks bright-white. The chair recedes below me.

'Sweet mother of Christ,' the Director says.

'I'm fine,' I tell them, standing. From the yellow Dean's expression, there's a brutal wind blowing from my direction. Academics' face has gone instantly old. Eight eyes have become blank discs that stare at whatever they see.

'Good God,' whispers Athletics.

'Please don't worry,' I say. 'I can explain.' I soothe the air with a casual hand.

Both my arms are pinioned from behind by the Director of Comp., who wrestles me roughly down, on me with all his weight. I taste floor.

'What's *wrong?*'

I say '*Nothing* is wrong.'

'It's all *right!* I'm *here!*' the Director is calling into my ear.

'Get help!' cries a Dean.

My forehead is pressed into parquet I never knew could be so cold. I am arrested. I try to be perceived as limp and pliable. My face is mashed flat; Comp.'s weight makes it hard to breathe.

'Try to listen,' I say very slowly, muffled by the floor.

'What in God's name are those . . . ,' one Dean cries shrilly, '. . . those *sounds?*'

There are clicks of a phone console's buttons, shoes' heels moving, pivoting, a sheaf of flimsy pages falling.

'*God!*'

'*Help!*'

The door's base opens at the left periphery: a wedge of the halogen hall-light, white sneakers and a scuffed Nun Bush. 'Let him *up!*' That's deLint.

'There is nothing wrong,' I say slowly to the floor. 'I'm in here.'

I'm raised by the crutches of my underarms, shaken toward what he must see as calm by a purple-faced Director: 'Get a *grip*, son!'

DeLint at the big man's arm: '*Stop* it!'

'I am not what you see and hear.'

Distant sirens. A crude half nelson. Forms at the door. A young Hispanic woman holds her palm against her mouth, looking.

'I'm not,' I say.

* * *

You have to love old-fashioned men's rooms: the citrus scent of deodorant disks in the long porcelain trough; the stalls with wooden doors in frames of cool marble; these thin sinks in rows, basins supported by rickety alphabets of exposed plumbing; mirrors over metal shelves; behind all the voices the slight sound of a ceaseless trickle, inflated by echo against wet porcelain and a cold tile floor whose mosaic pattern looks almost Islamic at this close range.

The disorder I've caused revolves all around. I've been half-dragged, still pinioned, through a loose mob of Administrative people by the Comp. Director—who appears to have thought variously that I am having a seizure (prying open my mouth to check for a throat clear of tongue), that I am somehow choking (a textbook Heimlich that left me whooping), that I am psychotically out of control (various postures and grips designed to transfer that control to him)—while about us roil deLint, trying to restrain the Director's restraint of me, the varsity tennis coach restraining deLint, my mother's half-brother speaking in rapid combinations of polysyllables to the trio of Deans, who variously gasp, wring hands, loosen neckties, waggle digits in C.T.'s face, and make *pases* with sheaves of now-pretty-clearly-superfluous application forms.

I am rolled over supine on the geometric tile. I am concentrating docilely on the question why U.S. restrooms always appear to us as infirmaries for public distress, the place to regain control. My head is cradled in a knelt Director's lap, which is soft, my face being swabbed with dusty-brown institutional paper towels he received from some hand out of the crowd overhead, staring with all the blankness I can summon into his jowls' small pocks, worst at the blurred jaw-line, of scarring from long-ago acne. Uncle Charles, a truly unparalleled slinger of shit, is laying down an enfilade of same, trying to mollify men who seem way more in need of a good brow-mopping than I.

'He's fine,' he keeps saying. 'Look at him, calm as can be, lying there.'

'You didn't see what *happened* in there,' a hunched Dean responds through a face webbed with fingers.

'Excited, is all he gets, sometimes, an excitable kid, impressed with—'

'But the *sounds* he made.'

'Undescribable.'

'Like an animal.'

'*Sub*animalistic noises and sounds.'

'Nor let's not forget the *gestures*.'

'Have you ever gotten *help* for this boy Dr. Tavis?'

'Like some sort of animal with something in its mouth.'

'This boy is damaged.'

'Like a stick of butter being hit with a mallet.'

'A writhing animal with a knife in its eye.'

'What were you possibly *about,* trying to enroll this—'

'And his *arms.*'

'You didn't see it, Tavis. His arms were—'

'Flailing. This sort of awful reaching drumming wriggle. *Waggling,*' the group looking briefly at someone outside my sight trying to demonstrate something.

'Like a time-lapse, a flutter of some sort of awful . . . growth.'

'Sounded most of all like a drowning goat. A goat, drowning in something viscous.'

'This strangled series of bleats and—'

'Yes they *waggled.*'

'So suddenly a bit of excited waggling's a crime, now?'

'You, sir, are in trouble. You are *in trouble.*'

'His face. As if he was strangling. Burning. I believe I've seen a vision of hell.'

'He has some trouble communicating, he's communicatively challenged, no one's denying that.'

'The boy needs *care.*'

'Instead of caring for the boy you send him here to *enroll, compete?*'

'Hal?'

'You have not in your most dreadful fantasies dreamt of the amount of *trouble* you have bought yourself, Dr. so-called Headmaster, *educator.*'

'. . . were given to understand this was all just a formality. You took him aback, is all. Shy—'

'And you, White. You sought to *recruit* him!'

'—and terribly impressed and excited, in there, without us, his support system, whom you asked to leave, which if you'd—'

'I'd only seen him play. On court he's gorgeous. Possibly a genius. We had no idea. The brother's in the bloody NFL for God's sake. Here's a top player, we thought, with Southwest roots. His stats were off the chart. We watched him through the whole WhataBurger last fall. Not a waggle or a noise. We were watching ballet out there, a mate remarked, after.'

'Damn right you were watching ballet out there, White. This boy is a balletic athlete, a player.'

'Some kind of athletic savant then. Balletic compensation for deep problems which *you* sir choose to disguise by muzzling the boy in there.'

An expensive pair of Brazilian espadrilles goes by on the left and enters a stall, and the espadrilles come around and face me. The urinal trickles behind the voices' small echoes.

'—haps we'll just be on our way,' C.T. is saying.

'The integrity of my sleep has been forever compromised, sir.'

'—think you could pass off a damaged applicant, fabricate credentials and shunt him through a kangaroo-interview and inject him into all the rigors of college life?'

'Hal here *functions,* you ass. Given a supportive situation. He's fine when he's by himself. Yes he has some trouble with excitability in conversation. Did you once hear him try to deny that?'

'We witnessed something only marginally *mammalian* in there, sir.'

'Like hell. Have a look. How's the excitable little guy doing down there, Aubrey, does it look to you?'

'You, sir, are quite possibly ill. This affair is not concluded.'

'What *ambulance?* Don't you guys *listen?* I'm telling you there's—'

'Hal? Hal?'

'Dope him up, seek to act as his mouthpiece, muzzling, and now he lies there catatonic, staring.'

The crackle of deLint's knees. 'Hal?'

'—inflate this publicly in any distorted way. The Academy has distinguished alumni, litigators at counsel. Hal here is provably competent. Credentials out the bazoo, Bill. The boy reads like a vacuum. *Digests* things.'

I simply lie there, listening, smelling the paper towel, watching an espadrille pivot.

'There's more to life than sitting there interfacing, it might be a newsflash to you.'

And who could not love that special and leonine roar of a public toilet?

Not for nothing did Orin say that people outdoors down here just scuttle in vectors from air conditioning to air conditioning. The sun is a hammer. I can feel one side of my face start to cook. The blue sky is glossy and fat with heat, a few thin cirri sheared to blown strands like hair at the rims. The traffic is nothing like Boston. The stretcher is the special type, with restraining straps at the extremities. The same Aubrey deLint I'd dismissed for years as a 2-D martinet knelt gurneyside to squeeze my restrained hand and say 'Just hang in there, Buckaroo,' before moving back into the administrative fray at the ambulance's doors. It is a special ambulance, dispatched from I'd rather not dwell on where, with not only paramedics but some kind of psychiatric M.D. on board. The medics lift gently and are handy with straps. The M.D., his back up against the ambulance's side, has both hands up in dispassionate mediation between the Deans and C.T., who keeps stabbing skyward with his cellular's antenna as if it were a sabre, outraged that I'm being needlessly ambulanced off to some Emergency Room against my will and interests. The issue whether the damaged even have interested wills is shallowly hashed out as some sort of ultra-mach fighter too high overhead to hear slices the sky from south to north. The M.D. has both hands up and is patting the air to signify dispassion. He has a big blue jaw. At the only other emergency room I have ever been in, almost exactly one year back, the psychiatric stretcher was wheeled in and then parked beside the waiting-room chairs. These chairs were molded orange plastic; three of them down the row were occupied by different people all of whom were holding empty prescription bottles and perspiring freely. This would have been bad enough, but in the end chair, right up next to the strap-secured head of my stretcher, was a T-shirted woman with barnwood skin and a trucker's cap and a bad starboard list who began to tell me, lying there restrained and immobile, about how she had seemingly overnight suffered a sudden and anomalous gigantism in her right breast, which she referred to as a titty; she had an almost parodic Québecois accent and described the 'titty's' presenting history and possible diagnoses for almost twenty minutes before I was rolled away. The jet's movement and trail seem incisionish, as if white meat behind the blue were exposed and widening in the wake of the blade. I once saw the word *KNIFE* finger-written on the steamed mirror of a nonpublic bathroom. I have become an infantophile. I am forced to roll my closed eyes either up or to the side to keep the red cave from bursting into flames from the sunlight. The street's passing traffic is constant and seems to go 'Hush, hush, hush.' The sun, if your fluttering eye catches it even slightly, gives you the blue and red floaters a flashbulb gives you. 'Why *not?* Why *not?* Why not *not*, then, if the best reasoning you can contrive is why not?' C.T.'s voice, receding with outrage. Only the gallant stabs of his antenna are now visible, just inside my sight's right frame. I will be conveyed to an Emergency Room of some kind, where I will be detained as long as I do not respond to questions, and then, when I do respond to questions, I will be sedated; so it will be inversion of standard travel, the ambulance and ER: I'll make the journey first, then depart. I think very briefly of the late Cosgrove Watt. I think of the hypophalangial Grief-Therapist. I think of the Moms, alphabetizing cans of soup in the cabinet over the microwave. Of Himself's umbrella hung by its handle from the edge of the mail table just inside the Headmaster's House's foyer. The bad ankle hasn't ached once this whole year. I think of John N. R. Wayne, who would have won this year's WhataBurger, standing watch in a mask as Donald Gately and

I dig up my father's head. There's very little doubt that Wayne would have won. And Venus Williams owns a ranch outside Green Valley; she may well attend the 18's Boys' and Girls' finals. I will be out in plenty of time for tomorrow's semi; I trust Uncle Charles. Tonight's winner is almost sure to be Dymphna, sixteen but with a birthday two weeks under the April 15 deadline; and Dymphna will still be tired tomorrow at 0830, while I, sedated, will have slept like a graven image. I have never before faced Dymphna in tournament play, nor played with the sonic balls the blind require, but I watched him barely dispatch Petropolis Kahn in the Round of 16, and I know he is mine.

It will start in the E.R., at the intake desk if C.T.'s late in following the ambulance, or in the green-tiled room after the room with the invasive-digital machines; or, given this special M.D.-supplied ambulance, maybe on the ride itself: some blue-jawed M.D. scrubbed to an antiseptic glow with his name sewn in cursive on his white coat's breast pocket and a quality desk-set pen, wanting gurneyside Q&A, etiology and diagnosis by Socratic method, ordered and point-by-point. There are, by the *O.E.D. VI*'s count, nineteen nonarchaic synonyms for *unresponsive,* of which nine are Latinate and four Saxonic. I will play either Stice or Polep in Sunday's final. Maybe in front of Venus Williams. It will be someone blue-collar and unlicensed, though, inevitably—a nurse's aid with quick-bit nails, a hospital security guy, a tired Cuban orderly who addresses me as *jou*—who will, looking down in the middle of some kind of bustled task, catch what he sees as my eye and ask So yo then man what's *your* story?

*Emmeline Chang's short story considers the love between fathers and sons, the way in which that love so often manifests itself as rage, and how both love and rage find their expression in competitive athletics, sometimes simultaneously.*

# Forty, Love

## Emmeline Chang

I am going to see my father for the first time in ten years. Whether he commanded it or requested it, I don't know, because the news came through my mother, as all news of my father has since I was thirty. A stroke.

When she first told me, the word didn't register. It was tennis I thought of. Me, a nervous and wiry fifteen, waiting. Legs apart, knees bent, my upper body swaying from side to side. Watching my father. The ball flying, fear and movement—stumbling into position, yanking my arm back. Stroke. The moment of contact. Relief.

My mother cleared her throat, and I came back to the present: me in London, in an Islington flat, my mother in Fairbridge, Connecticut. I thought of my sister confined to bed with a problem pregnancy in L.A. and imagined my mother moving from room to room, alone against the blue-scrolled wallpaper, cream carpets, and heavy furniture. My father bent and broken in their king-size bed. Guilt flooded me.

"Mom. Are you okay?"

"Well," she said. "Yes, I am fine." She paused. "He would like you to come home."

Did I want to? Yes, like all sons who are raised to be dutiful. No, like any person who has made the painful but necessary decision to cut off a relationship. But when I tried to cut off the filial feeling towards my father, my feelings of responsibility towards my mother welled up, doubled or tripled in strength like new creepers pushing through the ground after old ones have been tamped down, smothered.

So here I am, outside the tall brick house with its porch flanked by white columns. Sitting in my car, hoping that I won't see my mother's shadow moving behind the curtains. Because then the guilt would begin to trickle, and I would have to go in.

What will he look like, after so many years? I remember seeing my mother last summer, searching for clues to his appearance in her own. New York was bustling past our sidewalk table, but all I noticed were the deepened curves of her laugh lines, the fragile set of her collarbone, the pale muscle of her upper arms. Yes, her skin was thinner, more lined. I imagined deeper thought lines on his forehead, age spots on his chest. Had his muscles thinned and weakened? But she looked fit. She was taking care of herself. Surely my father, who had to be the best at everything, was exercising aggressively.

I look out at the house. Apparently I was wrong. I sigh. Around me, the car is damp with the vapor from my breath. It is chilly. I take my leather gloves from my coat pocket, stroke their smooth folds. The supple surfaces and pungent scent ease my nerves. Touching the gloves, I always feel an assurance; I feel the ease of quality and comfort and success, how those things can be shaped into something I hold in my hands. It's like the way I feel when I finish a workout with my trainer and sense the long muscles of my arms, the loose strength beneath my satisfied fatigue. Outside, only the occasional car turns onto the street; the Friday evening rush hour is over. Dusk is deepening the color of the sky above the houses, the quiet oaks and elms. The engine purrs. It's only a rental car, but it's the same model I drive in London. I press down ever so slightly on the gas pedal. It seems I need the sound of a well-tuned BMW to tell me that I am a successful man.

In earlier years, I needed my father to tell me. Why else would I have let him drill me like that, hour after hour, day after day? Even now, when I look at the house, those high school days come back to me. I feel it in every muscle. My arms, legs, back, even my eyes—fatigue fills every fiber.

I remember hot, sunny days, the shadows of the net and posts sharp against the surface of the court. "Volley! Volley!" he shouted. "Why don't you run for it?" He sliced his racket downward. I swung and missed, cursed my muscles. The ball smashed into the ground beyond me and bounced on, fast and hard.

I kill the engine and jerk the door open. The house waits for me. I stride toward it. I was determined then, and I'm determined now. But now I'm forty, I'm not cowed by him, and I know this is just a weekend, not a match whose outcome will determine my future.

"Mi-chael!" my mother cries when she opens the door. "Already past seven o'clock. We were waiting." She looks composed but more fragile than before, her hair swept back and curled under, a crown of white beginning to show beneath the black strands. "Why are you so late?" she says. I imagine him in the dark hush of the family room behind us, listening.

"Work." My eyes slide past her. A wood safety gate blocks off the wide, curving stairway. The Chinese-style urns are gone from the foyer. Meanwhile, my voice goes on as if things were normal, too loud for this subdued house. "You know the New York office. As soon as you get in from out of town, it's meeting after meeting . . ." It's true, but it's also true that I didn't have to arrange those meetings. "I'm sorry, Ma. You're alone with him all the time."

"No, the home-help workers and the speech therapist, they come." She unfolds a paper from her sweater pocket, touches an imaginary pair of glasses, and shifts into a stance that suggests a stout, chesty woman. "All raht, Missus Kim, Ah've prepared a list of words your husband have trouble with. *Ig*norance, *arg*uments, de*ci*sions . . ." She folds the paper, and her stance returns to normal.

I force a smile. "That accent is great, Ma. And your body movements." It's a good thing she has her acting. I don't think a subservient Asian woman could have survived with my father, but my mother wasn't like that—she headed the mostly white PTA, organized fund-raisers for the local theater, even acted in their plays. Has this stroke taken too large a toll on her independence? I touch her arm. "This therapist sounds helpful."

"Yes, very helpful, this Carol Beth lady," my mother says. "I just do small things. Practice the words with him. We practice Korean words, too. Also I help him change clothes. Put everything on the right side so he will notice it. He has a little bit of left-side neglect."

*Left-side neglect.* I imagine all the other terms I've never heard, a whole thick medical file of them. My mother smiles at me, her eyes still light inside their gentle folds of skin. "A few days ago I have to put special pads in his underwear—not exactly like the young, romantic days." She covers her small, lipsticked mouth with her hand for a moment—just a fleeting second of vulnerability that makes me think, *Korean wife*—and then she slaps my bottom gently. "Go. You have been a bad son so many years. See if he has a plan for how you can make it up."

My father had a plan for everything, which was *forward, upward. Forward and upward, faster and harder.* Direction and discipline had gotten him from his father's stationery store to medical school to a country-club membership and the most respected surgical practice in Fairbridge. He was a solid man with a heavy chest and shoulders, a man who got up at five every morning to do a hundred push-ups and swim a mile in our backyard swimming pool. My sister, Annette, and I were caterpillars before the force of his breath and will. Despite the demands of his practice, he drilled us in spelling and multiplication, then algebra, the butterfly stroke and chemistry, tennis and calculus and the SATs—even French, which he couldn't speak. I endured this, sweating and panting, 'til bedtime, while my sister, the girl child, glided off by mid-evening to "help Mom with the housework" or "help Mom prepare for her show." I can still remember those drills. Hour after hour. Serves, volleys, drives, backhands. The sky darkened and the wind cooled while I sprinted for the ball, trying to make out the yellow-green smudge in the falling dusk. Afterward I labored under the glow of my fluorescent lamp, working math problems in blunt pencil on the rough, acidic paper of the SAT prep books. My father sat beside me with a stack of medical journals. I felt his heat and bulk, breathed the muffling odor of kimchee and beer. Sometimes fatigue filled me like hot air. I struggled to focus on the page and hold my eyes open. Then a loud snap shocked me awake: my father slapping the desk with his journal. "Concentrate! Keep working!" I stared at the page, my eyes watering. Mute anger and obedience roiled inside me. I was numb; I was a soldier stumbling forward. My father was a force that could not be stopped.

But a body is a machine. And it can only be pushed so far.

I pause in the family-room doorway. The sofas and coffee table are gone; a twin bed and dark TV have replaced the antique Korean-style writing table that sat along the far wall. Only the lacquered altar and leather reclining chair are left. Silence lies over the room like a husk. I can barely look at the circle of lamplight in the corner.

"Mi-chael?" My father's voice cracks the stillness.

"Yes." I step forward, and the habit of respect bows my head. At the edge of my vision I can see his feet propped on the reclining chair's footrest. He wears gray hospital socks with non-skid stripes across the sole. To the side I see the thin metallic legs of a walker. I think of the strong thighs that carried him across the court, bounding toward whatever spot I sent the ball to.

"Well. So now you final-ly—" The sounds are slack, yet also forced; his muscles have struggled to make the sounds. "You finally come to your father," he says. I force myself to look at him.

He is wrapped in a blanket. Above it, his face pokes out. *He is ruined,* I think. He is a proud Indian chief with black eyes that stare out from beyond a paralyzed droop of skin. His hair sticks out in gray and white tufts.

"I'm sorry, Dad." The words come from my mouth before I'm aware of them. Sorry? Is this what I feel, when he insulted my wife and said my son should not be born? Even the word "Dad" sounds strange, wrong for our formal, removed relationship.

"No," he says.

"No? What do you mean?"

He shakes his head. His mouth tries to form a word. He struggles to shape the necessary muscles, then lifts his hand in a short, dismissive wave.

"Come on. You have to explain what you mean."

His eyes look out at me. Nothing.

"I don't understand." Does he mean, *No, you're not sorry?* Or, *No, I do not accept an apology?* I have come all this way, I am not even sure I want to talk to him again, but he cannot reject me without saying why. If this is a rejection. "Dad, I don't understand *No.*"

I stare into his unblinking eyes. There is anger there. I recognize it. The same anger that burned across the court when I screwed up a shot.

"Dad, tell me!"

His mouth tightens. Nothing else. He will not make an effort to tell me. He will let me feel the full weight of his stare; he is going to let that *No* hang there, a force I can't counter.

"Dad!" I put my hand on his shoulder and shake. "You Have To Tell Me. *I. Don't. Understand.*"

"Michael!"

I whirl when I hear my mother's voice. Drop my arm in shame.

"What are you doing?" There is shock, disbelief—disappointment—in her eyes.

"I was just trying to understand him. He was saying something—"

"Do you understand that your father is sick?"

"I do. Of course."

She looks at me as if I'm someone she doesn't know. I drop my eyes and turn and walk from the room, defeated.

I know this is not the way to return. Whether I want to vent a righteous anger, undo the things that happened years ago, or seek absolution, I have not done it. And cannot, like this. I never knew how to deal with my father. I could stumble along and do my best to keep time with his onward press, but I could never leave the forced march. Of course, I had my own hopes. During my sophomore year of high school, I wanted an after-school job to pay for a car, gas, dates with the girls I would take out in my car. I had never before succeeded at swaying my father, but this time I was determined. I laid out logical arguments, pointed at the straight A's on my report card, mapped out schedules to show that a job would not interfere with my studying or my sports.

He brushed it aside: "We provide for you so you don't waste your time. Anywhere you want to go, your mother can take you. You concentrate on studying and working hard."

I didn't let up.

"You are being ridiculous!" my father finally exclaimed, looking up from the spread pages of my calculus homework. "You put a job and a car ahead of everything else. How will you ever succeed in life? You aren't even serious enough at tennis to be good."

I stared down at the handwritten equations. "I'm getting better," I insisted. "I am."

"Hah. You think that is good enough?" He picked up my latest test and slapped it down in front of me as if to say, *Only a 92.* "At tennis I can beat you straight, no points for you." He stared at my stubborn face. "What do you say about that?"

I flushed. "You've had more practice!"

"Practice, then. You practice until you can beat me—with no points for me. If you can, I let you get a car and a job. Provided your grades don't drop."

I practiced all fall and winter. I stayed after school to practice on the courts and spent hours at the concrete backboard down the road. I remember leaves skittering across the asphalt there, the sting of wind against my curled hands, evenings when I tasted the first snowflakes before I quit. When winter came, I moved to the Y. Forehand drives, backhand slices, volleys, drop shots, rushes to the net. I practiced serves, topspin lobs, hitting the same spot five times in a row. Icicles melted, and water trickled from the eaves. I enlisted the tennis-team captain in my mission. In my accelerated math class, we finished differential calculus and moved on to integrals. By March, I thought I had a chance. In April, the first blossoms appeared on the trees outside the school, and I beat the tennis-team captain for the tenth time. Finally, at the end of April, I faced my father on the court.

There he was, the man who had been setting the standards for me all my life. He was all solid chest and arms and thighs. Thick locks of hair pushed out from behind his sweatband. My body seemed suddenly to be made of wrists and oversized feet. He bounced a ball with his racket and laid down the rules. I had one game to beat him. I would have the first serve. As long as one person kept winning consecutive points, we would keep score as usual. But, as soon as the other took back the serve, the score would reset: love, love. We would play until someone lost.

I nodded, turned my racket in my sweating hands.

I can still feel those moments. I toss the ball up. My racket connects, and the ball cuts through the air, a direct line to the spot I want. My father's eyes widen, but he reacts, returns the serve. The ball comes to me and I stretch out to meet it. My racket carves the air, clean and strong, and *thwock*—the ball sails back across the court. Once, then again, and then once more. Perfect placement, every time. My father runs, pivots, leans for a shot—he plays as well as I've ever seen him play. But I win the point.

"Fifteen, love," I say. I try to keep my voice calm, but inside I'm leaping and bounding. *You see, you see, you see how I've improved. I can do this, you know I can.*

We play, and the blue sky comes down to meet the court. My muscles open, my arm hums with power, the ball sings through the air.

"Thirty, love," I say. And then, "Forty, love."

Game point. The day shimmers around me; we are playing on a game board perfectly balanced at the top of the world. Behind me, the hours of practice slope away. Ahead, the future rises to meet me and I can see my car, my girlfriend, my life. I look at my father. He is strong, tan. He is the best doctor in the county, and I love him immensely. Then I see the nervous way he grips his racket, the way he swipes at his brow. He is afraid, I see. And proud, so proud of me, prouder than he has ever been. But still, he is determined.

Something in me twists. I don't think I can bear it, to see this man who stands so proud, who came from Korea to work in his father's store, who pulled himself through college and med school and pulled his whole family with him—I don't think I can bear to see this man defeated.

I gather myself in. I toss the ball, bring my racket through the air. But this time my racket wavers, the ball lands just beyond my intended spot. Still, I play well. I play with all my skill, all my body. But my father wins the point. And the score resets: love, love.

From there it is downhill. I win back the serve. I win a point, then another. But I can't keep it going, can't keep my father from coming back in. We are fifteen, love. Thirty, love. And the score resets. The score resets, again and again. The sun streaks the sky with brilliant color and sets. The sky darkens. I ask if we should go home. *No,* my father says, *keep going! You want this, you can't give up.* My arm hurts. I begin to hold it between points. And despite the deepening chill in the air, my throat is so parched it's hard to breathe. *Dad,* I say. *I think we should stop. Maybe we can try this another day.* But my father serves the ball again. *Where is your willpower?* he growls. *Where is your will to succeed?* I hit a backhand. Another. I try to slice and my racket veers; the ball smacks into the net. *Please,* I say. I can see by my watch that it's 9:00. Only a lone streetlamp casts light in our direction. I picture my mother and sister at the table before untouched bowls of kimchee. My father is indefatigable, invincible. Soon 9:30 passes, and then 10:00. I trip and see my elongated shadow stumble across the court. We aren't even stopping to rest between points. I'm sore and tired, hungry, angry; I don't care anymore. It's 10:45; the score has just reset one more time. I don't know how to end this game, it's clear I won't get the car or job or anything else I dreamed of, and I just want a way to go home. I wonder if he is doing this to end the bet, to make sure I never stand up for myself again. *Please,* I say, one last time. *Let's go home.* My father stares at me as if he hasn't heard and serves the ball again. And then I do something I am ashamed of to this day. I stumble forward and hit the ball into the net. *What was that?!* my father roars, but I don't look at him. *Your serve,* I say, and toss him the ball. The ball comes smashing towards me. I can't jump out of its way—I can't be as blatant as that—and with that thought I swing, wildly. The ball bounces off the side of my racket and rolls into the fence. Thirty love. Forty love. *This is it,* my father shouts. The ball flies over the net, bounces into the service court, and rises towards me. My father has run to the net; he is holding his racket as he stares at me, slack-jawed; and I know that a quick turn of my racket will put it where he can never return it. I run toward the ball, raise my racket in surrender, and watch it sail past me, out of bounds.

My father said nothing as he watched the ball go. Then he dropped his racket arm and shook his head. I'll never forget the way he looked at me as we left the court. I have not played tennis since that day.

In the morning I make myself hurry down to the family room. My mother is standing by my father's reclining chair, balancing a plastic basin on the hospital sidearm table. I stop. My father is rubbing his face with a washcloth. With his eyes squeezed shut and his glasses off, he looks vulnerable, like a boy. I feel the air leaving me. I drop into a chair beside him. It may be that I had to come home, but I can feel just as well that there is no point. The weekend stretches out before me like a dusty road.

My mother takes the washcloth from my father, then lifts the basin. Her shoulders sag forward. The suggestion of fatigue makes me ashamed. I stand up to take the basin from her. I will be the dutiful son. I will help my mother. I will get through.

"No, I am okay." My mother stops me with one hand and takes the basin into the powder room.

I lean over to pour my father a glass of water. "Do you need anything?" I ask.

He lowers his head towards the sidearm table. I pull a tissue from its box and give it to him.

"No?" I move my hand toward his glasses. "These? The phone?" He shakes his head. "Or this?" The soft cloth for his glasses. The TV remote. A device made of a breathing spout, a tube marked with millimeter lines, and a squared-off handle with a smiley-face lodged inside. "What do you want?"

My father lowers his head further and gestures beneath the sidearm table with one hand. I bend down and see a translucent plastic container with a round, snap-on lid.

"Yes, yes. This," my father says, and I pick it up.

"What is it?" I say, but he doesn't answer. He makes another gesture, impatient, and I give it to him. "I'm sorry, I don't understand," I say.

Behind me, my mother says, "He doesn't want you to look." My father is already lifting the sheet draped across his lap and sliding the container underneath. I turn away, not knowing whether I should reach for the container when he finishes, or pretend that it doesn't exist. I turn the TV on and flip past golf, a cooking channel, some Saturday morning cartoons, trying not to hear the sound of liquid streaming against plastic. Then I feel callous and turn back for the container. My father ignores me and hands the container to my mother. I look away, occupy myself with rearranging the items on his table. From the powder room comes the sound of liquid pouring, then the toilet's flush. When my mother comes out, she has a pink flower in her hand.

"For the hero," she says, holding it out to my father.

"A cripple," he retorts. "Not a hero."

"Your father is a temporary crippled crank," she says to me, but she is smiling. She kisses him on the mouth and slips the flower into his hand. She isn't wearing her usual pink nail polish and rings, but her nails are neatly clipped and glossed. Her stretchy pink jacket curves in neatly at the waist. Three weeks of helping him, and she still looks so composed. Pramila would have locks of hair straggling around her ears, a stained sweatshirt that went with her hangnails, but not her Lady Rolex. Pramila squeezes dozens of accomplishments into each day, but she is rarely organized.

"Silly," my mother says to him as she straightens up. My father's lips twitch, and he struggles to smile with both sides of his mouth. He stops, self-conscious, and puts the flower behind his ear. When her eyes meet his, he bends in a slight bow. My mother flushes and raises her hand to her mouth.

*They love each other.* In all these years, I have never truly seen this, too distracted with cars and jobs and my own choices in life. I feel a twinge: Now it is too late for me to absorb their wisdom and good habits. I will go back to Pramila, the friction of our callused lives, the distance that's widened into a decision to divorce. In sickness and in health, we vowed. But I have failed. Pramila will never take care of me like this.

We were married overseas. Pramila and I were posted in London the year I was thirty. I knew the time was right: We had been together for more than a year, the main-office gossip mill was across the ocean, and her London family had given me the nod. But before I proposed, I wanted to call my father.

"I thought you might decide this," he said. "But really, I do not think it is a good idea."

"Listen, Dad. Just come out and spend the holidays with us." I had a vision of Pramila stepping into the candlelit entrance of an old church, snowflakes on her eyelashes, laughing and glowing from the cold as she pushed back the fur-trimmed hood of her coat; and I ached with wanting my parents to see this, too. "Pramila's like you in a lot of ways—intense, really driven—"

"I'm sorry, Michael. We have many things to do here."

"Just the holidays, Dad. Some family time. Christmas."

"I don't think so."

I tried to swallow my frustration. I leaned my forehead against the window sash. Across the street, two Pakistani teenagers were standing outside the kebab place. One of them stood with his shoulder sticking out, vulnerable. The pose reminded me of Pramila's youngest brother.

"Then we'll come visit you," I said.

"No," he said. "I do not want you to. I cannot—what is the word?—condone this marriage."

"You can't—" I felt as if I had been punched in the stomach. That he would be so direct. That he would not even give it a chance. "I'm getting married. And you don't even want to meet my wife." My voice was flat. "Okay, then."

There was silence, and then my father spoke. "Michael. Believe me." I could hear the emotion in his voice. "I am thinking of you."

He was thinking of me. If only he could understand. "Dad, I hear you. But listen to yourself. You're being racist."

"No. Of course we would like if you marry a Korean American, someone with the same background." He paused. "But if you don't like Korean ladies, I prefer you marry a white."

"That's enough, Dad."

"Michael, I know your emotions are involved. But I have experience, I am an outsider. I tell you, society is not so simple—"

I hung up the phone. My hand was shaking. I needed some air. I pushed the window wide open. A constable came out of the coffee shop on our side of the street and glanced at the Pakistani kids. They slouched defiantly; the constable gave them a warning look. I turned away. I detested politics, but it was clear. The British were a bunch of bastards high on their power and feelings of superiority, and the Americans were just a friendlier version of the same thing. You only had to remember the condescending way soldiers had talked about Korea when they returned from the war. How could my father take part? The phone rang, and I grabbed it.

"Yes?"

"Listen, Michael. I know you don't like what I say, but I say it anyway. It is not just that your wife is darker, your children will be darker, too."

"Yes, I'm aware of that."

"You know what I experience when I come to America. I'm sure Mommy tell you—"

"Thanks, Dad. But I don't want to hear how my kids with Pramila shouldn't be born. And I don't want them hearing that from their grandfather."

"So you have already decided. You don't even ask my opinion."

"Believe me, no one has to seek your opinion. You're ready to volunteer it whether we—"

"Michael, don't talk to your parents that way. Your mother and I—"

"Leave Mom out of this."

"Mommy is my wife."

"And Pramila's going to be mine," I say.

It was after this conversation that I decided. He was an insidious growth seeping from my bones, taking over my muscles and my blood. Some things have to be sliced out. Sometimes it's incredibly painful. Sometimes you think you'll die. But it has to be done. How, though, do you remove someone from your life? If they've shaped you so deeply, they are everywhere. In places, in situations. No matter how far you go.

"Oh, Mike, look. Wouldn't a game be perfect now?" That was Pramila as we were walking one afternoon. Our son had just turned six, and we had left him with a baby-sitter for the first time. Our first full day alone in years. She turned to me, her eyes dark and shining. "The weather, Mike. Look. The sky. And look at that court."

"Pramila. You know how I feel about it."

"Come on, just a few strokes. Nothing serious."

"I'll pass."

She eyed me. "I'm telling you, you really need to talk about your father. Get it out." She pushed a few wisps of hair from her face. "I'm here, you know."

"There's nothing to talk about."

"Sure there is. You can't even walk onto a court and swat a ball back and forth."

"I *know* what it is," I said. "I've analyzed all that. I just don't play tennis anymore."

"Fine." She shrugged. "Don't try to clear up the things that stunt you." She turned from the tennis court and began striding down the sidewalk.

"Stunt me?" I said, angrily. I caught up to her. "Look, if you're going to insult me . . ." I felt stupid hurrying alongside her. "Listen, you're the one who's with such a stunted, emotionally maimed husband."

"I know," she said.

* * *

Caring for a stroke survivor is work that goes on and on. I drape a towel around my father's neck. My mother hands me the electric razor and I shave him, trying to go over all of his cheeks and jaws and chin. I imagine the razor vibrating against the nerves on his left side, loosening the fibers that thread back into his stubborn brain. My father winces and I jerk the razor away, guilty.

My mother sets the basin in front of my father again and hands him a toothbrush; he brushes. Thank God he's right-handed, I think. My mother brings a tray laden with round white bowls: soft rice, salted seaweed, marinated soybeans, golden mushrooms steeped in sesame oil, green onions in hot sauce, anchovies. He mashes spoonfuls of food against the inside of his bowl before bringing them to his mouth. I'm relieved to see that he eats by himself, but it's hard to watch his awkward efforts.

We bring him a shirt from the closet and help him put it on. The shirt is a soft flannel; all the buttons have been replaced by Velcro strips. I turn on the TV, help him shift when he's uncomfortable. My mother directs most of these things, and I am thankful, because at least this way my ignorance is obscured. I'm reminded of how Pramila directed me in taking care of Philip. He was so small I was afraid I might hurt him just by touching him the wrong way. I remember feeling that he was so much mine, so much ours—I would shelter him, feed him with my body if I had to. With Philip there is none of the ambivalence I feel with my father. And still, this is the son I brought to tears.

He is eight years old, and he has had training wheels for two years now. Far too long, in my view. So I took him to the park. Pramila came with me, something she's rarely done of late.

"Today's the day," I said. Philip looked at me, scared. He knew what I meant, and he watched with wide eyes as I unscrewed the bolts and detached the small wheels from the sides of his bike. As I removed them, the wheels seemed sad and vulnerable: for a moment, I wondered if I were doing the right thing.

"All right, Philip. Up you go." I watched as he straddled the seat and stretched his legs and toes to touch the ground. "Right. You can let go now."

Pramila watched silently.

"Go," I said. "Philip, go." He looked at me, scared, then glanced at Pramila. She smiled encouragement. He screwed up his face. I could tell he was gathering courage. I held my breath. He picked up a foot.

*Yes,* I thought. I closed my eyes, and then I heard him push off, heard the whir of bicycle spokes in the breeze.

"Philip . . ." Pramila said. Her voice was high, strangled. My eyes popped open. There was my son, running in strange tiptoe fashion, swaying from one toe to the other, the bike pulled along beneath.

"Philip!" I shouted. "Stop it. Put your feet up. There's nothing to be scared of!" But my son kept toeing his way down the road. "Philip, god-damnit. Pedal! *Pedal!*"

When he stopped, my son was in tears. Pramila gathered him into her arms, turned her back on me, and began walking in the direction of our flat. And I stood there squinting into the afternoon sun, burning with anger and fear, and love.

During my father's midafternoon nap, the phone rings. My mother answers.

"Oh," she says. "Nice to hear from you. Are you two finished eating dinner? You must be so busy, taking care of everything by yourself." I stiffen. My father is blinking awake. Pramila and I live in such thick silence, I'm shocked that she's even called. Perhaps it's for my mother's sake. The two of them have always tried to build a normal in-law relationship, and over the years they've gotten fairly close, though knowing each other almost entirely through phone calls has put a certain formality into the way they speak. I try to read my mother's body language, her words. Is it possible Pramila is changing her mind? My mother knows about the decision; maybe she can do something magical to bring Pramila back. Maybe with me far away, Pramila will remember how much she likes my mother, how she wouldn't want to lose a mother-in-law.

My father struggles to readjust his blanket. He frowns at me, as if he is adding the situation up in his mind. Surely he's wondering why Pramila doesn't stop talking to my mother, why she isn't asking to speak to her own husband. My mother has promised not to tell him, but still—what has he figured out? What has she let slip? I move towards my mother, trying to signal subtly for the phone. She smiles at me and continues talking. She nods at something Pramila has said, laughs, waves for me to wait. I stare out into the room, then realize I am tapping my foot. I stop myself, give my mother another significant look.

"Well, I think Michael is ready to talk to you," she says. Then, "Oh. Not even for a minute? Oh, of course. Of course you must be very busy."

Heat rises in my face. I can't even look at my father. How can Pramila do this to me? For the first time, the divorce begins to seem real.

I can barely look at my mother when she hangs up the phone.

"She is just so busy," my mother says. "Going crazy. She just wanted to find out how Daddy was. Or maybe she is just paying you back for so many business trips." My mother smiles. "In the past I think of doing the same thing to your father when he stayed at the office too long."

She pinches my cheek affectionately. "Spend more time with her." I smile, and try to make it look real.

"Right," I say. "Maybe I have to make an appointment to spend time with her if she's so busy." I wonder if our joking has covered up anything.

"Oh!" my mother says. "Speaking of appointment." "She glances at her watch and looks around for her purse. It takes me a moment to realize what she is doing.

"You're going out?" I try to conceal my horror.

"First time in three weeks!" My mother smiles. "I need a break from this old man. I have to color my hair so I don't look like his old wife."

"Mom, you can't." The naked urgency in my voice shocks me.

"Oh, Michael. I give you and your father a chance for a reunion." She touches my cheek: a joke, a reassurance, a piece of motherly advice. Then she leaves.

After the door closes, silence takes over the house. My father hitches himself forward. I can feel him looking at me.

"Well," I say. "There must be something better on TV." Professional wrestling has been playing silently for the last half hour.

"What is the situation?" my father says. I ignore him, turn up the sound with the remote, but he raises his voice. "Your wife does not talk to you?"

A commentator yammers into the space between us.

My father pushes his chin forward, as if he has to stick his neck out to raise the volume of his voice. "You know, in marriage there must be flexibility."

On the chair arm, his hand is still wide and tanned. Once it could grip a tennis racket and squeeze until I hurt looking at it. This man knows nothing about flexibility. I restrain myself from talking.

"Look at me," he says. "You have no respect."

Respect, I think. He had no respect for me. His will washed over me, and neither my body nor my mind was strong enough to stop that wave. Now I have become like him. I have drowned my wife and child.

"I know what you are thinking. Blaming me." The old force is in his voice. "You are shortsighted. Why struggle with me? My life is over. I did my job in the world. Now this has happened, maybe some people say, a tragedy. I say, what tragedy? I finished my job. Can you say the same thing?"

Tears come to my eyes. I can't look at him. I can't cry in front of him. I cross the room and press my forehead to the cold window. The sports announcer goes on and on, then abruptly mutes.

Behind me, I hear my father's rasping breath. Then his voice. "I am not your enemy. Face your life."

There is a long silence in which I pray for this moment to disappear. Finally it is too much.

"Excuse me," I say into my chest. I duck out of the room. I wonder if he heard me. It's wrong to leave him alone; even the thought of it burns shame into me, but I continue hurrying down the hall. I pause only to yank the closet door open, reach in, and pull out the thing I know will be there.

I speed down the road in my BMW. The sunroof is open, and I am driving under a high spring sky. Only treetops break the blue sky far above. My friends and I used to call this a tennis sky. I round the curve of the road, accelerate up the hill, and let momentum carry the car through a turn. Then it's into the parking lot, where I brake and yank my high school racket from the backseat. The old backboard is there, the same dirty white concrete with a crooked crack running down to the asphalt. A scruffy tennis ball, gray with neglect, is half-buried in the grass along the asphalt's edge.

I serve the ball high and hard, making myself run when it shoots back on the rebound. It's a dead bounce, without that sweet spock of sound, but I make up for it by smashing the ball back extra hard. It's me and the wall. I slam the ball, again and again. My arms thrum with the force of my strokes. I can't get it out, can't drive the feeling out of my gut. I swing and hit again and again. Until finally the ball smacks against the wall, half-bounces and dies in midair. I run for it, fall and skin my knee. The ball rolls into the grass.

"Shit!" I fling my racket. Aluminum clangs against concrete. "Shit! Fucking shit to hell!" I drop my head into my knees, shuddering, almost sobbing, under the spinning sky.

When I push open the back door and edge inside, the house is silent. My ear strains for breathing, voices, footsteps. There is nothing. Finally I summon my courage and walk into the family room. My father is on the floor. He is curled there, motionless, one hand stretched toward an overturned bowl of food. A cry rises in my throat, and I bound across the room.

"I'm sorry, I'm sorry." I pull him, drag him up, lift him into the reclining chair. He is incredibly heavy, as if his bones were filled with all the weight of my heart. "I'm sorry," I whisper. The other words push against my chest like a river: *I am bad, I was weak, I have not learned how to do it either. Help me. Please.*

But all I can say is "I'm sorry. I'm so sorry. I know. I know. Forgive me." I run my hands over him, frightened, pleading to the gods that there be no bleeding, no broken bones.

My father says nothing, but his eyes are dark and wet. When I finally settle him back in the chair, we stare at each other like two men who have never learned to talk.

Then we hear the garage door opening. A moment later, the back door opens and my mother enters the room. Smiling, glowing, her hair a burnished coppery black. She sees us, looks from one to the other.

"What happened? Is something wrong?"

I look at my father, waiting for his sentence. He looks back at me for a long moment. Then he looks down at his lap.

"Nothing," he says.

"Nothing?" my mother says, staring at the fallen bowl, the spilled food. "What do you mean?" She looks at me. I shake my head. My father keeps his eyes in his lap. Finally my mother bends and picks up the bowl.

That evening I sit in my old bedroom. I feel the walls of the house around me like an empty box, and I wonder, what will it be like after my father's death? I see my mother sitting in the living room while dust falls around her like ash. See myself in England, wandering through rooms filled with strong leather couches, glass-topped tables, and my father's heavy-muscled ghost. He will be with me for the rest of my life. I stand up suddenly. This will not go on.

Downstairs in the kitchen, I close the door that leads into my father's sickroom and pick up the phone. I dial. And wait, gripping the hard plastic of the receiver. I brace myself for her irritation, her voice rising in anger. *It's 3 A.M. here—couldn't it wait?* The phone rings. I imagine its shrill insistence in the dark rooms, Philip whimpering in his sleep, Pramila pushing hair out of her face as she gropes for the phone. I can almost smell her warm, sleepy body. Suddenly I miss her so much it aches. I take a breath. The machine picks up. Startled, I hang up.

*Stupid!* I pound my thigh. Of course the machine picked up. It's 3 A.M.

I take a breath and dial again. Surely she will pick up this time. The phone has awakened her; she will know a call at this time must be urgent. I ready myself. One ring. Two. What will I say? The machine picks up. Pramila's clear, confident voice tells me to leave a message. The machine beeps, high-pitched and efficient. I open my mouth, but fear closes my throat. There's an empty hiss as the tape unrolls on the other end of the line.

"Pramila," I croak. "Are you there? Pramila." She does not pick up. She must be awake. "*Pramila.*" I raise my voice, then glance nervously at the door to the sick room. "Pramila, look, I—" I have no idea what to say. "Pramila, please. It's me." My voice cracks, and I fall silent. I am suspended on the line. I imagine her playing the tape back, listening to all my awkward pauses. "Pramila," I say one last time. And then the silence is too much for me and I hang up.

For long moments afterward I stand in the kitchen, staring past the rectangles of moonlight on the counter. The apples in the fruit bowl shine faintly. In the microwave's glossy surface, I glimpse myself, tense and unhappy.

From beyond the front of the house, a distant siren sounds. I turn towards it half-consciously, walk across the room. When I ease the door of the sick room open, I see the glow of the corner lamp on my father's closed eyelids. I let out a sigh of relief and move closer. The siren fades until the only sound in the room is the whistle of my father's breath. I stop by the bed. In the dim light, he looks old. His muscles are set in tired folds. I touch the edge of his sleeve. His arm is splayed out against the sheet so that I think of a hospital room, IV needles, a deathbed. I sink into the bedside chair, suddenly drained. All the emotion has run out of me; there is nothing left. I sit there for a long time, until finally I get up and go upstairs, to bed.

Sunday afternoon. In high school, when I still played tennis, my father and I used to watch matches together on Sunday afternoons. Today I have turned the TV on, and we are watching again.

"Look, Dad. It's Michael Chang." Another Michael. An Asian-American who has survived the swells of advice and expectation, who rides the wave of success with strength and balance. Still, what do I know about Michael Chang's inner life? What do I know of anyone's? We watch him return a serve with ease. My father nods slowly, noting the moves, the technique.

"Great backhand," I say.

"Yes . . . it is good."

Even Michael Chang can't get an unstinting compliment. Michael dashes across the court and sends the ball flying into his opponent's far corner.

"Strong legs," I say. "He runs down every ball." I glance over at my father.

He blinks, struggles with a word. "Strong will," he says.

I nod. We watch the game. From the kitchen, we hear my mother's knife against the cutting board, her voice as she hums a low tune. Behind us, the clock ticks. The men on screen hit the ball back and forth.

My father gives a low whistle of appreciation. I turn. His eyes move rhythmically from side to side; side to side they move, with the ball. The motions are so tiny and perfect, so easy. I am so moved I want to cry.

"Dad, I think he's going to win, don't you?" There is an almost absurd joy in my voice, just barely suppressed. The simplicity of my father's eye movements, the controlled ease of Michael Chang's strokes, the sun slanting onto our laps—it's almost too much to bear.

"Bachennfurth," my father says.

"What, Dad?" I lean in.

"B-back," he says. "Back and forth."

"Back and forth," I repeat. In front of us, the game continues. We watch the ball bounce back and forth. It takes me back to childhood, to afternoons when I walked into the room and stopped to watch my father watch the games. Across the small screen two people move, and in between, a speck goes back and forth: *Click,* then *clack. Click,* then *clack*—it makes a V so shallow and wide, I always think it will fly off the screen. It's hypnotic, I think—if you forget the details and strategy and results, it's almost meditation. Together, we sit. In front of us, the ball bounces from one side to the other. Back and forth, back and forth, like the ticking of a clock.

*Vladimir Nabokov, who for a time made his living as a teacher of tennis, was responsible for some of the most beautiful passages ever written about the game. During* Lolita's *pivotal tennis-playing scenes, the teenaged title character emerges as if from a chrysalis, a surprisingly graceful and charming young woman who is undeniably on the cusp of maturity—and independence.*

*This excerpt takes place at a hotel in Colorado visited by Lolita and stepfather Humbert Humbert, during their second cross-country odyssey together. While his nymphet plays mixed doubles, someone plays a practical joke on Humbert, the significance of which is not yet clear. From this point forward, however, Lolita will be* Lolita's *protagonist, and the novel's silver-tongued narrator will merely react.*

# From *Lolita*

## Vladimir Nabokov

By permitting Lolita to study acting I had, fond fool, suffered her to cultivate deceit. It now appeared that it had not been merely a matter of learning the answers to such questions as what is the basic conflict in "Hedda Gabler," or where are the climaxes in "Love Under the Lindens," or analyze the prevailing mood of "Cherry Orchard"; it was really a matter of learning to betray me. How I deplored now the exercises in sensual simulation that I had so often seen her go through in our Beardsley parlor when I would observe her from some strategic point while she, like a hypnotic subject or a performer in a mystic rite, produced sophisticated versions of infantile make-believe by going through the mimetic actions of hearing a moan in the dark, seeing for the first time a brand new young stepmother, tasting something she hated, such as buttermilk, smelling crushed grass in a lush orchard, or touching mirages of objects with her sly, slender, girl-child hands. Among my papers I still have a mimeographed sheet suggesting:

Tactile drill. Imagine yourself picking up and holding: a pingpong ball, an apple, a sticky date, a new flannel-fluffed tennis ball, a hot potato, an ice cube, a kitten, a puppy, a horseshoe, a feather, a flashlight.

Knead with your fingers the following imaginary things: a piece of bread, india rubber, a friend's aching temple, a sample of velvet, a rose petal.

You are a blind girl. Palpate the face of: a Greek youth,

Cyrano, Santa Claus, a baby, a laughing faun, a sleeping stranger, your father.

But she had been so pretty in the weaving of those delicate spells, in the dreamy performance of her enchantments and duties! On certain adventurous evenings, in Beardsley, I also had her dance for me with the promise of some treat or gift, and although these routine leg-parted leaps of hers were more like those of a football cheerleader than like the languorous and jerky motions of a Parisian *petit rat,* the rhythms of her not quite nubile limbs had given me pleasure. But all that was nothing, absolutely nothing, to the indescribable itch of rapture that her tennis game produced in me—the teasing delirious feeling of teetering on the very brink of unearthly order and splendor.

Despite her advanced age, she was more of a nymphet than ever, with her apricot-colored limbs, in her sub-teen tennis togs! Winged gentlemen! No hereafter is acceptable if it does not produce her as she was then, in that Colorado resort between Snow and Elphinstone, with everything right: the white wide little-boy shorts, the slender waist, the apricot midriff, the white breast-kerchief whose ribbons went up and encircled her neck to end behind in a dangling knot leaving bare her gaspingly young and adorable apricot shoulder blades with that pubescence and those lovely gentle bones, and the smooth, downward-tapering back. Her cap had a white peak. Her racket had cost me a small fortune. Idiot, triple idiot! I could have filmed her! I would have had her now with me, before my eyes, in the projection room of my pain and despair!

She would wait and relax for a bar or two of white-lined time before going into the act of serving, and often bounced the ball once or twice, or pawed the ground a little, always at ease, always rather vague about the score, always cheerful as she so seldom was in the dark life she led at home. Her tennis was the highest point to which I can imagine a young creature bringing the art of make-believe, although I daresay, for her it was the very geometry of basic reality.

The exquisite clarity of all her movements had its auditory counterpart in the pure ringing sound of her every stroke. The ball when it entered her aura of control became somehow whiter, its resilience somehow richer, and the instrument of precision she used upon it seemed inordinately prehensile and deliberate at the moment of clinging contact. Her form was, indeed, an absolutely perfect imitation of absolutely topnotch tennis—without any utilitarian results. As Edusa's sister, Electra Gold, a marvelous young coach, said to me once while I sat on a pulsating hard bench watching Dolores Haze toying with Linda Hall (and being beaten by her): "Dolly has a magnet in the center of her racket guts, but why the heck is she so polite?" Ah, Electra, what did it matter, with such grace! I remember at the very first game I watched being drenched with an almost painful convulsion of beauty assimilation. My Lolita had a way of raising her bent left knee at the ample and springy start of the service cycle when there would develop and hang in the sun for a second a vital web of balance between toed foot, pristine armpit, burnished arm and far back-flung racket, as she smiled up with gleaming teeth at the small globe suspended so high in the zenith of the powerful and graceful cosmos she had created for the express purpose of falling upon it with a clean resounding crack of her golden whip.

It had, that serve of hers, beauty, directness, youth, a classical purity of trajectory, and was, despite its spanking pace, fairly easy to return, having as it did no twist or sting to its long elegant hop.

That I could have had all her strokes, all her enchantments, immortalized in segments of celluloid, makes me moan to-day with frustration. They would have been so much more than the snapshots I burned! Her overhead volley was related to her service as the envoy is to the ballade; for she had been trained, my pet, to patter up at once to the net on her nimble, vivid, white-shod feet. There was nothing to choose between her forehand and backhand drives: they were mirror images of one another—my very loins still tingle with those pistol reports repeated by crisp echoes and Electra's cries. One of the pearls of Dolly's game was a short half-volley that Ned Litam had taught her in California.

She preferred acting to swimming, and swimming to tennis; yet I insist that had not something within her been broken by me—not that I realized it then!—she would have had on the top of her perfect form the will to win, and would have become a real girl champion. Dolores, with two rackets under her arm, in Wimbledon. Dolores endorsing a Dromedary. Dolores turning professional. Dolores acting a girl champion in a movie. Dolores and her gray, humble, hushed husband-coach, old Humbert.

There was nothing wrong or deceitful in the spirit of her game—unless one considered her cheerful indifference toward its outcome as the feint of a nymphet. She who was so cruel and crafty in everyday life, revealed an innocence, a frankness, a kindness of ball-placing, that permitted a second-rate but determined player, no matter how uncouth and incompetent, to poke and cut his way to victory. Despite her small stature, she covered the one thousand and fifty-three square feet of her half of the court with wonderful ease, once she had entered into the rhythm of a rally and as long as she could direct that rhythm; but any abrupt attack, or sudden change of tactics on her adversary's part, left her helpless. At match point, her second serve, which—rather typically—was even stronger and more stylish than her first (for she had none of the inhibitions that cautious winners have), would strike vibrantly the harp-cord of the net—and ricochet out of court. The polished gem of her dropshot was snapped up and put away by an opponent who seemed four-legged and wielded a crooked paddle. Her dramatic drives and lovely volleys would candidly fall at his feet. Over and over again she would land an easy one into the net—and merrily mimic dismay by drooping in a ballet attitude, with her fore-locks hanging. So sterile were her grace and whipper that she could not even win from panting me and my old-fashioned lifting drive.

I suppose I am especially susceptible to the magic of games. In my chess sessions with Gaston I saw the board as a square pool of limpid water with rare shells and stratagems rosily visible upon the smooth tes-sellated bottom, which to my confused adversary was all ooze and squid-cloud. Similarly, the initial tennis coaching I had inflicted on Lolita—prior to the revelations that came to her through the great Californian's lessons—remained in my mind as oppressive and distressful memo-ries—not only because she had been so hopelessly and irritatingly irri-tated by every suggestion of mine—but because the precious symmetry of the court instead of reflecting the harmonies latent in her was utterly jumbled by the clumsiness and lassitude of the resentful child I mis-taught. Now things were different, and on that particular day, in the pure air of Champion, Colorado, on that admirable court at the foot of steep stone stairs leading up to Champion Hotel where we had spent the night, I felt I could rest from the nightmare of unknown betrayals within the innocence of her style, of her soul, of her essential grace.

She was hitting hard and flat, with her usual effortless sweep, feed-ing me deep skimming balls—all so rhythmically coordinated and overt as to reduce my footwork to, practically, a swinging stroll—crack players will understand what I mean. My rather heavily cut serve that I had been taught by my father who had learned it from Decugis or Borman, old friends of his and great champions, would have seriously troubled my Lo, had I really tried to trouble her. But who would upset such a lucid dear? Did I ever mention that her bare arm bore the 8 of vaccination? That I loved her hopelessly? That she was only fourteen?

An inquisitive butterfly passed, dipping, between us.

Two people in tennis shorts, a red-haired fellow only about eight years my junior, with sunburnt bright pink shins, and an indolent dark girl with a moody mouth and hard eyes, about two years Lolita's senior, appeared from nowhere. As is common with dutiful tyros, their rackets were sheathed and framed, and they carried them not as if they were the natural and comfortable extensions of certain specialized muscles, but hammers or blunderbusses or wimbles, or my own dreadful cum-bersome sins. Rather unceremoniously seating themselves near my pre-cious coat, on a bench adjacent to the court, they fell to admiring very vocally a rally of some fifty exchanges that Lo innocently helped me to foster and uphold—until there occurred a syncope in the series causing her to gasp as her overhead smash went out of court, whereupon she melted into winsome merriment, my golden pet.

I felt thirsty by then, and walked to the drinking fountain; there Red approached me and in all humility suggested a mixed double. "I am Bill Mead," he said. "And that's Fay Page, actress. Maffy On Say"— he added (pointing with his ridiculously hooded racket at polished Fay who was already talking to Dolly). I was about to reply "Sorry, but—" (for I hate to have my filly involved in the chops and jabs of cheap bunglers), when a remarkably melodious cry diverted my attention: a bell-boy was tripping down the steps from the hotel to our court and making me signs. I was wanted, if you please, on an urgent long distance call— so urgent in fact that the line was being held for me. Certainly. I got into my coat (inside pocket heavy with pistol) and told Lo I would be back in a minute. She was picking up a ball—in the continental foot-racket way which was one of the few nice things I had taught her,—and smiled—she smiled at me!

An awful calm kept my heart afloat as I followed the boy up to the hotel. This, to use an American term, in which discovery, retribution, torture, death, eternity appear in the shape of a singularly repulsive nutshell, was *it*. I had left her in mediocre hands, but it hardly mattered now. I would fight, of course. Oh, I would fight. Better destroy everything than surrender her. Yes, quite a climb.

As the desk, a dignified, Roman-nosed man, with, I suggest, a very obscure past that might reward investigation, handed me a message in his own hand. The line had not been held after all. The note said:

"Mr. Humbert. The head of Birdsley (sic!) School called. Summer residence—Birdsley 2-8282. Please call back immediately. Highly important."

I folded myself into a booth, took a little pill, and for about twenty minutes tussled with space-spooks. A quartet of propositions gradually became audible: soprano, there was no such number in Beardsley; alto, Miss Pratt was on her way to England; tenor, Beardsley School had not telephoned; bass, they could not have done so, since nobody knew I was, that particular day, in Champion, Colo. Upon my stinging him, the Roman took the trouble to find out if there had been a long distance call. There had been none. A fake call from some local dial was not excluded. I thanked him. He said: You bet. After a visit to the purling men's room and a stiff drink at the bar, I started on my return march. From the very first terrace I saw, far below, on the tennis court which seemed the size of a school child's ill-wiped slate, golden Lolita playing in a double. She moved like a fair angel among three horrible Boschian cripples. One of these, her partner, while changing sides, jocosely slapped her on her behind with his racket. He had a remarkably round head and wore incongruous brown trousers. There was a momentary flurry—he saw me, and throwing away his racket—mine!—scuttled up the slope. He waved his wrists and elbows in would-be comical imitation of rudimentary wings, as he climbed, bow-legged, to the street, where his gray car awaited him. Next moment he and the grayness were gone. When I came down, the remaining trio were collecting and sorting out the balls.

"Mr. Mead, who was that person?"

Bill and Fay, both looking very solemn, shook their heads.

That absurd intruder had butted in to make up a double, hadn't he, Dolly?

Dolly. The handle of my racket was still disgustingly warm. Before returning to the hotel, I ushered her into a little alley half-smothered in fragrant shrubs, with flowers like smoke, and was about to burst into ripe sobs and plead with her imperturbed dream in the most abject manner for clarification, no matter how meretricious, of the slow awfulness enveloping me, when we found ourselves behind the convulsed Mead twosome—assorted people, you know, meeting among idyllic settings in old comedies. Bill and Fay were both weak with laughter—we had come at the end of their private joke. It did not really matter.

Speaking as if it really did not really matter, and assuming, apparently, that life was automatically rolling on with all its routine pleasures, Lolita said she would like to change into her bathing things, and spend the rest of the afternoon at the swimming pool. It was a gorgeous day. Lolita!

# Part II

# Women's Tennis

*A perfect combination of violent action taking place in an atmosphere of total tranquility*

— Billie Jean King

*Ellen Gilchrist's short story takes the reader on a journey of sorts with an all-too recognizable group she calls the Lawn Tennis Club Ladies: up to the gates marked Members Only, across the red-in-tooth-and-claw savannah that is Getting In and Staying In, and ultimately into the polar vastness of one Club Lady's heart.*

# In the Land of Dreamy Dreams

## Ellen Gilchrist

On the third of May, 1977, LaGrande McGruder drove out onto the Huey P. Long Bridge, dropped two Davis Classics and a gut-strung PDP tournament racket into the Mississippi River, and quit playing tennis forever.

"That was it," she said. "That was the last goddamn straw." She heaved a sigh, thinking this must be what it feels like to die, to be through with something that was more trouble than it was worth.

As long as she could remember LaGrande had been playing tennis four or five hours a day whenever it wasn't raining or she didn't have a funeral to attend. In her father's law office was a whole cabinet full of her trophies.

After the rackets sank LaGrande dumped a can of brand-new Slazenger tennis balls into the river and stood for a long time watching the cheerful, little, yellow constellation form and re-form in the muddy current.

"Jesus Fucking A Christ," she said to herself. "Oh, well," she added, "maybe now I can get my arms to be the same size for the first time in my life."

LaGrande leaned into the bridge railing, staring past the white circles on her wrists, souvenirs of twenty years of wearing sweatbands in the fierce New Orleans sunlight, and on down to the river where the little yellow constellation was overtaking a barge.

"That goddamn little new-rich Yankee bitch," she said, kicking the bridge with her leather Tretorns.

There was no denying it. There was no undoing it. At ten o'clock that morning LaGrande McGruder, whose grandfather had been president of the United States Lawn Tennis Association, had cheated a crippled girl out of a tennis match, had deliberately and without hesitation made a bad call in the last point of a crucial game, had defended the call against loud protests, taken a big drink of her Gatorade, and proceeded to win the next twelve games while her opponent reeled with disbelief at being done out of her victory.

At exactly three minutes after ten that morning she had looked across the net at the impassive face of the interloper who was about to humiliate her at her own tennis club and she had changed her mind about honor quicker than the speed of light. "Out," she had said, not giving a damn whether the serve was in or out. "Nice try."

"It couldn't be out," the crippled girl said. "Are you sure?"

"Of course I'm sure," LaGrande said. "I wouldn't have called it unless I was sure."

"Are you positive?" the crippled girl said.

"For God's sake," LaGrande said, "look, if you don't mind, let's hurry up and get this over with. I have to be at the country club for lunch." That ought to get her, LaGrande thought. At least they don't let Jews into the country club yet. At least that's still sacred.

"Serving," the crippled girl said, trying to control her rage.

LaGrande took her position at the back of the court, reached up to adjust her visor, and caught the eye of old Claiborne Redding, who was sitting on the second-floor balcony watching the match. He smiled and waved. How long has he been standing there, LaGrande wondered. How long has that old fart been watching me? But she was too busy to worry about Claiborne now. She had a tennis match to save, and she was going to save it if it was the last thing she ever did in her life.

The crippled girl set her mouth into a tight line and prepared to serve into the forehand court. Her name was Roxanne Miller, and she had traveled a long way to this morning's fury. She had spent thousands of dollars on private tennis lessons, hundreds of dollars on equipment, and untold time and energy giving cocktail parties and dinner parties for the entrenched players who one by one she had courted and black-mailed and finagled into giving her matches and return matches until finally one day she would catch them at a weak moment and defeat them. She kept a mental list of such victories. Sometimes when she went to bed at night she would pull the pillows over her head and lie there imagining herself as a sort of Greek figure of justice, sitting on a marble chair in the clouds, holding a scroll, a little parable of conquest and re-venge.

It had taken Roxanne five years to fight and claw and worm her way into the ranks of respected Lawn Tennis Club Ladies. For five years she had dragged her bad foot around the carefully manicured courts of the oldest and snottiest tennis club in the United States of America.

For months now her ambitions had centered around LaGrande. A victory over LaGrande would mean she had arrived in the top echelons of the Lawn Tennis Club Ladies.

A victory over LaGrande would surely be followed by invitations to play in the top doubles games, perhaps even in the famous Thursday foursome that played on Rena Clark's private tennis court. Who knows, Roxanne dreamed, LaGrande might even ask her to be her doubles partner. LaGrande's old doubles partners were always retiring to have babies. At any moment she might need a new one. Roxanne would be there waiting, the indefatigable handicapped wonder of the New Orleans tennis world.

She had envisioned this morning's victory a thousand times, had seen herself walking up to the net to shake LaGrande's hand, had planned her little speech of condolence, after which the two of them would go into the snack bar for lunch and have a heart-to-heart talk about rackets and balls and backhands and forehands and volleys and lobs.

Roxanne basked in her dreams. It did not bother her that LaGrande never returned her phone calls, avoided her at the club, made vacant replies to her requests for matches. Roxanne had plenty of time. She could wait. Sooner or later she would catch LaGrande in a weak moment.

That moment came at the club's 100th Anniversary Celebration. Everyone was drunk and full of camaraderie. The old members were all on their best behavior, trying to be extra nice to the new members and pretend like the new members were just as good as they were even if they didn't belong to the Boston Club or the Southern Yacht Club or Comus or Momus or Proteus.

Roxanne cornered LaGrande while she was talking to a famous psychiatrist-player from Washington, a bachelor who was much adored in tennis circles for his wit and political connections.

LaGrande was trying to impress him with how sane she was and hated to let him see her irritation when Roxanne moved in on them.

"When are you going to give me that match you promised me?" Roxanne asked, looking wistful, as if this were something the two of them had been discussing for years.

"I don't know," LaGrande said. "I guess I just stay so busy. This is Semmes Talbot, from Washington. This is Roxanne, Semmes. I'm sorry. I can't remember your last name. You'll have to help me."

"Miller," Roxanne said. "My name is Miller. Really now, when will you play with me?"

"Well, how about Monday?" LaGrande heard herself saying. "I guess I could do it Monday. My doubles game was canceled." She looked up at the doctor to see if he appreciated how charming she was to everyone, no matter who they were.

"Fine," Roxanne said. "Monday's fine. I'll be here at nine. I'll be

counting on it so don't let me down." She laughed. "I thought you'd
never say yes. I was beginning to think you were afraid I'd beat you."

"Oh, my goodness," LaGrande said, "anyone can beat me, I don't
take tennis very seriously anymore, you know. I just play enough to keep
my hand in."

"Who was that?" Semmes asked when Roxanne left them. "She certainly has her nerve!"

"She's one of the new members," LaGrande said. "I really try so
hard not to be snotty about them. I really do believe that every human
being is just as valuable as everyone else, don't you? And it doesn't matter a bit to me what anyone's background is, but some of the new people
are sort of hard to take. They're so, oh, well, so *eager.*"

Semmes looked down the front of her silk blouse and laughed happily into her aristocratic eyes. "Well, watch out for that one," he said.
"There's no reason for anyone as pretty as you to let people make you
uncomfortable."

Across the room Roxanne collected Willie and got ready to leave
the party. She was on her way home to begin training for the match.

Willie was glad to leave. He didn't like hanging around places
where he wasn't wanted. He couldn't imagine why Roxanne wanted to
spend all her time playing tennis with a bunch of snotty people.

Roxanne and Willie were new members. Willie's brand-new 15 million dollars and the New Orleans Lawn Tennis Club's brand-new
$700,000 dollar mortgage had met at a point in history, and Willie's
application for membership had been approved by the board and rail-
roaded past the watchful noses of old Claiborne Redding and his bud-
dies. Until then the only Jewish member of the club had been a
globetrotting Jewish bachelor who knew his wines, entertained lav-
ishly at Antoine's, and had the courtesy to stay in Europe most of the
time.

Willie and Roxanne were something else again. "What in the hell
are we going to do with a guy who sells ties and a crippled woman who
runs around Audubon Park all day in a pair of tennis shorts," Claiborne
said, pulling on a pair of the thick white Australian wool socks he wore
to play in. The committee had cornered him in the locker room.

"The membership's not for him," they said. "He doesn't even play.
You'll never see him. And she really isn't a cripple. One leg is a little bit
shorter than the other one, that's all."

"I don't know," Claiborne said. "Not just Jews, for God's sake, but
Yankee Jews to boot."

"The company's listed on the American Stock Exchange, Claiborne.
It was selling at 16fi this morning, up from 5. And he buys his insurance

from me. Come on, you'll never see them. All she's going to do is play a little tennis with the ladies."

Old Claiborne rued the day he had let himself be talked into Roxanne and Willie. The club had been forced to take in thirty new families to pay for its new building and some of them were Jews, but, as Claiborne was fond of saying, at least the rest of them tried to act like white people.

Roxanne was something else. It seemed to him that she lived at the club. The only person who hung around the club more than Roxanne was old Claiborne himself. Pretty soon she was running the place. She wrote *The Lawn Tennis Newsletter.* She circulated petitions to change the all-white dress rule. She campaigned for more court privileges for women. She dashed in and out of the bar and the dining room making plans with the waiters and chefs for Mixed Doubles Nights, Round Robin Galas, Benefit Children's jamborees, Saturday Night Luaus.

Claiborne felt like his club was being turned into a cruise ship.

On top of everything else Roxanne was always trying to get in good with Claiborne. Every time he settled down on the balcony to watch a match she came around trying to talk to him, talking while the match was going on, remembering the names of his grandchildren, complimenting him on their serves and backhands and footwork, taking every conceivable liberty, as if at any moment she might start showing up at their weddings and debuts.

Claiborne thought about Roxanne a lot. He was thinking about her this morning when he arrived at the club and saw her cream-colored Rolls-Royce blocking his view of the Garth Humphries Memorial Plaque. He was thinking about her as he got a cup of coffee from a stand the ladies had taken to setting up by the sign-in board. This was some more of her meddling, he thought, percolated coffee in Styrofoam cups with plastic spoons and some kind of powder instead of cream.

At the old clubhouse waiters had brought steaming cups of thick chicory-flavored café au lait out onto the balcony with cream and sugar in silver servers.

Claiborne heaved a sigh, pulled his pants out of his crotch, and went up to the balcony to see what the morning would bring.

He had hardly reached the top of the stairs when he saw Roxanne leading LaGrande to a deserted court at the end of the property. My God in Heaven, he thought, how did she pull that off? How in the name of God did she get hold of Leland's daughter?

Leland McGruder had been Claiborne's doubles partner in their youth. Together they had known victory and defeat in New Orleans and

Jackson and Monroe and Shreveport and Mobile and Atlanta and as far away as Forest Hills during one never to be forgotten year when they had thrown their rackets into a red Ford and gone off together on the tour.

Down on the court LaGrande was so aggravated she could barely be civil. How did I end up here, she thought, playing second-class tennis against anyone who corners me at a party.

LaGrande was in a bad mood all around. The psychiatrist had squired her around all weekend, fucked her dispassionately in someone's *garçonnierre,* and gone back to Washington without making further plans to see her.

She bounced a ball up and down a few times with her racket, thinking about a line of poetry that kept occurring to her lately whenever she played tennis. "Their only monument the asphalt road, and a thousand lost golf balls."

"Are you coming to Ladies Day on Wednesday?" Roxanne was saying, "We're going to have a great time. You really ought to come. We've got a real clown coming to give out helium balloons, and we're going to photograph the winners sitting on his lap for the newsletter. Isn't that a cute idea?"

"I'm afraid I'm busy Wednesday," LaGrande said, imagining balloons flying all over the courts when the serious players arrived for their noon games. "Look," she said, "let's go on and get started. I can't stay too long."

They set down their pitchers of Gatorade, put on their visors and sweatbands, sprayed a little powdered resin on their hands, and walked out to their respective sides of the court.

Before they hit the ball four times LaGrande knew something was wrong. The woman wasn't going to warm her up! LaGrande had hit her three nice long smooth balls and each time Roxanne moved up to the net and put the ball away on the sidelines.

"How about hitting me some forehands," LaGrande said. "I haven't played in a week. I need to warm up."

"I'll try," Roxanne said, "I have to play most of my game at the net, you know, because of my leg."

"Well, stay back there and hit me some to warm up with," LaGrande said, but Roxanne went right on putting her shots away with an assortment of tricks that looked more like a circus act than a tennis game.

"Are you ready to play yet?" she asked. "I'd like to get started before I get too tired."

"Sure," LaGrande said. "Go ahead, you serve first. There's no reason to spin a racket over a fun match." Oh, well, she thought, I'll just go ahead and slaughter her. Of course, I won't lob over her head, I don't suppose anyone does that to her.

Roxanne pulled the first ball out of her pants. She had a disconcerting habit of sticking the extra ball up the leg of her tights instead of keeping it in a pocket. She pulled the ball out of her pants, tossed it expertly up into the air, and served an ace to LaGrande's extreme backhand service corner.

"Nice serve," LaGrande said. Oh, well, she thought, everyone gets one off occasionally. Let her go on and get overconfident. Then I can get this over in a hurry.

They changed courts for the second serve. Roxanne hit short into the backhand court. LaGrande raced up and hit a forehand right into Roxanne's waiting racket. The ball dropped neatly into a corner and the score was 30-love.

How in the shit did she get to the net so fast, LaGrande thought. Well, I'll have to watch out for that. I thought she was supposed to be crippled.

Roxanne served again, winning the point with a short spinning forehand. Before LaGrande could gather her wits about her she had lost the first game.

Things went badly with her serve and she lost the second game. While she was still recovering from that she lost the third game. Calm down, she told herself. Get hold of yourself. Keep your eye on the ball. Anticipate her moves. It's only because I didn't have a chance to warm up. I'll get going in a minute.

Old Claiborne stood watching the match from a secluded spot near the door to the dining room, watching it with his heart in his throat, not daring to move any farther out onto the balcony for fear he might distract LaGrande and make things worse.

Why doesn't she lob, Claiborne thought. Why in the name of God doesn't she lob? Maybe she thinks she shouldn't do it just because one of that woman's legs is a little bit shorter than the other.

He stood squeezing the Styrofoam cup in his hand. A small hole had developed in the side, and drops of coffee were making a little track down the side of his Fred Perry flannels, but he was oblivious to everything but the action on the court.

He didn't even notice when Nailor came up behind him. Nailor was a haughty old black man who had been with the club since he was a young boy and now was the chief groundskeeper and arbiter of manners among the hired help.

Nailor had spent his life tending Rubico tennis courts without once having the desire to pick up a racket. But he had watched thousands of tennis matches and he knew more about tennis than most players did.

He knew how the little fields of energy that surround men and women move and coalesce and strike and fend off and retreat and attack and conquer. That was what he looked for when he watched tennis. He wasn't interested in the details.

If it was up to Nailor no one but a few select players would ever be allowed to set foot on his Rubico courts. The only time of day when he was really at peace was the half hour from when he finished the courts around 7:15 each morning until they opened the iron gates at 7:45 and the members started arriving.

Nailor had known LaGrande since she came to her father's matches in a perambulator. He had lusted after her ass ever since she got her first white tennis skirt and her first Wilson autograph racket. He had been the first black man to wax her first baby-blue convertible, and he had been taking care of her cars ever since.

Nailor moonlighted at the club polishing cars with a special wax he had invented.

Nailor hated the new members worse than Claiborne did. Ever since the club had moved to its new quarters and they had come crowding in bringing their children and leaving their paper cups all over the courts he had been thinking of retiring.

Now he was watching one of them taking his favorite little missy to the cleaners. She's getting her little booty whipped for sure this morning, he thought. She can't find a place to turn and make a stand. She don't know where to start to stop it. She's got hind teat today whether she likes it or not and I'm glad her daddy's not here to watch it.

Claiborne was oblivious to Nailor. He was trying to decide who would benefit most if he made a show of walking out to the balcony and taking a seat.

He took a chance. He waited until LaGrande's back was to him, then walked out just as Roxanne was receiving serve.

LaGrande made a small rally and won her service, but Roxanne took the next three games for the set. "I don't need to rest between sets unless you do," she said, walking up to the net. "We really haven't been playing that long. I really don't know why I'm playing so well. I guess I'm just lucky today."

"I just guess you are," LaGrande said. "Sure, let's go right on. I've got a date for lunch." Now I'll take her, she thought. Now I'm tired of being polite. Now I'm going to beat the shit out of her.

Roxanne picked up a ball, tossed it into the air, and served another ace into the backhand corner of the forehand court.

Jesus Fucking A Christ, LaGrande thought. She did it again. Where in the name of God did that little Jewish housewife learn that shot.

LaGrande returned the next serve with a lob. Roxanne ran back, caught it on the edge of her racket and dribbled it over the net.

Now LaGrande lost all powers of reason. She began trying to kill the ball on every shot. Before she could get hold of herself she had lost three games, then four, then five, then she was only one game away from losing the match, then only one point.

This is it, LaGrande thought. Armageddon.

Roxanne picked up the balls and served the first one out. She slowed herself down, took a deep breath, tossed up the second ball and shot a clean forehand into the service box.

"Out," La Grande said. "Nice try."

"It couldn't be out," Roxanne said, "are you sure?"

"Of course I'm sure," LaGrande said. "*I wouldn't have called it unless I was sure.*"

Up on the balcony Old Claiborne's heart was opening and closing like a geisha's fan. He caught LaGrande's eye, smiled and waved, and, turning around, realized that Nailor was standing behind him.

"Morning, Mr. Claiborne," Nailor said, leaning politely across him to pick up the cup. "Looks like Mr. Leland's baby's having herself a hard time this morning. Let me bring you something nice to drink while you watch."

Claiborne sent him for coffee and settled back in the chair to watch LaGrande finish her off, thinking, as he often did lately, that he had outlived his time and his place. "I'm not suited for a holding action," he told himself, imagining the entire culture of the white Christian world to be stretched out on some sort of endless Maginot Line besieged by the children of the poor carrying portable radios and boxes of fried chicken.

Here Claiborne sat, on a beautiful spring morning, in good spirits, still breathing normally, his blood coursing through his veins on its admirable and accustomed journeys, and only a few minutes before he had been party to a violation of a code he had lived by all his life.

He sat there, sipping his tasteless coffee, listening to the Saturday lawn mowers starting up on the lawn of the Poydras Retirement Home, which took up the other half of the square block of prime New Orleans real estate on which the new clubhouse was built. It was a very exclusive old folks' home, with real antiques and Persian rugs and a board of directors made up of members of the New Orleans Junior League. Some of the nicest old people in New Orleans went there to die.

Claiborne had suffered through a series of terrible luncheons at the Poydras Home in an effort to get them to allow the tennis club to unlock one of the gates that separated the two properties. But no matter how the board of directors of the Lawn Tennis Club pleaded and bargained and implored, the board of directors of the Poydras Home stoutly refused to allow the tennis-club members to set foot on their lawn to retrieve the balls that flew over the fence. A ball lost to the Poydras Home was a ball gone forever.

The old-fashioned steel girders of the Huey P. Long Bridge hung languidly in the moist air. The sun beat down on the river. The low-hanging clouds pushed against each other in fat cosmic orgasms.

LaGrande stood on the bridge until the constellation of yellow balls was out of sight around a bend in the river. Then she drove to her house on Philip Street, changed clothes, got in the car, and began to drive aimlessly up and down Saint Charles Avenue, thinking of things to do with the rest of her life.

She decided to cheer herself up. She turned onto Carrollton Avenue and drove down to Gus Mayer.

She went in, found a saleslady, took up a large dressing room, and bought some cocktail dresses and some sun dresses and some summer skirts and blouses and some pink linen pants and a beige silk Calvin Klein evening jacket.

Then she went downstairs and bought some hose and some makeup and some perfume and some brassieres and some panties and a blue satin Christian Dior gown and robe.

She went into the shoe department and bought some Capezio sandals and some Bass loafers and some handmade espadrilles. She bought a red umbrella and a navy blue canvas handbag.

When she had bought one each of every single thing she could possibly imagine needing she felt better and went on out to the Country Club to see if anyone she liked to fuck was hanging around the pool.

*"Adults at Home" is a story for anyone who's ever wondered how it must feel to be Mark McEnroe or the other Williams sisters: the older ones, who flank mother Oracene in the players' box. If there were a joke that began, "How is tennis like a soap opera?" Marcy Dermansky's short story would be the punchline.*

# Adults at Home

## Marcy Dermansky

The afternoon my little sister won her first U.S. Open, I was also busy, having strenuous sex with David Solemn, a man I'd met earlier that morning at Dunkin Donuts. We did it on the white living room carpet in my parents' new Connecticut house while the match was broadcast live on the big screen TV. David kept pace with the rallies, moving fast when Amy served and volleyed, thrusting hard for first serves and over-heads.

"Your sister hits the shit out of the ball," he said.

My sister, Amy Luna, rising tennis star, took the second set at love. She rocked back and forth on the heels of her sneakers during the closing ceremonies, grinned throughout her older opponent's retirement speech as the defeated former champion bid farewell to her loyal fans. Amy threw her racquet high in the air, filled her hands with the monstrous trophy and a cardboard replica of the check for the sum of $750,000.

The camera panned to my parents, wearing new white linen outfits, hugging, kissing—lips on lips, hands in each other's hair. I watched, my mouth agape. All year long my mother had told me about her divorce lawyer. She talked about equitable property settlements and wanted to know if I'd started looking for an apartment. She took an inventory of the furniture, offered me the old living room sofa and matching armchair, a new set of white ceramic dishes from Pottery Barn. "I'm fine here," I said, though I wasn't, and my mother sighed loudly before asking me to return a stack of overdue library books.

Amy handed her trophy to a ball girl and took the microphone. She spun around, around and around, taking in the crowd, the applause. Everyone at Arthur Ashe Stadium was on their feet. Amy giggled. John McEnroe, a commentator for NBC, cooed about her infectious charm. He rambled on about her amazing poise on the court and the adorable slope of her nose, comparing it to the distinctive Nike stripe. They all loved her, adored her. She was seventeen. Her legs were long and skinny and nicely curved. She had a flat chest, a long blond ponytail.

David Solemn stared at the TV.

"She's so cute," he said.

I stared at David Solemn. He was a good-looking man, even without clothes. I ran my hand through his thinning hair but he didn't respond. I shut my eyes. Amplified by three-feet high speakers, Dolby surround sound, my world-famous, vain, selfish, giggling sister cleared her throat.

"I'm so happy," she began.

The next day, my family sat me down at the long oak table in the dining room. Amy wore the red velvet miniskirt that signified victory. Dad ran the palms of his hands over his new laptop. My mother drank a Bloody Mary.

"Why don't you start?" Dad said, looking to Amy. "Put the ball in play, so to speak."

Amy giggled.

"It's nothing personal, Rebecca," she said. "But I just hate looking at you in the morning, seeing how sad you are. I think about you being too broke to go to the movies or to pay for your own groceries and I feel guilty for how great my life is. Dad says I can't give you any of my money or I would. I'd write you a check for $20,000 today, but Dad says that you have to earn your own way. Anyhow, you're ruining the best time of my life. *Sixty Minutes* is coming for an interview tomorrow and I don't want you living here in this house. It's embarrassing. I'm ashamed of you."

"Hmm," Dad said, opening his laptop. "Is that it?"

"Yep," said Amy, giving Dad a hearty nod. "I said it all."

"Lacking in sensitivity, but to the point."

Amy grinned. "Just like my game. No mercy."

"Why not $100,000?" I said to Amy. "Why not $200,000?"

Mom coughed.

Dad started pressing buttons on the keyboard.

"Your mother has decided to let me speak for the both of us," he said. "I've prepared a speech."

I looked to Mom for support. She'd finished her Bloody Mary and was chewing celery.

"I typed this up, Rebecca," Dad said, "because I wanted to make sure I didn't forget anything."

Dad put his hand on Mom's. She grimaced and then seemed to re-think her decision, smiling and deliberately covering his hand with hers. Dad lifted her hand to his lips and kissed it. Amy rolled her eyes.

"As you know," he said, "our marriage has been strained. We've had problems. Who could have believed we'd get through your mother's affair with Amy's tennis pro? My unfortunate dalliances with secretaries are also common knowledge. Your mother and I have been through plenty. Too much.

"I almost lost my business to the recession, and we were all unhappy then. You probably remember. You had to give up your flute lessons, ceramics class, even summer camp. We sacrificed. Your mother and I double-mortgaged the old house to pay for Amy's lessons. Your mother continues to clip coupons. Everything she buys, she buys on sale, even though I tell her these are the salad days. We could live on the interest of Amy's winnings alone, not to mention the endorsements.

"Do you know what has held us together? During the hard times? The glue of the Luna family? Amy's tennis.

"Amy's tennis. I wanted to leave, admit my failure and start a new life, but I couldn't give up, for years, because I had to pay for Amy's tennis lessons. She had that kind of promise you can't ignore. So you had to go to a state school instead of Swarthmore because I couldn't afford tuition and the tennis academy. I asked you if you would give up a prestigious education for your sister and you did.

"Well, I look at you now, living at home, wandering around the house in your leggings after quitting that wonderful job on Wall Street, and I wonder if we let you make the wrong choice. My heart breaks for you, Rebecca."

Dad looked up from his computer and smiled at Mom. He drank from her empty Bloody Mary glass. Amy stretched her arms over her head. When she saw me watching her, she smiled.

"We've made it," said Dad. "Your sister is a start. She won the goddamned U.S. Open. We bought this new house in Connecticut. Your mother and I completed our therapy with a marriage counselor and we've resolved our anger. I can honestly say that we've worked through our problems. We are through with the lies, the infidelity. The Luna family is at the light at the end of the tunnel and we deserve happiness. But to get to this solid ground, we've come to a painful realization."

Dad took a big breath.

"It's you, Rebecca. You are ruining our marriage. Three years ago you moved back home for what was supposed to be a summer. You've shown no signs of wanting to leave. You spread your dirty dishes all over the house. You borrow your mother's new car and return it with an empty gas tank.

"You've become a walking, aching mess and without our help, I don't think you know how to help yourself. We all love you, Rebecca—your mother, and Amy, and me, your Daddy. We all love you. You don't need to win a Grand Slam to win your parents' love. We love you as much as we love your sister. And it's because we love you that we've decided you can't live here any longer. We want you to leave the house today. Before we back down in our resolve. You have to live your own life. We all know that you can do it."

Tears streamed down my mother's cheeks. Amy rolled her wrists in small, concentric circles. I waited for what came next, the finale, the money. The money! Of course, the money. My parents knew I had no money. Where could I go without any money? Did they want me sleeping in a homeless shelter in New Haven? I couldn't even afford a weekend at Motel 6. Dad shut the computer down and left the room. Amy put her hands on top of her head. She looked at me and shrugged her shoulders.

"Tough luck, huh?" she said.

When I was eight years old, not long after my sister's birth, I stopped talking. My parents took me to a specialist in Manhattan. The tests revealed no physical impediment, but the bills were more than my parents could afford and we had to move to a smaller apartment. Dad yelled at Mom. Amy slept soundly in her crib. I hid in my bedroom closet.


David Solemn was thirty-five. He was an artist. For the last twelve years, he had lived at home. The Solemns had long ago stopped asking when he was going to move out. Instead, his mother got her own apartment in New York. She visited on weekends.

David had given up on finding a job or a girlfriend. So when I called him from the Dunkin Donuts where we had met only the day before, there was no hesitation in his offer.

I moved right in.

During the week, when Mrs. Solemn was gone, I cooked dinners for David and his father. In October, I even made a practice run at Thanksgiving. I did the turkey, the stuffing, cranberries and sweet potatoes and string beans sprinkled with slivered almonds. Gravy made from scratch. For dessert, there was homemade apple pie and vanilla ice cream. "Now this is a girl," David's father had said. When we were done, the three of us went upstairs and watched a TV movie—three adults, sprawled across the fluffy, white comforter on the Solemn's king-sized bed. I gave Mr. Solemn a kiss goodnight before David and I went off to bed.

I'd been living in the Solemn house for over a month when Mrs. Solemn invited me out to the back porch for a chat.

"I'm sixty years old, Rebecca," she said. "So when I tell you something, don't think that I don't know. Let's say you're an artist. If you are an artist and you live your entire life without making that art you might as well be dead."

She looked at me knowingly.

I knew Jackie Solemn was taking art classes. But I had no interest in making art. I wasn't ready to commit suicide either. I liked to cook but I didn't tell this to Mrs. Solemn.

"Oh," I said. "That's how my sister feels about tennis."

Mrs. Solemn shook her head. "Your tennis playing sister doesn't interest me." She put her hands on both sides of my face. "I'm talking about you. Living in my house, living in your unemployed adult boyfriend's parents' house. I feel like I can talk to you freely because you're not my child. Doesn't this situation trouble you?"

Most people, Mrs. Solemn included, will let you down. They put so much stock in employment. Making money. Working. In a previous incarnation, I'd done that. I had the fast-track job in the big city and five days a week, I wore the good clothes and sat diligently in front of a computer, performing the tasks that I was assigned, my head aching, black spots clouding my field of vision, until the clock struck five—and even then, I often put in overtime. Living this kind of life, you're too zonked out to be properly miserable. I rode the subway, paid rent, paid the electric bill and the phone bill, parceled the remaining dividends to the dry cleaners, the deli by my office where I bought lunch, the Vietnamese place where I got spring rolls and steamed vegetables and rice for dinner. Vacations, I went to the Caribbean with coworkers from the office, drank too much, and had drunken sex with relatively good-looking strangers.

My life, as I am supposed to believe, had value then.

"I like living here," I told Mrs. Solemn.

Mrs. Solemn tilted her head back gazing at the peeling white paint of the porch ceiling. A dog barked down the street; I listened longingly to the sounds of Sunday football on TV inside the house.

"I used to worry that David wouldn't wake up in the mornings," she said. "Sometimes, when he slept late into the afternoon, I'd vacuum outside of his door to wake him up. I'd cook bacon to lure him downstairs. I'd knock on the door, wake him up. I lived in dread of opening up the door to find my dead son."

Like David and his father, I was relieved when Mrs. Solemn left at the end of her weekends.

Our lives were simple.

David made art during the day in the basement, elaborate cartoons based on his life, the quest to end tension and the simultaneous search for the perfect girlfriend. He'd been looking for this perfect woman for years. He even took one of the more beautiful candidates to Hawaii, bought her the jewelry she pointed to in store windows. David was tall and handsome and charming and talented and smart, the whole package, but most women want a man who has a job and doesn't live at home. A man who doesn't twitch.

Mr. Solemn worked in the attic. He was a distributor of rawhide bones and chews. On busy days, I went upstairs and helped out, answered the phones and helped with the invoicing.

I felt I was *it*, the perfect girlfriend. My love for David was so large, my affection for Mr. Solemn so pure. I wanted nothing. In their chaotic, three-story house, there were no maids to complain about the wet towels on the floor. No long-legged, bouncing sister, running into the kitchen for a Gatorade. No more breathless stories of trips to Paris and London, or tedious recounts of misplayed points. Better still, there were no three o'clock calls from my father, checking up on the day's job search.

Mr. Solemn gave me $200 each week to spend on groceries. I cooked and cleaned and I was happy. Evenings, the three of us went to the movies. Sometimes we rented them. Other nights Mr. Solemn worked late, and David and I cuddled in the living room, reading in front of the fireplace. Mr. Solemn always finished by the eleven o'clock news. We would meet together on the big bed at the end of the day.

Of all these good things, what I loved most was watching *General Hospital* with David. At 2:52 every afternoon, Monday through Friday, I'd start popping the popcorn on the gas stove. By 2:54, I'd be melting the butter. At 2:56, I'd put three ice cubes into tall, frosted glasses and pour the Diet Coke. At 2:57, David would appear from the basement. We would carry the popcorn and Diet Cokes up to the den, and still have two full minutes to settle down, kiss, munch on the popcorn until the show started.

We had the same favorite character, Carly Roberts. Carly had come to Port Charles to ruin the life of her birth mother, Bobbie Jones. Within months, Carly was able to seduce Bobbie's husband, family man and neurosurgeon Tony Jones. Soon Carly found out she was pregnant. She didn't know if the baby was Tony's or AJ Quartermaine's, the young, good-looking, wealthy, recovering alcoholic, eligible bachelor on the show.

Ours was a happiness most people are too scared to try.

There are four months between the U.S. Open and the next big international tournament, the Australian Open. Amy hated to practice;

she often refused to train between events. She was bored. There was no other reason for her to show up at David Solemn's house on one particularly warm and beautiful Saturday afternoon, driving a gleaming, white Mercedes convertible.

David and I were sitting on lawn chairs in the late afternoon sun, eating turkey sandwiches, while inside the house Mr. Solemn and Jackie Solemn discussed their dying marriage.

"Cool car, huh?" Amy called out.

She wore black, mirrored sunglasses, a scoop neck pastel pink T-shirt, a pink leather jacket, and shiny pink lip gloss. "I only have a learner's permit, so I'm not supposed to drive. I'm seventeen years old but I've been so busy with tennis I haven't had the time to get my license." She smiled at David. "My name is Amy Luna. I'm Rebecca's little sister. I'm appalled that she hasn't invited me over. I've been wanting to meet you, the mysterious boyfriend. Come out for a drive."

"No," I said, fingering the barely eaten sandwich on my lap. "We're busy."

David leapt to his feet.

We went to the Connecticut coast, David at the wheel, driving ninety miles an hour down the interstate, Amy next to him in the front seat, laughing, her blond hair flying behind her, crying, "Faster, faster." I closed my eyes, gripping the fastened seat belt.

At the beach, the blue sky had turned gray. The strip of sand where the waves broke was littered with thick white foam and dead jellyfish. Amy sprinted, showing off her speed, jumping over the glutinous corpses.

"Look at me," she giggled. "Look."

I thought about taking a rock hammer to her forehead.

"I'm jumping for my life," she cried. "I'm chasing ground strokes down the line."

Then David started running after her, tackling her from behind so that they both fell into the sand. Amy giggled and shrieked and David tickled her ribs. He slipped a handful of sand down her pink T-shirt. I walked behind them, quiet, hands jammed in my jeans pockets.

"Leonardo DiCaprio didn't even know who I was," I heard Amy telling David when she was back on her feet. "He doesn't watch sports. Supposedly he has a girlfriend, some model, but I don't think it's going to last. He took my phone number, but he's back in Hollywood. John McEnroe's having a big bash next weekend out at the Hamptons. He's always flirting with me. I promised to hit the ball around with his kids. You should come."

"Cool," David said.

He looked good that day. For weeks, David hadn't been doing all that great. He'd been slouching. And the twitching was worse, his legs, even his eyebrows. He'd lost interest in *General Hospital*, leaving halfway through the show. But with the infectious Amy Luna around, his body remained straight and still. His skin glowed.

"Let's go out for cappuccinos," Amy said. "I had the best cappuccino when I was in Italy last May for the Italian Open. Connecticut blows."

David nodded his head. I knew for a fact that he had never once left the country. He put his arms around Amy's shoulders, guiding her back to the Mercedes. I poked at a dead jellyfish with a long stick, looking into its bulging, vacant eyes. When they're alive, jellyfish are magical, arms long and luminescent and shimmering neon, pink and purple. It was insane to have thought I was the perfect girlfriend. Pathetic.

The local news showed footage of a six-week-old puppy at the ASPCA, the kind that breaks your heart, small enough to fit on the face of a tennis racquet—big, soulful eyes.

"We could use a dog in this house," Mr. Solemn said.

"I've never had a dog," I said.

It was shameful. I could hear the longing in my voice. I was feeling sorry for myself because David had just called. Amy had got drunk on tequila shots at John McEnroe's big charity gala in the Hamptons. She passed out in the guestroom, and McEnroe had invited David to stay for the weekend.

"Never, Rebecca?" Mr. Solemn said. "You've never known a dog's crazy love?"

I hadn't. I hadn't known a lot of things. I'd had my parents' love for the entire eight years until golden Amy was born. But maybe not. Maybe my parents were too busy cheating on each other to notice when I started to crawl or took my first steps. My Dad said I didn't need to win a Slam for his love, but once I moved into the Solemn's house, he never called. Not once. Mr. Solemn was a warm, honest man, and the next day, after I made breakfast, we went straight to the ASPCA. The crying began when I found out the puppy, the one I was going to love with all my heart after David dumped me, had been adopted earlier that morning. So Mr. Solemn led me back to the car and then drove onward, leading us to the mall. I don't think he had any plans for the day.

After the Gap, we headed to the food court, collapsing at a secluded table next to the waterfall. Mr. Solemn summoned the energy to buy us frozen yogurt waffle cones while I slumped over the table, head on my elbows, crying onto my knuckles. When I closed my eyes, I found myself thinking about *General Hospital.*

Things hadn't worked out so well for Carly Roberts. After her baby was born, she told Bobbie that she, Carly, was her long-lost daughter, that her newborn son was Bobbie's grandchild. After so many months of build-up, Carly's secret was disclosed in front of the major players on the show, in the dining room of the Port Charles hotel. Outside there was a blizzard, the worst in years. And Bobbie rejected them both, Carly and the baby. She seemed lonelier than ever. You couldn't be more alone than Bobbie.

Mr. Solemn returned. He patted my hand.

"It's a good thing about the pup." He slid a waffle cone through my fingers, and didn't let go until he could feel my grip around the cone. "Now that I think of it, I couldn't bear to go through the housebreaking again."

I nodded, picking a strawberry off the smooth yogurt with my tongue. Tears continued to stream down my cheeks.

"Our last dog was in love with David," he said. "He had no use for me or Jackie. The nutty thing actually went on a hunger strike when David went to college, literally starved himself to death. After that we stuck to cats. That is until Boots got run over by the mail truck. Then Jackie decided it was bad luck with pets for the Solemns and called a moratorium. I'd forgotten. Yes, the pup would have been a big mistake."

"My mother never wanted pets," I said. "She said cleaning up after me and my sister was enough. I won a goldfish once at a school fair but Amy and her tennis friends flushed it down the toilet."

"I'm so sorry, Rebecca," Mr. Solemn said. "It sure is a pleasure having you around. As far as I am concerned, you can stay for as long as you like. I always thought it would be easier with a daughter."

It wasn't necessary for me to stop crying. Whenever I thought I was done, Mr. Solemn only had to say the next lovely thing.

"What do you say about going to the Body Shop?" he asked. Mr. Solemn started to gather up the dark blue Gap shopping bags, two to each hand. "I noticed you're low on bubble bath. How is your car running these days?"

Lying alone at night, waiting for David to get back from Amy's warm-up sessions in Florida, I closed my eyes, trying to remember us when we were first together. Memories of us at Dunkin Donuts at three in the morning when we couldn't sleep. Glazed chocolate donuts. Instead, I saw Carly Roberts.

"You've got to do something," she said. "Fast."

I rolled over, hugging my pillow. David and I had stopped having sex weeks ago, but we slept in the same bed, side by side, David's arm tossed over my shoulders.

"Mr. Solemn is sweet," Carly said. "But you can't live on a couple of outfits. And the Gap. Come on. He should have taken you to Nordstrom's. He's a putz like Tony Jones, that pathetic excuse of a middle-aged neurosurgeon I used to think I loved. Your good father figure misses his wife. Pretty soon he's going to start making the moves on you."

I shook my head. The world was not as terrible a place as Carly believed. Mr. Solemn checked the oil in my car. He put fluid into the power steering gauge; he tightened the fan belts. My mother's old Nissan ran quieter, smoother than it had in years.

"Your loser boyfriend is doing it with your sister," Carly said. "Don't take that kind of treatment from a man. You've got wiles."

Carly had wiles. She grew up scrappy and angry. I grew up too quiet for anger. I was the one who hid in the closet while my parents fought. A couple of times, I'd fallen asleep and they didn't find me until the next morning.

I turned on the light and pulled out a notebook. I'd make a shopping list. David Solemn would be home for dinner the next day. I would make one of his favorites: spinach lasagna, maybe, or broiled salmon with garlic mashed potatoes. There would be salad. I'd bake Tollhouse cookies, filling the house with that wonderful, warm aroma of melting chocolate. He would never want to leave.

I'd just taken the cookies out of the oven when Mom showed up at the Solemn house. She sat at the kitchen table, hands around the glass of milk I'd poured her, watching intently as I slid the warm cookies off the cookie sheet onto a red platter.

"Look at you," she said. "I didn't even know you could bake."

The spinach was in a strainer in the sink, waiting to be washed, dried, chopped. I shrugged and handed her a warm chocolate chip cookie. Mom nibbled around the edges.

"You put in pecans," she said. She dipped her cookie in the milk.

David would be home in three hours and I had tons of cooking to do. I planned to change the sheets on our bed. I heard the dryer going in the basement. I had tried to plan the day perfectly but Mom was screwing everything up.

"I used to worry that she was involved with John McEnroe," Mom said. "As if that weren't bad enough. She's just a teenager, but what can I do? She has millions in the bank. Millions. I can't control her. She wants your David on the sidelines. When she could hire anybody.

Anybody. Your Dad doesn't care as long as she keeps winning. I'm sick about it."

Mom looked pale. Her black cardigan was covered in lint; her hair was flat, dirty. I wondered how the revitalized marriage was going. My father had made promises before. They would be going to Australia soon to watch Amy play. The year before, they'd gone snorkeling in the Great Barrier Reef after Amy got knocked out in the round of sixteen.

"Do you want a hug?" Mom said.

"No," I said, and took a step back. "What are you talking about?"

"I think you should move back home."

I noticed Mr. Solemn standing in the doorway. Normally he made noise when entering a room. It was the middle of the afternoon; he was supposed to be working.

"Your father agreed," Mom said. "He promised not to bother you about the job. We can redecorate your bedroom."

Mr. Solemn looked at the floor. "I'll miss you, Rebecca," he said.

"I'm making dinner." I went to the refrigerator and began removing ingredients: vine-ripened tomatoes, ricotta cheese, mozzarella. "You can stay for dinner, Mom. You can meet David."

Mom laid her chocolate chip cookie on the table. She walked over to me, carrying her glass of milk.

"You poor, delusional girl," she said. "He's not coming back. He's with your sister in Australia, helping her get ready for the Open. Amy says it's love. She goes and picks your unsuitable boyfriend to love."

Mr. Solemn took the bag of tomatoes out of my hand, the cheese from the other, and put them on the chopping block.

"I don't know what to say," he said. "I thought I raised him better."

Mom shook my shoulders. "Wake up, Rebecca," she said. "Pack your things. I'm taking you home."

I thought about Carly Roberts. After the baby was born, after Tony left her and AJ threatened to sue for full custody, Carly took her baby to Jason Morgan, the brain-damaged, kind-hearted Port Charles mobster. They ended up safe and protected in his luxurious penthouse.

"Wiles," Carly said.

I looked at Mr. Solemn. "I want to stay," I said. "There's salad. I bought artichoke hearts for the salad."

"Which way is your bedroom?" Mom tugged at my arm. "I'll help you pack."

"There are croutons," I said. I shook Mom off, and pointed to the pantry.

"Rebecca, wake up," Mom said, and when I didn't budge, she flung her glass of milk at me. I felt the milk splatter across my face and run down the front of my T-shirt, make a puddle on my clean floor. I sucked on the ends of my dripping hair as Mom walked slowly towards the door. Mr. Solemn rushed to the counter for paper towels.

I would set the table with place mats. I would use the good crystal.

*This short story by the fearless novelist, critic, and story writer Margaret Atwood begins with tennis, then wanders far afield: halfway around the world, where it collides with history.*

# The Man from Mars

## Margaret Atwood

A long time ago Christine was walking through the park. She was still wearing her tennis dress; she hadn't had time to shower and change, and her hair was held back with an elastic band. Her chunky reddish face, exposed with no softening fringe, looked like a Russian peasant's, but without the elastic band the hair got in her eyes. The afternoon was too hot for April; the indoor courts had been steaming, her skin felt poached.

The sun had brought the old men out from wherever they spent the winter: she had read a story recently about one who lived for three years in a manhole. They sat weedishly on the benches or lay on the grass with their heads on squares of used newspaper. As she passed, their wrinkled toadstool faces drifted towards her, drawn by the movement of her body, then floated away again, uninterested.

The squirrels were out, too, foraging; two or three of them moved towards her in darts and pauses, eyes fixed on her expectantly, mouths with the ratlike receding chins open to show the yellowed front teeth. Christine walked faster, she had nothing to give them. People shouldn't feed them, she thought; it makes them anxious and they get mangy.

Halfway across the park she stopped to take off her cardigan. As she bent over to pick up her tennis racquet again someone touched her on her freshly bared arm. Christine seldom screamed; she straightened up suddenly, gripping the handle of her racquet. It was not one of the old men, however; it was a dark-haired boy of twelve or so.

"Excuse me," he said. "I search for Economics Building. Is it there?" He motioned towards the west.

Christine looked at him more closely. She had been mistaken: he was not young, just short. He came a little above her shoulder, but then, she was above the average height; "statuesque," her mother called it when she was straining. He was also what was referred to in their family as "a person from another culture": oriental without a doubt, though perhaps not Chinese. Christine judged he must be a foreign student and gave him her official welcoming smile. In high school she had been president of the United Nations Club; that year her school had been picked

91

to represent the Egyptian delegation at the Mock Assembly. It had been an unpopular assignment—nobody wanted to be the Arabs—but she had seen it through. She had made rather a good speech about the Palestinian refugees.

"Yes," she said, "that's it over there. The one with the flat roof. See it?"

The man had been smiling nervously at her the whole time. He was wearing glasses with transparent plastic rims, through which his eyes bulged up at her as though through a goldfish bowl. He had not followed where she was pointing. Instead he thrust towards her a small pad of green paper and a ballpoint pen.

"You make map," he said.

Christine set down her tennis racquet and drew a careful map. "We are here," she said, pronouncing distinctly. "You go this way. The building is here." She indicated the route with a dotted line and an X. The man leaned close to her, watching the progress of the map attentively; he smelled of cooked cauliflower and an unfamiliar brand of hair grease. When she had finished Christine handed the paper and pen back to him with a terminal smile.

"Wait," the man said. He tore the piece of paper with the map off the pad, folded it carefully and put it in his jacket pocket; the jacket sleeves came down over his wrists and had threads at the edges. He began to write something; she noticed with a slight feeling of revulsion that his nails and the ends of his fingers were so badly bitten they seemed almost deformed. Several of his fingers were blue from the leaky ballpoint.

"Here is my name," he said, holding the pad out to her.

Christine read an odd assemblage of Gs, Ys and Ns, neatly printed in block letters. "Thank you," she said.

"You now write *your* name," he said, extending the pen.

Christine hesitated. If this had been a person from her own culture she would have thought he was trying to pick her up. But then, people from her own culture never tried to pick her up; she was too big. The only one who had made the attempt was the Moroccan waiter at the beer parlour where they sometimes went after meetings, and he had been direct. He had just intercepted her on the way to the Ladies' Room and asked and she said no; that had been that. This man was not a waiter though, but a student; she didn't want to offend him. In his culture, whatever it was, this exchange of names on pieces of paper was probably a formal politeness, like saying thank you. She took the pen from him.

"That is a very pleasant name," he said. He folded the paper and placed it in his jacket pocket with the map.

Christine felt she had done her duty. "Well, goodbye," she said. "It was nice to have met you." She bent for her tennis racquet but he had already stooped and retrieved it and was holding it with both hands in front of him, like a captured banner.

"I carry this for you."

"Oh no, please. Don't bother, I am in a hurry," she said, articulating clearly. Deprived of her tennis racquet she felt weaponless. He started to saunter along the path; he was not nervous at all now, he seemed completely at ease.

"*Vous parlez français?*" he asked conversationally.

"*Oui, un petit peu,*" she said. "Not very well." How am I going to get my racquet away from him without being rude? she was wondering.

"*Mais vous avez un bel accent.*" His eyes goggled at her through the glasses: was he being flirtatious? She was well aware that her accent was wretched.

"Look," she said, for the first time letting her impatience show, "I really have to go. Give me my racquet, please."

He quickened his pace but gave no sign of returning the racquet. "Where you are going?"

"Home," she said. "My house."

"I go with you now," he said hopefully.

"*No,*" she said: she would have to be firm with him. She made a lunge and got a grip on her racquet; after a brief tug of war it came free.

"Goodbye," she said, turning away from his puzzled face and setting off at what she hoped was a discouraging jog-trot. It was like walking away from a growling dog: you shouldn't let on you were frightened. Why should she be frightened anyway? He was only half her size and she had the tennis racquet, there was nothing he could do to her.

Although she did not look back she could tell he was still following. Let there be a streetcar, she thought, and there was one, but it was far down the line, stuck behind a red light. He appeared at her side, breathing audibly, a moment after she reached the stop. She gazed ahead, rigid.

"You are my friend," he said tentatively.

Christine relented: he hadn't been trying to pick her up after all, he was a stranger, he just wanted to meet some of the local people; in his place she would have wanted the same thing.

"Yes," she said, doling him out a smile.

"That is good," he said. "My country is very far."

Christine couldn't think of an apt reply. "That's interesting," she said. "*Très interessant.*" The streetcar was coming at last; she opened her purse and got out a ticket.

"I go with you now," he said. His hand clamped on her arm above the elbow.

"You . . . stay . . . *here*," Christine said, resisting the impulse to shout but pausing between each word as though for a deaf person. She detached his hand—his hold was quite feeble and could not compete with her tennis biceps—and leapt off the curb and up the streetcar steps, hearing with relief the doors grind shut behind her. Inside the car and a block away she permitted herself a glance out a side window. He was standing where she had left him; he seemed to be writing something on his little pad of paper.

When she reached home she had only time for a snack, and even then she was almost late for the Debating Society. The topic was, "Resolved: That War Is Obsolete." Her team took the affirmative and won.


Christine came out of her last examination feeling depressed. It was not the exam that depressed her but the fact that it was the last one: it meant the end of the school year. She dropped into the coffee shop as usual, then went home early because there didn't seem to be anything else to do.

"Is that you, dear?" her mother called from the living room. She must have heard the front door close. Christine went in and flopped on the sofa, disturbing the neat pattern of cushions.

"How was your exam, dear?" her mother asked.

"Fine," said Christine flatly. It had been fine; she had passed. She was a not a brilliant student, she knew that, but she was conscientious. Her professors always wrote things like "A serious attempt" and "Well thought out but perhaps lacking in *élan*" on her term papers; they gave her Bs, the occasional B+. She was taking Political Science and Economics, and hoped for a job with the Government after she graduated; with her father's connections she had a good chance.

"That's nice."

Christine felt, resentfully, that her mother had only a hazy idea of what an exam was. She was arranging gladioli in a vase; she had rubber gloves on to protect her hands as she always did when engaged in what she called "housework." As far as Christine could tell her housework consisted of arranging flowers in vases: daffodils and tulips and hyacinths through gladioli, irises and roses, all the way to asters and mums. Sometimes she cooked, elegantly and with chafing-dishes, but she thought of it as a hobby. The girl did everything else. Christine thought it faintly sinful to have a girl. The only ones available now were either foreign or pregnant; their expressions usually suggested they were being taken advantage of somehow. But her mother asked what they would do otherwise; they'd either have to go into a Home or stay in their own countries, and Christine had to agree this was probably true. It was hard, anyway, to argue with her mother. She was so delicate, so preserved-looking, a harsh breath would scratch the finish.

"An interesting young man phoned today," her mother said. She had finished the gladioli and was taking off her rubber gloves. "He asked to speak with you and when I said you weren't in we had quite a little chat. You didn't tell me about him, dear." She put on the glasses which she wore on a decorative chain around her neck, a signal that she was in her modern, intelligent mood rather than her old-fashioned whimsical one.

"Did he leave his name?" Christine asked. She knew a lot of young men but they didn't often call her; they conducted their business with her in the coffee shop or after meetings.

"He's a person from another culture. He said he would call back later."

Christine had to think a moment. She was vaguely acquainted with several people from other cultures, Britain mostly; they belonged to the Debating Society.

"He's studying Philosophy in Montreal," her mother prompted. "He sounded French."

Christine began to remember the man in the park. "I don't think he's French, exactly," she said.

Her mother had taken off her glasses again and was poking absent-mindedly at a bent gladiolus. "Well, he sounded French." She meditated, flowery sceptre in hand. "I think it would be nice if you had him to tea."

Christine's mother did her best. She had two other daughters, both of whom took after her. They were beautiful; one was well married already and the other would clearly have no trouble. Her friends consoled her about Christine by saying, "She's not fat, she's just big-boned, it's the father's side," and "Christine is so healthy." Her other daughters had never gotten involved in activities when they were at school, but since Christine could not possibly ever be beautiful even if she took off weight, it was just as well she was so athletic and political, it was a good thing she had interests. Christine's mother tried to encourage her interests whenever possible. Christine could tell when she was making an extra effort, there was a reproachful edge to her voice.

She knew her mother expected enthusiasm but she could not supply it. "I don't know, I'll have to see," she said dubiously.

"You look tired, darling," said her mother. "Perhaps you'd like a glass of milk."

Christine was in the bathtub when the phone rang. She was not prone to fantasy but when she was in the bathtub she often pretended she was a dolphin, a game left over from one of the girls who used to bathe her when she was small. Her mother was being bell-voiced and gracious in the hall; then there was a tap at the door.

"It's that nice young French student, Christine," her mother said.

"Tell him I'm in the bathtub," Christine said, louder than necessary. "He isn't French."

She could hear her mother frowning. "That wouldn't be very polite, Christine. I don't think he'd understand."

"Oh, all right," Christine said. She heaved herself out of the bathtub, swathed her pink bulk in a towel and splattered to the phone.

"Hello," she said gruffly. At a distance he was not pathetic, he was a nuisance. She could not imagine how he had tracked her down: most likely he went through the phone book, calling all the numbers with her last name until he hit on the right one.

"It is your friend."

"I know," she said. "How are you?"

"I am very fine." There was a long pause, during which Christine had a vicious urge to say, "Well, goodbye then," and hang up; but she was aware of her mother poised figurinelike in her bedroom doorway. Then he said, "I hope you also are very fine."

"Yes," said Christine. She wasn't going to participate.

"I come to tea," he said.

This took Christine by surprise, "You do?"

"Your pleasant mother ask me. I come Thursday, four o'clock."

"Oh," Christine said, ungraciously.

"See you then," he said, with the conscious pride of one who has mastered a difficult idiom.

Christine set down the phone and went along the hall. Her mother was in her study, sitting innocently at her writing desk.

"Did you ask him to tea on Thursday?"

"Not exactly, dear," her mother said. "I did mention he might come round to tea *some*time, though."

"Well, he's coming Thursday. Four o'clock."

"What's wrong with that?" her mother said serenely. "I think it's a very nice gesture for us to make. I do think you might try to be a little more co-operative." She was pleased with herself.

"Since you invited him," said Christine, "you can bloody well stick around and help me entertain him. I don't want to be left making nice gestures all by myself."

"Christine, *dear*," her mother said, above being shocked. "You ought to put on your dressing gown, you'll catch a chill."

After sulking for an hour Christine tried to think of the tea as a cross between an examination and an executive meeting; not enjoyable, certainly, but to be got through as tactfully as possible. And it *was* a nice gesture. When the cakes her mother had ordered arrived from *The Patisserie* on Thursday morning she began to feel slightly festive; she even resolved to put on a dress, a good one, instead of a skirt and blouse. After all, she had nothing against him, except the memory of the way he had grabbed her tennis racquet and then her arm. She suppressed a quick impossible vision of herself pursued around the living room, fending him off with thrown sofa cushions and vases of gladioli; nevertheless she told the girl they would have tea in the garden. It would be a treat for him, and there was more space outdoors.

She had suspected her mother would dodge the tea, would contrive to be going out just as he was arriving: that way she could size him up and then leave them alone together. She had done things like that to Christine before; the excuse this time was the Symphony Committee. Sure enough, her mother carefully mislaid her gloves and located them with a faked murmur of joy when the doorbell rang. Christine relished for weeks afterwards the image of her mother's dropped jaw and flawless recovery when he was introduced: he wasn't quite the foreign potentate her optimistic, veil-fragile mind had concocted.

He was prepared for celebration. He had slicked on so much hair cream that his head seemed to be covered with a tight black patent-leather cap, and he had cut the threads off his jacket sleeves. His orange tie was overpoweringly splendid. Christine noticed, however, as he shook her mother's suddenly-braced white glove that the ballpoint ink on his fingers was indelible. His face had broken out, possibly in anticipation of the delights in store for him; he had a tiny camera slung over his shoulder and was smoking an exotic-smelling cigarette.

Christine led him through the cool flowery softly-padded living room and out by the French doors into the garden. "You sit here," she said. "I will have the girl bring tea."

This girl was from the West Indies. Christine's parents had been enraptured with her when they were down at Christmas and had brought her back with them. Since that time she had become pregnant, but Christine's mother had not dismissed her. She said she was slightly disappointed but what could you expect, and she didn't see any real difference between a girl who was pregnant before you hired her and one who got that way afterwards. She prided herself on her tolerance; also there was a scarcity of girls. Strangely enough, the girl became progressively less easy to get along with. Either she did not share Christine's mother's view of her own generosity, or she felt she had gotten away with something and was therefore free to indulge in contempt. At first Christine had tried to treat her as an equal. "Don't call me 'Miss

Christine,' " she had said with an imitation of light, comradely laughter. "What you want me to call you then?" the girl had said, scowling. They had begun to have brief, surly arguments in the kitchen, which Christine decided were like the arguments between one servant and another. Her mother's attitude towards each of them was similar; they were not altogether satisfactory but they would have to do.

The cakes, glossy with icing, were set out on a plate and the teapot was standing ready; on the counter the electric kettle boiled. Christine headed for it, but the girl, till then sitting with her elbows on the kitchen table and watching her expressionlessly, made a dash and intercepted her. Christine waited until she had poured the water into the pot. Then, "I'll carry it out, Elvira," she said. She had just decided she didn't want the girl to see her visitor's orange tie; already, she knew, her position in the girl's eyes had suffered because no one had yet attempted to get *her* pregnant.

"What you think they pay me for, Miss Christine?" the girl said insolently. She swung towards the garden with the tray; Christine trailed her, feeling lumpish and awkward. The girl was at least as big as she was but in a different way.

"Thank you, Elvira," Christine said when the tray was in place. The girl departed without a word, casting a disdainful backwards glance at the frayed jacket sleeves, the stained fingers. Christine was now determined to be especially kind to him.

"You are very rich," he said.

"No," Christine protested, shaking her head, "we're not." She had never thought of her family as rich; it was one of her father's sayings that nobody made any money with the Government.

"Yes," he repeated, "you are very rich." He sat back in his lawn chair, gazing about him as though dazed.

Christine set his cup of tea in front of him. She wasn't in the habit of paying much attention to the house or the garden; they were nothing special, far from being the largest on the street; other people took care of them. But now she looked where he was looking, seeing it all as though from a different height: the long expanses, the border flowers blazing in the early-summer sunlight, the flagged patio and walks, the high walls and the silence.

He came back to her face, sighing a little. "My English is not good," he said, "but I improve."

"You do," Christine said, nodding encouragement.

He took sips of his tea, quickly and tenderly as though afraid of injuring the cup. "I like to stay here."

Christine passed him the cakes. He took only one, making a slight face as he ate it; but he had several more cups of tea while she finished the cakes. She managed to find out from him that he had come over on a church fellowship—she could not decode the denomination—and was studying Philosophy or Theology, or possibly both. She was feeling well-disposed towards him: he had behaved himself, he had caused her no inconvenience.

The teapot was at last empty. He sat up straight in his chair, as though alerted by a soundless gong. "You look this way, please," he said. Christine saw that he had placed his miniature camera on the stone sundial her mother had shipped back from England two years before. He wanted to take her picture. She was flattered, and settled herself to pose, smiling evenly.

He took off his glasses and laid them beside his plate. For a moment she saw his myopic, unprotected eyes turned towards her, with something tremulous and confiding in them she wanted to close herself off from knowing about. Then he went over and did something to the camera, his back to her. The next instant he was crouched beside her, his arm around her waist as far as it could reach, his other hand covering her own hands which she had folded in her lap, his cheek jammed up against hers. She was too startled to move. The camera clicked.

He stood up at once and replaced his glasses, which glittered now with a sad triumph. "Thank you, Miss," he said to her. "I go now." He slung the camera back over his shoulder, keeping his hand on it as though to hold the lid on and prevent escape. "I send to my family; they will like."

He was out the gate and gone before Christine had recovered; then she laughed. She had been afraid he would attack her, she could admit it now, and he had; but not in the usual way. He had raped, *rapeo, rapere, rapui, to seize and carry off,* not herself but her celluloid image, and incidentally that of the silver tea service, which glinted mockingly at her as the girl bore it away, carrying it regally, the insignia, the official jewels. Christine spent the summer as she had for the past three years: she was the sailing instructress at an expensive all-girls camp near Algonquin Park. She had been a camper there, everything was familiar to her; she sailed almost better than she played tennis.

The second week she got a letter from him, postmarked Montreal and forwarded from her home address. It was printed in block letters on a piece of the green paper, two or three sentences. It began, "I hope you are well," then described the weather in monosyllables and ended, "I am fine." It was signed, "Your friend." Each week she got another of these letters, more or less identical. In one of them a colour print was enclosed: himself, slightly cross-eyed and grinning hilariously, even more spindly than she remembered him against her billowing draperies, flowers exploding around them like firecrackers, one of his hands an

equivocal blur in her lap, the other out of sight; on her own face, astonishment and outrage, as though he was sticking her in the behind with
his hidden thumb.

She answered the first letter, but after that the seniors were in training for the races. At the end of the summer, packing to go home, she
threw all the letters away.

When she had been back for several weeks she received another of
the green letters. This time there was a return address printed at the
top which Christine noted with foreboding was in her own city. Every
day she waited for the phone to ring; she was so certain his first attempt
at contact would be a disembodied voice that when he came upon her
abruptly in mid-campus she was unprepared.

"How are you?"

His smile was the same, but everything else about him had deterio-
rated. He was, if possible, thinner; his jacket sleeves had sprouted a lush
new crop of threads, as though to conceal hands now so badly bitten
they appeared to have been gnawed by rodents. His hair fell over his
eyes, uncut, ungreased; his eyes in the hollowed face, a delicate triangle
of skin stretched on bone, jumped behind his glasses like hooked fish.
He had the end of a cigarette in the corner of his mouth, and as they
walked he lit a new one from it.

"I'm fine," Christine said. She was thinking, I'm not going to get involved again, enough is enough, I've done my bit for internationalism.
"How are you?"

"I live here now," he said. "Maybe I study Economics."

"That's nice." He didn't sound as though he was enrolled anywhere.

"I come to see you."

Christine didn't know whether he meant he had left Montreal in
order to be near her or just wanted to visit her at her house as he had
done in the spring; either way she refused to be implicated. They were
outside the Political Science building. "I have a class here," she said.
"Goodbye." She was being callous, she realized that, but a quick chop
was more merciful in the long run, that was what her beautiful sisters
used to say.

Afterwards she decided it had been stupid of her to let him find out
where her class was. Though a timetable was posted in each of the colleges: all he had to do was look her up and record her every probable
movement in block letters on his green notepad. After that day he
never left her alone.

Initially he waited outside the lecture rooms for her to come out.
She said hello to him curtly at first and kept on going, but this didn't
work; he followed her at a distance, smiling his changeless smile. Then

she stopped speaking altogether and pretended to ignore him, but it made no difference, he followed her anyway. The fact that she was in some way afraid of him—or was it just embarrassment?—seemed only to encourage him. Her friends started to notice, asking her who he was and why he was tagging along behind her; she could hardly answer because she hardly knew.

As the weekdays passed and he showed no signs of letting up, she began to jog-trot between classes, finally to run. He was tireless, and had an amazing wind for one who smoked so heavily: he would speed along behind her, keeping the distance between them the same, as though he were a pull-toy attached to her by a string. She was aware of the ridiculous spectacle they must make, galloping across campus, something out of a cartoon short, a lumbering elephant stampeded by a smiling, emaciated mouse, both of them locked in the classic pattern of comic pursuit and flight; but she found that to race made her less nervous than to walk sedately, the skin on the back of her neck crawling with the feel of his eyes on it. At least she could use her muscles. She worked out routines, escapes: she would dash in the front door of the Ladies' Room in the coffee shop and out the back door, and he would lose the trail, until he discovered the other entrance. She would try to shake him by detours through baffling archways and corridors, but he seemed as familiar with the architectural mazes as she was herself. As a last refuge she could head for the women's dormitory and watch from safety as he was skidded to a halt by the receptionist's austere voice: men were not allowed past the entrance.

Lunch became difficult. She would be sitting, usually with other members of the Debating Society, just digging nicely into a sandwich, when he would appear suddenly as though he'd come up through an unseen manhole. She then had the choice of barging out through the crowded cafeteria, sandwich half-eaten, or finishing her lunch with him standing behind her chair, everyone at the table acutely aware of him, the conversation stilting and dwindling. Her friends learned to spot him from a distance; they posted lookouts. "Here he comes," they would whisper, helping her collect her belongings for the sprint they knew would follow.

Several times she got tired of running and turned to confront him. "What do you want?" she would ask, glowering belligerently down at him, almost clenching her fists; she felt like shaking him, hitting him.

"I wish to talk with you."

"Well, here I am," she would say. "What do you want to talk about?"

But he would say nothing; he would stand in front of her, shifting his feet, smiling perhaps apologetically (though she could never pinpoint the exact tone of that smile, chewed lips stretched apart over the nicotine-yellowed teeth, rising at the corners, flesh held stiffly in place for an invisible photographer), his eyes jerking from one part of her face to another as though he saw her in fragments.

Annoying and tedious though it was, his pursuit of her had an odd result: mysterious in itself, it rendered her equally mysterious. No one had ever found Christine mysterious before. To her parents she was a beefy heavyweight, a plodder, lacking in flair, ordinary as bread. To her sisters she was the plain one, treated with an indulgence they did not give to each other: they did not fear her as a rival. To her male friends she was the one who could be relied on. She was helpful and a hard worker, always good for a game of tennis with the athletes among them. They invited her along to drink beer with them so they could get into the cleaner, more desirable Ladies and Escorts side of the beer parlour, taking it for granted she would buy her share of the rounds. In moments of stress they confided to her their problems with women. There was nothing devious about her and nothing interesting.

Christine had always agreed with these estimates of herself. In childhood she had identified with the false bride or the ugly sister; whenever a story had begun, "Once there was a maiden as beautiful as she was good," she had known it wasn't her. That was just how it was, but it wasn't so bad. Her parents never expected her to be a brilliant social success and weren't overly disappointed when she wasn't. She was spared the manoeuvring and anxiety she witnessed among others her age, and she even had a kind of special position among men: she was an exception, she fitted none of the categories they commonly used when talking about girls; she wasn't a cock-teaser, a cold fish, an easy lay or a snarky bitch; she was an honorary person. She had grown to share their contempt for most women.

Now, however, there was something about her that could not be explained. A man was chasing her, a peculiar sort of man, granted, but still a man, and he was without doubt attracted to her, he couldn't leave her alone. Other men examined her more closely than they ever had, appraising her, trying to find out what it was those twitching bespectacled eyes saw in her. They started to ask her out, though they returned from these excursions with their curiosity unsatisfied, the secret of her charm still intact. Her opaque dumpling face, her solid bear-shaped body became for them parts of a riddle no one could solve. Christine sensed this. In the bathtub she no longer imagined she was a dolphin; instead she imagined she was an elusive water-nixie, or sometimes, in moments of audacity, Marilyn Monroe. The daily chase was becoming a habit; she even looked forward to it. In addition to its other benefits she was losing weight.

All these weeks he had never phoned her or turned up at the

house. He must have decided however that his tactics were not having the desired result, or perhaps he sensed she was becoming bored. The phone began to ring in the early morning or late at night when he could be sure she would be there. Sometimes he would simply breathe (she could recognize, or thought she could, the quality of his breathing), in which case she would hang up. Occasionally he would say again that he wanted to talk to her, but even when she gave him lots of time nothing else would follow. Then he extended his range: she would see him on her streetcar, smiling at her silently from a seat never closer than three away; she could feel him tracking her down her own street, though when she would break her resolve to pay no attention and would glance back he would be invisible or in the act of hiding behind a tree or hedge.

Among crowds of people and in daylight she had not really been afraid of him; she was stronger than he was and he had made no recent attempt to touch her. But the days were growing shorter and colder, it was almost November, often she was arriving home in twilight or a darkness broken only by the feeble orange streetlamps. She brooded over the possibility of razors, knives, guns; by acquiring a weapon he could quickly turn the odds against her. She avoided wearing scarves, remembering the newspaper stories about girls who had been strangled by them. Putting on her nylons in the morning gave her a funny feeling. Her body seemed to have diminished, to have become smaller than his.

Was he deranged, was he a sex maniac? He seemed so harmless, yet it was that kind who often went berserk in the end. She pictured those ragged fingers at her throat, tearing at her clothes, though she could not think of herself as screaming. Parked cards, the shrubberies near her house, the driveways on either side of it, changed as she passed them from unnoticed background to sinister shadowed foreground, every detail distinct and harsh: they were places a man might crouch, leap out from. Yet every time she saw him in the clear light of morning or afternoon (for he still continued his old methods of pursuit), his aging jacket and jittery eyes convinced her that it was she herself who was the tormentor, the persecutor. She was in some sense responsible; from the folds and crevices of the body she had treated for so long as a reliable machine was emanating, against her will, some potent invisible odour, like a dog's in heat or a female moth's, that made him unable to stop following her.

Her mother, who had been too preoccupied with the unavoidable fall entertaining to pay much attention to the number of phone calls Christine was getting or to the hired girl's complaints of a man who hung up without speaking, announced that she was flying down to New York for the weekend; her father decided to go too. Christine panicked:

she saw herself in the bathtub with her throat slit, the blood drooling
out of her neck and running in a little spiral down the drain (for by this
time she believed he could walk through walls, could be everywhere at
once). The girl would do nothing to help; she might even stand in the
bathroom door with her arms folded, watching. Christine arranged to
spend the weekend at her married sister's.

When she arrived back Sunday evening she found the girl close to
hysterics. She said that on Saturday she had gone to pull the curtains
across the French doors at dusk and had found a strangely contorted
face, a man's face, pressed against the glass, staring at her from the garden. She claimed she had fainted and had almost had her baby a month
too early right there on the living room carpet. Then she had called the
police. He was gone by the time they got there but she had recognized
him from the afternoon of the tea; she had informed them he was a
friend of Christine's.

They called Monday evening to investigate, two of them. They were
very polite, they knew who Christine's father was. Her father greeted
them heartily; her mother hovered in the background, fidgeting with
her porcelain hands, letting them see how frail and worried she was.
She didn't like having them in the living room but they were necessary.

Christine had to admit he'd been following her around. She was relieved he'd been discovered, relieved also that she hadn't been the one
to tell, though if he'd been a citizen of the country she would have
called the police a long time ago. She insisted he was not dangerous, he
had never hurt her.

"That kind don't hurt you," one of the policemen said. "They just
kill you. You're lucky you aren't dead."

"Nut cases," the other one said.

Her mother volunteered that the thing about people from another
culture was that you could never tell whether they were insane or not
because their ways were so different. The policeman agreed with her,
deferential but also condescending, as though she was a royal halfwit
who had to be humoured.

"You know where he lives?" the first policeman asked. Christine had
long ago torn up the letter with his address on it; she shook her head.

"We'll have to pick him up tomorrow then," he said. "Think you can
keep him talking outside your class if he's waiting for you?"

After questioning her they held a murmured conversation with her
father in the front hall. The girl, clearing away the coffee cups, said if
they didn't lock him up she was leaving, she wasn't going to be scared
half out of her skin like that again.

Next day when Christine came out of her Modern History lecture
he was there, right on schedule. He seemed puzzled when she did not

begin to run. She approached him, her heart thumping with treachery and the prospect of freedom. Her body was back to its usual size; she felt herself a giantess, self-controlled, invulnerable.

"How are you?" she asked, smiling brightly.

He looked at her with distrust.

"How have you been?" she ventured again. His own perennial smile faded; he took a step back from her.

"This the one?" said the policeman, popping out from behind a notice board like a Keystone Kop and laying a competent hand on the worn jacket shoulder. The other policeman lounged in the background; force would not be required.

"Don't *do* anything to him," she pleaded as they took him away. They nodded and grinned, respectful, scornful. He seemed to know perfectly well who they were and what they wanted.

The first policeman phoned that evening to make his report. Her father talked with him, jovial and managing. She herself was now out of the picture; she had been protected, her function was over.

"What did they *do* to him?" she asked anxiously as he came back into the living room. She was not sure what went on in police stations.

"They didn't do anything to him," he said, amused by her concern. "They could have booked him for Watching and Besetting, they wanted to know if I'd like to press charges. But it's not worth a court case: he's got a visa that says he's only allowed in the country as long as he studies in Montreal, so I told them to just ship him down there. If he turns up here again they'll deport him. They went around to his rooming house, his rent's two weeks overdue; the landlady said she was on the point of kicking him out. He seems happy enough to be getting his back rent paid and a free train ticket to Montreal." He paused. "They couldn't get anything out of him though."

"*Out* of him?" Christine asked.

"They tried to find out why he was doing it; following you, I mean." Her father's eyes swept her as though it was a riddle to him also. "They said when they asked him about that he just clammed up. Pretended he didn't understand English. He understood well enough, but he wasn't answering."

Christine thought this would be the end, but somehow between his arrest and the departure of the train he managed to elude his escort long enough for one more phone call.

"I see you again," he said. He didn't wait for her to hang up.

Now that he was no longer an embarrassing present reality, he could be talked about, he could become an amusing story. In fact, he was the only amusing story Christine had to tell, and telling it preserved both for herself and for others the aura of her strange allure. Her friends and the men who continued to ask her out speculated about his motives. One suggested he had wanted to marry her so he could remain in the country; another said that oriental men were fond of well-built women: "It's your Rubens quality."

Christine thought about him a lot. She had not been attracted to him, rather the reverse, but as an idea only he was a romantic figure, the one man who had found her irresistible; though she often wondered, inspecting her unchanged pink face and hefty body in her full-length mirror, just what it was about her that had done it. She avoided whenever it was proposed the theory of his insanity: it was only that there was more than one way of being sane.

But a new acquaintance, hearing the story for the first time, had a different explanation. "So he got you, too," he said, laughing. "That has to be the same guy who was hanging around our day camp a year ago this summer. He followed all the girls like that. A short guy, Japanese or something, glasses, smiling all the time."

"Maybe it was another one," Christine said.

"There couldn't be two of them, everything fits. This was a pretty weird guy."

"What . . . *kind* of girls did he follow?" Christine asked.

"Oh, just anyone who happened to be around. But if they paid any attention to him at first, if they were nice to him or anything, he was unshakeable. He was a bit of a pest, but harmless."

Christine ceased to tell her amusing story. She had been one among many, then. She went back to playing tennis, she had been neglecting her game.

A few months later the policeman who had been in charge of the case telephoned her again.

"Like you to know, Miss, that fellow you were having the trouble with was sent back to his own country. Deported."

"What for?" Christine asked. "Did he try to come back here?" Maybe she had been special after all, maybe he had dared everything for her.

"Nothing like it," the policeman said. "He was up to the same tricks in Montreal but he really picked the wrong woman this time—a Mother Superior of a convent. They don't stand for things like that in Quebec—had him out of here before he knew what happened. I guess he'll be better off in his own place."

"How old was she?" Christine asked, after a silence.

"Oh, around sixty, I guess."

"Thank you very much for letting me know," Christine said in her

best official manner. "It's such a relief." She wondered if the policeman
had called to make fun of her.

She was almost crying when she put down the phone. What *had* he
wanted from her then? A Mother Superior. Did she really look sixty, did
she look like a mother? What did convents mean? Comfort, charity?
Refuge? Was it that something had happened to him, some intolerable
strain just from being in this country; her tennis dress and exposed legs
too much for him, flesh and money seemingly available everywhere but
withheld from him wherever he turned, the nun the symbol of some
final distortion, the robe and veil reminiscent to his near-sighted eyes of
the women of his homeland, the ones he was able to understand? But
he was back in his own country, remote from her as another planet; she
would never know.

He hadn't forgotten her though. In the spring she got a postcard
with a foreign stamp and the familiar block-letter writing. On the front
was a picture of a temple. He was fine, he hoped she was fine also, he was
her friend. A month later another print of the picture he had taken in
the garden arrived, in a sealed manila envelope otherwise empty.

Christine's aura of mystery soon faded; anyway, she herself no
longer believed in it. Life became again what she had always expected.
She graduated with mediocre grades and went into the Department of
Health and Welfare; she did a good job, and was seldom discriminated
against for being a woman because nobody thought of her as one. She
could afford a pleasant-sized apartment, though she did not put much
energy into decorating it. She played less and less tennis; what had been
muscle with a light coating of fat turned gradually into fat with a thin
substratum of muscle. She began to get headaches.

As the years were used up and the war began to fill the newspapers
and magazines, she realized which eastern country he had actually
been from. She had known the name but it hadn't registered at the
time, it was such a minor place; she could never keep them separate in
her mind.

But though she tried, she couldn't remember the name of the city,
and the postcard was long gone—had he been from the North or the
South, was he near the battle zone or safely far from it? Obsessively she
bought magazines and pored over the available photographs, dead vil-
lagers, soldiers on the march, colour blowups of frightened or angry
faces, spies being executed; she studied maps, she watched the late-
night newscasts, the distant country and terrain becoming almost more
familiar to her than her own. Once or twice she thought she could recognize him but it was no use, they all looked like him.

Finally she had to stop looking at the pictures. It bothered her too much, it was bad for her; she was beginning to have nightmares in which he was coming through the French doors of her mother's house in his shabby jacket, carrying a packsack and a rifle and a huge bouquet of richly coloured flowers. He was smiling in the same way but with blood streaked over his face, partly blotting out the features. She gave her television set away and took to reading nineteenth-century novels instead; Trollope and Galsworthy were her favourites. When, despite herself, she would think about him, she would tell herself that he had been crafty and agile-minded enough to survive, more or less, in her country, so surely he would be able to do it in his own, where he knew the language. She could not see him in the army, on either side; he wasn't the type; and to her knowledge he had not believed in any particular ideology. He would be something nondescript, something in the background, like herself. Perhaps he had become an interpreter.

*In this excerpt from Tara McCarthy's novel* Never Tear Us Apart: My Life with Flora and Fauna Sparks, *celebrity journalist Sloan Madden recalls one of her first encounters with an . . .* unusual *pair of teenage pop stars whose authorized biography she has been commissioned to write.*

# Deuce

## Tara McCarthy

Brian woke up aroused and almost made me late for breakfast with the twins. He begged me to bring him along—I was never more popular than during the time I knew the twins—but I firmly refused.

"It'd be unprofessional," I said.

He faked a pout. "You're no fun."

I kissed him hard. "Now I know you don't mean that."

He slapped me on the ass as I left the bed. "No, I don't suppose I do."

It wasn't the first time Brian and I had gone back to drink from the fountain over the years, but this was the only time that my susceptibility to his charm and unflagging sexual appetite would really cause trouble. I hadn't had sex in so long that the attention of this man who couldn't get enough of me cast a spell. I might have been a cynical, hardened, single bitch when I'd stepped off the plane from New York City, but I was naming the kids by the time I revved the engine on my red rental car the morning after.

As I consulted the directions Brian had printed for me from Map Quest—he'd looked so cute sitting at his computer in the buff—I thought maybe, just maybe, he was no longer the lothario he'd once been. Maybe he was ready to settle down and have babies. Maybe I was, too. Just maybe this strange turn of events involving the Sparks sisters— namely their unanticipated request that I abandon my magazine feature and write their biography—was only one of two incentives to stay on the West Coast for a while. I'd been in L.A. less than twenty-four hours and already it seemed possible that the life I'd always imagined, the one that was just the right guy and the right gig away, was upon me. At the ripe old age of thirty-five, I was ready for it. More than ready. In fact, I was so desperate for it that I didn't give a second thought that morning to the "Always" peel-away I spotted in Brian's trash bin.

I'd agreed to meet Flora and Fauna at their country club to discuss the book I'd been asked to write. As I steered through the shadowy roads of Bel-Air, the suggestion of mansions behind towering green walls of shrubbery seduced me further. I couldn't help but think that if the book I was to write sold even a fraction of the number of records Flora and Fauna had sold to date, I'd be rich before long. The twins had been dominating the *Billboard* charts ever since "I'm Beside Myself" had hit the airwaves two years previous—and their upcoming Grammy sweep and third album, *Girl Wonder*, were about to secure their place as the premiere teen-pop queens of the new millennium. As if tempting the Fates, I turned on the radio and, sure enough, there they were, on the third station to pop up on the scanner. With the volume high and the windows low, I put on my shades and sang along:

*"With our hearts in time and your hand in mine I'm beside myself with love."*

At the club, I entrusted my car to a valet and entered the main building. I found the restaurant easily and told the maître d' that I was meeting the Sparks party, which I'd presumed would include Fred. Whether as father or manager, he'd likely have a contract of some sort for me to sign.

The maître d' reached for a slip of paper on the reservations podium. "That would make you Sloan Madden," he said.

"Indeed it would," I said, remembering just then to take off my sunglasses and feeling, I'm embarrassed to admit, pretty damn important.

"They've left a message," said the maître d'. "They've asked that you meet them on the tennis courts." He fussed with the reservations book without apparent purpose.

I scanned the near-empty restaurant and thought I spotted Ben Stiller's wife. "I'm sorry," I said, thinking, *Marcia! Marcia! Marcia!* "But what are they doing on the tennis courts?"

"Uh . . ." he began—and with the tone he took, he might as well have said "duh"—"they're playing tennis."

I thought, *Of course they are.*

They were rich and famous and fit; why should the fact that they were fused at the spine prevent them from enjoying a popular leisure activity? Any number of sports might have been impossible for pygopagus Siamese twins; cycling, say, or luge. But tennis? Sure. Why not? I'd been more surprised when I'd learned that Flora and Fauna had a rock-climbing wall at The Joint, their massive, custom-designed, notoriously symmetrical Beverly Hills home.

As I made my way through labyrinthine garden pathways leading to the courts, I came upon a middle-aged couple. When they turned and saw me, the man shoved a camera under his jacket. They rushed past and disappeared around a curve and I stepped up to the spot they'd evacuated. Through Bird of Paradise plumes, I found a clear view of

Flora (hair in high pigtails) and Fauna (with a low ponytail) and felt a strong urge to give chase; I'd tackle the shutterbug, confiscate his film, and save the twins from what I imagined to be the freaky experience of happening upon pictures of yourself you'd never known were taken. The sight of the twins, however, rendered me paralyzed just as it had the day before, and I was suddenly grateful I'd first met them poolside, in bikinis and sarongs. I would not—repeat, *would not*—pass out this time.

Dressed in matching white, pleated tennis skirts and pink-and-white striped T-shirts, the girls wielded rackets confidently and alternately returned balls being hurled at them by a machine. Their blond hair jumped animatedly with each movement, and when they turned to allow Flora to practice her backhand without whacking her sister, I could see that her tee was tied in a knot to expose her navel; Fauna's top was tucked in tight. A wiry man crouched behind them seemed to be murmuring encouragement, though I was too far away to hear.

I took a few deep breaths once I realized my heart was racing; despite all the videos and photos I'd seen over the years, the actual sight of them still had the power to quicken my pulse. So I stood and watched them from that secret place, willing myself to become somehow used to the fact that they weren't just identical twins standing too close. I needed to grow accustomed to their movements, more arachnidan than human, so I wouldn't have to cope with this kind of shock every time I saw them. Surely it would wear on them as much as it would on me.

My nerves finally calmed, I pressed on and found my way to court level, where Fred Sparks was sitting under a sun umbrella near the net. He gestured wordlessly to a second lawn chair beside him, and I stepped around a small red cooler so that I could sit down. On account of the hour—just 10:00 A.M.—I noted the can of Budweiser in Fred's hand, but it wouldn't be long before I would have a hard time picturing him without one no matter the time of day.

"Hey, Sloan!"

I looked up to see Fauna wiping sweat from her brow. "You play?"

"No. Not really."

Flora pushed her way out from behind her sister, rotating their bodies to the left with a little dip and step that looked like a cute line-dancing move. "I don't believe you," she said, swinging her racket like a pendulum. "Come on. We'll kick your butt."

I looked at Fred—*Could they be serious?*—and his eyes met mine sharply. The look on his face was one I would see many times during the next several months. It was the look of a weary but fierce man defying someone—*anyone, go on*—to deny his daughters what they wanted. Suddenly, I wanted to know everything about this man who had raised these seemingly well-adjusted conjoined twins. Would he have had those lines and those grays had the egg fully separated? Would he have been as supportive of his girls if they hadn't made him a millionaire ten times over? Would he have let their mother back into his bed if she'd resurfaced after all those years? Would he invite *me* into it, to move against his lanky body, once he'd had enough Budweisers? The fact that he had seventeen-year-old daughters didn't necessarily make him much older than I was, but he looked it.

"Well," said Fauna, "Are you coming?"

I severed Fred's stare and got up. "Alright," I intoned, with a skeptical lilt, "but be warned. I spent a year on the tennis team of the local swimming club when I was twelve."

"Oooh," said Flora.

"Our knees are shaking," said Fauna.

And so their teacher, who swiftly introduced himself as Ralph and just as swiftly steered the serving machine off the court, handed me a racket and a ball. I walked to the far end of the court and toed the line. I touched ball to my racket with extended arms, then hefted the fuzzy sphere over my head and swung.

I missed.

"Oh yeah," Flora said dryly. "We're in trouble."

I chased after the ball clumsily, like a kangaroo with poor depth perception, and finally bent to swat at it a few times before it mercifully came to rest. "I haven't played in years," I said as I picked up the ball and returned to the baseline. "Cut me some slack."

"We're sorry," said Fauna, covering her mouth to hide her laughter. When I dropped the ball again, Flora doubled over—I thought, *That's got to hurt*—and let out one more loud cackle before straightening both torso and expression.

"Sorry," she said, but she was apologizing to me, not to her sister, so maybe it didn't hurt at all.

This time, instead of attempting an overhead serve, I opted for a simpler approach. I bounced the ball and sent it soaring over the net on the upswing. The twins moved left in a quick cross-step and Fauna easily made the return. Apparently she was left-handed and Flora right. I wondered whether that was by birth or necessity as I rushed forward, just barely catching the lime-green globe with an upward stroke that sent it way high, back over the girls' heads. They moved down-court in sure, syncopated steps, like a horse trotting effortlessly backwards.

Flora called, "I got it," then switched her racket to her left hand— her inside hand—and sent the ball back over their heads from behind. Fauna had to duck to avoid getting elbowed in the ear.

I tried to duplicate their easy backward movement to get to the ball this time, but my feet wouldn't cooperate. I fell hard on my ass.

The girls rushed the net.

"Are you okay?"

"Are you hurt?"

My pride more wounded than anything—*When did I become such a spaz?*—I started to get up. In an instant, Fred was helping me to my feet with the steady arms that had broken my fall the day before.

"At least you stayed conscious this time" he said as I brushed off the seat of my shorts. He smelled like beer and freesia.

"We can stop," Fauna said.

"No, it's okay," I said. I never did much like losing. But neither did I like giving up. Besides, it wasn't like I'd any intention of actually trying to *beat* the girls. At that moment, anyway, I pitied them far too much for that. It would be a few months before I would begin to fathom that I might one day stop feeling so sorry for them, might stop hiding my true nature in an attempt to protect them—from the world, from their plight, from the way that my life, so ridiculously individualistic, threw that plight into high relief. Though it's true I was about to have my first spectacular lapse in generosity.

"Why don't you serve," I said, tossing a ball over the net. I walked beyond the service line, turned, and assumed a bent-knee stance. I swayed back and forth with my racket at the ready between my legs. Out of long-forgotten habit, I spun it in my hands.

"Check it out," Flora said to her sister, as Fauna prepared to serve. "Sloan's doing an impersonation of a tennis player."

"Oh, so that's how it's going to be?" I realized I hadn't yet had a cigarette that morning. "We're talking trash?"

"Is that what you old people call it?" Flora asked.

And with that Fauna served and I darted right. The ball I sent back barely crossed the net, so the girls had to rush forward, which they did with success. I was right in their faces to continue the rally, though, and hit the ball hard over Fauna's left shoulder. It bounced just inside the sideline.

"Lucky break," Flora said as she pulled a ball out of her pocket.

"Yeah, well, I hate to tell you"—I was getting short of breath—"but you're not exactly Venus and Serena."

Fauna's eyes snapped to mine and I felt a flash of guilt and fear.

"Yeah, well, you're no Jennifer Capriati over there," Flora said. She squeezed her racket between her knobby knees so she could adjust a pigtail with her free hands.

I let air enter my lungs.

"We've only just started taking lessons," said Fauna.

Then I heard a male voice:

"Sloan? Sloan Madden?"

The twins looked up toward the path behind me and I turned. It was Brian.

He came forward with a shocked smile. "It *is* you. My God, it's been years. How the hell are you? You look *great*."

I just stared at him, thinking, *What on earth could he be up to?* Thinking, *That color green makes his eyes look really blue.*

"Don't tell me you don't remember me," he said, baring his unnaturally white teeth. "Brian Understahl? We went to college together?"

*Yeah, and you had me bent me over your bureau not two hours ago.* My face felt hot. My insides clenched. I had no idea at the time that this was merely my first lesson in a course that would take several months to complete; in the end, it would teach me that what was true in bed was true out of it, too. Brian got what Brian wanted.

"Sloan?" Fred called. "You know this guy?" He was out of his seat and coming closer.

"Yeah," I called. "It's okay."

Brian waved, said "How do you do," and Fred receded.

"I'm so sorry to barge in," my lover continued, turning back to the twins. "It's just Sloan over here, well, I saw her from the path up there and I guess I always wondered what happened to her." He stepped toward the girls and held out a hand. "I'm Brian."

It was only then that I noticed he'd brought props: He was actually holding a tennis racket.

"Nice to meet you," Flora said, shaking Brian's hand. "I'm Flora."

"And I'm Fauna," said her sister.

"But of course I already knew that," Brian said, winking at Flora and bowing to kiss Fauna's hand.

I thought, *Oh give me a break.*

"Sloan's going to write our biography," Fauna blurted, as if words could hide the blush that was deepening so as to rival her sister's tan.

"No kidding!" Brian beamed at me. "That's brilliant. I always knew you'd make it big. Anyway . . ." He pulled out his wallet. "Here's my card." He handed it to me. "Look me up. I'd love to do drinks."

"That'd be great," I said, because I had to say *something*.

"And hey, such an honor to meet you," he said, as he backed away. "I absolutely *love* your stuff." He looked at Flora, who seemed to have hiked her top even higher when no one was paying attention, and he actually licked his lips. Then he turned and smiled at Fauna, who was beaming in spite of herself.

"We could use a fourth," Flora said, pointing to his racket.

"Wish I could," he said. "But I've got a meeting. I'm a lowly little screenwriter and a director is deigning to buy me lunch." Then he declared in all seriousness: "You two should really be in pictures. In fact,

I've got just the project for you, now that I think of it." He nodded his head thoughtfully. "We should talk about it. Sloan has my info."

I thought, *Oh, he's goooood,* and he was gone.

"He's hot," said Flora, when I turned to face them again.

"You think?" I said, indulging a split-second of pride.

"Oh totally," said Fauna. "And super sweet."

Then Flora said, "I'd do him in a second," and I had to choke back my shock.

I looked toward Fred, who was out of earshot—but then Flora would have known that. What she didn't yet know was that I didn't like to be screwed with. Not by Brian. Not by her. And when I saw her poking her tongue around in her mouth—as if to foil the smirk that would have appeared otherwise—I knew she was screwing with me. I just didn't know why she'd chosen sexual bravado as her method.

"Wouldn't you?" she asked, swinging her racket again in a silent tick-tock.

I forced the beginning of a smile, then caught Fauna's eye. "What is she, writing a book?"

Fauna shrugged and Flora said, "I bet I could get him, too."

She bounced the ball she was holding in such a way that Fauna apparently knew to catch it on the rebound.

"So," Flora said, "are we going to play it out or what?"

"Absolutely," I said, as I watched them bounce a ball back and forth between their middle hands. "But I just realized that you two have an unfair advantage."

Flora's tongue went to work again inside her mouth. "And what might that be?"

"You've got two rackets."

So I guess I was through playing nice.

No longer able to control the wry smile tugging at the corners of her lip-glossed mouth, Flora tossed her racket courtside and put a hand on her hip. "Well, it took you long enough to figure *that* out."

And at that point I grew hell-bent on kicking their asses. Or at least Flora's; if I had to take Fauna down, too, then that was how it was going to be. There they were in all their freakiness—two perfect little bodies joined in a complex bundle of nerves and bone—but was I any less freaky? Did I deserve any less pity or consideration? For every time they'd been asked "Do you sleep at the same time?" I'd been asked, "Are you seeing anyone?" For every time a member of the press wanted to know, "Do you like the same boys?" a married friend of mine had suggested that maybe I was just a little bit too picky. (Come on, maybe just a little?) They had their big breasts and fame and fortune—and girlish optimism, God love them—and what did I have? A pack-a-day habit, a string of failed relationships, and a reputation as a career woman in spite of a career that never quite took off.

Flora and Fauna would never be seated at the singles' table at a wedding. They'd never run through their entire address book trying to find a friend who might go out with them so they could maybe meet someone new. Maybe, I thought at the time, the only thing we three really had in common was the fact that there existed people on the planet who were convinced we were lesbians—Flora and Fauna because of their forced proximity; me on account of my ghastly dry-spell.

But that was all behind me, and I wasn't turning back. I had a man in my corner for the first time in ages and I was going to do everything in my power to keep him there, his crazy schemes aside. After all, everyone in the free world wanted to meet the twins in person; why should Brian be any different? And really, I'd made it pretty easy for him, hadn't I?

So I ignored the knot forming in my stomach and concentrated on my game. Since the reality of my opponents was too distracting, I decided to pretend I was playing a top-of-the-line virtual reality game. I'd simply selected Siamese Twins—over, say, Kung Fu Fighters—from a menu of computer-generated opponents. The switch down to one racket had barely affected the twins' game, but I was starting to find my groove.

"Time out," I eventually said, when I was winded from what must have been a solid twenty minutes of play. "Who's keeping score, anyway?" I made my way to the chair beside Fred.

"You're so competitive," said Flora as she and Fauna followed me off the court and picked up bottles of water. Their nails were the same color pink.

"We should really get down to business," said Fred, who handed me my own water as he cracked open another Bud. "We promised Sloan here breakfast."

I thought, *Water? Cigarette? Water? Cigarette?*

"In a minute, Dad," Flora said, and she and her sister squirted water on each other's necks. As they walked back onto the court, Flora said, "Match point."

Taken aback, I said, "I honestly don't think so."

And she said, "Well, I do."

We both looked at Fauna, who could only shrug once more.

I poked fingers through my racket to adjust the strings as if that would make any difference at all. Since I'd stepped off the plane, my life had apparently gone on autopilot, and me, I was locked in cargo.

"You ready?" Flora shouted, and in spite of her earlier mockery, I assumed the position.

"As ready as I'll ever be," I answered.

"Actually, I think it's my turn to serve," Fauna said.

Flora rolled her eyes at her sister and handed her the racket. "Whatever," she said, folding her arms. "Just get it over with."

And with one swift serve she did.

When I got into my car an hour later—legal papers had been exchanged over a meal—I called Brian and didn't mince words: "What the fuck was that about?"

"I have no idea what you're talking about," he said.

"*They ought to be in pictures?*"

"Must have been my evil twin."

"You could have gotten me in trouble."

"Ah, but I didn't."

"Still . . ." But I didn't know what else to say.

He exhaled hard and let out a little moan. "Can we talk about it after you come over and let me eat your fabulous—"

Call waiting signaled another call. "Hold that thought," I said, lust replicating in my head.

"Hello?" I said, after clicking over.

"Sloan?"

"Yes."

"It's Fauna."

The fact that I'd only left her maybe ten minutes before confused me.

"You have to help me," she said, her voice far away and tinny.

"Where are you?"

"In the limo. Dad's gone off to take care of some other business and Flora just fell asleep."

"I don't understand." And I wanted to get back to Brian, so I could say something about his hard—.

"You have to help me," Fauna said again, interrupting my thought.

"You already said that," I snapped. "Help you with what?"

There was a crack and hiss on the line before she said the words that would keep me up that night and many other nights to come: "I want to record a solo album."

# Part III

# Men's Tennis

*You guys are the pits of the world!*
   —The Pretenders
    (paraphrasing John McEnroe),
    "Pack It Up"

*As in Ellen Gilchrist's story in Part II, "The Tennis Court" uses the country club (one located in Malaysia during the 1960s) as a metaphor for something larger: in this case, not merely a social class, but an entire culture—the world, even. British and Malaysian, American and Japanese meet on the courts of "the Club," and the results appear straightforward, at first. In the words of Paul Theroux's narrator, however, "Nothing in Ayer Hitam was ever so neat."*

# The Tennis Court

## Paul Theroux

Everyone hated Shimura; but no one really knew him: Shimura was Japanese. He was not a member of the Club. About every two weeks he would stop one night in Ayer Hitam on his way to Singapore. He spent the day in Singapore and stopped again on the way back. Using us—which was how Evans put it—he was avoiding two nights at an expensive hotel. I say he wasn't in our club; yet he had full use of the facilities, because he was a member of the Selangor Club in Kuala Lumpur and we had reciprocal privileges. Seeing his blue Toyota appear in the driveway, Evans always said, "Here comes the freeloader."

Squibb said, "I say, there's a nip in the air."

And Alec said, "Shoot him down."

I didn't join them in their bigoted litany. I liked Shimura. I was ashamed of myself for not actively defending him, but I was sure he didn't need my help.

That year there were hundreds of Japanese businessmen in Kuala Lumpur selling transistor radios to the Malays. It seemed a harmless enough activity, but the English resented them and saw them as poaching on what they considered an exclusively British preserve. Evans said, "I didn't fight the war so that those people could tell us how to run our club."

Shimura was a tennis player. On his fifth or sixth visit he had suggested, in a way his stuttering English had blunted into a tactless complaint, that the ball-boys moved around too much.

"They must stand quiet."

It was the only thing he had ever said, and it damned him. Typical Japanese attitude, people said, treating our ball-boys like prisoners of war. Tony Evans, chairman of the tennis committee, found it unforgivable. He said to Shimura, "There are courts in Singapore," but Shimura only laughed.

121

He seemed not to notice that he was hated. His composure was per-fect. He was a small dark man, fairly young, with ropes of muscle knot-ted on his arms and legs, and his crouch on the court made him seem four-legged. He played a hard darting game with a towel wound around his neck like a scarf; he barked loudly when he hit the ball.

He always arrived late in the afternoon, and before dinner played sev-eral sets with anyone who happened to be around. Alec had played him, so had Eliot and Strang; he had won every match. Evans, the best player in the Club, refused to meet him on the tennis court. If there was no one to play, Shimura hit balls against the wooden backboard, barking at the hard ones, and he practiced with such determination you could hear his grunts as far as the reading room. He ate alone and went to bed early. He spoke to no one; he didn't drink. I sometimes used to think that if he had spent some time in the bar, like the other temporary members who passed through Ayer Hitam, Shimura would have no dif-ficulty.

Alec said, "Not very clubbable."

"Ten to one he's fiddling his expenses," said Squibb.

Evans criticized his lob.

He could not have been hated more. His nationality, his size, his stinginess, his laugh, his choice of tennis partners (once he had played Eliot's sexually browsing wife)—everything told against him. He was aloof, one of the worst social crimes in Malaysia; he was identified as a parasite, and worst of all he seemed to hold everyone in contempt. Offenses were invented: he bullied the ball-boys, he parked his car the wrong way, he made noises when he ate.

It may be hard to be an American—I sometimes thought so when I remembered our beleaguered Peace Corps teachers—but I believe it was even harder to be a Japanese in that place. They had lost the war and gained the world; they were unreadable, impossible to know; more courtly than the Chinese, they used this courtliness to conceal. The Chinese were secretive bumblers and their silences could be hysterical; the Japanese gave nothing away; they never betrayed their frenzy. This contempt they were supposed to have: it wasn't contempt, it was a total absence of trust in anyone who was not Japanese. And what was perhaps more to the point, they were the opposite to the English in every way I could name.

The war did not destroy the English—it fixed them in fatal atti-tudes. The Japanese were destroyed and out of that destruction came different men; only the loyalties were old—the rest was new. Shimura, who could not have been much more than thirty, was one of these new men, a postwar instrument, the perfectly calibrated Japanese. In spite of what everyone said, Shimura was an excellent tennis player.

So was Evans, and it was he who organized the club game: How to get rid of Shimura?

Squibb had a sentimental tolerance for Malays and a grudging respect for the Chinese, but like the rest of the club members he had an absolute loathing for the Japanese. When Alec said, "I suppose we could always debag him," Squibb replied fiercely, "I'd like to stick a kukri in his guts."

"We could get him for an infraction," said Strang.

"That's the trouble with the obnoxious little sod," said Squibb. "He doesn't break the rules. We're lumbered with him for life."

The hatred was old. The word "Changi" was associated with Shimura. Changi was the jail in Singapore where the British were imprisoned during the war, after the fall of the city, and Shimura was held personally responsible for what had gone on there: the water torture, the rotan floggings, the bamboo rack, the starvation and casual violence the Japanese inflicted on people they despised because they had surrendered.

"I know what we ought to do," said Alec. "He wants his tennis. We won't give him his tennis. If we kept him off the courts we'd never see his face here again."

"That's a rather low trick," said Evans.

"Have you got a better one?" said Squibb.

"Yes," said Evans. "Play him."

"I wouldn't play him for anything," said Squibb.

"He'd beat you in any case," said Alec.

Squibb said, "But he wouldn't beat Tony."

"Not me—I'm not playing him. I suggest we get someone else to beat him," said Evans. "These Japs can't stand humiliation. If he was really beaten badly we'd be well rid of him."

I said, "This is despicable. You don't know Shimura—you have no reason to dislike that man. I want no part of this."

"Then bugger off!" shouted Squibb, turning his red face on me. "We don't need a bloody Yank to tell us—"

"Calm yourself," said Alec. "There's ladies in the bar."

"Listen," I said to Squibb, "I'm a member of this Club. I'm staying right here."

"What about Shimura?" said Alec.

"It's just as I say, if he was beaten badly he'd be humiliated," said Evans.

Squibb was looking at me as he said, "There are some little fuckers you can't humiliate."

But Evans was smiling.

*   *   *

The following week Shimura showed up late one afternoon, full of beans. He changed, had tea alone, and then appeared on the court with the towel around his neck and holding his racket like a sword. He chopped the air with it and looked around for a partner.

The court was still except for Shimura's busy shadow, and at the far end two ball-boys crouched with their sarongs folded between their knees. Shimura hit a few practice shots on the backboard.

We watched him from the rear verandah, sitting well back from the railing: Evans, Strang, Alec, Squibb, and myself. Shimura glanced up and bounced the racket against his palm. A ball-boy stood and yawned and drew out a battered racket. He walked toward Shimura, and though Shimura could not possibly have heard it there were four grunts of approval from the verandah.

Raziah, the ball-boy, was slender; his flapping blue sports shirt and faded wax-print sarong made him look careless and almost comic. He was taller than Shimura and, as Shimura turned and walked to the net to meet him, the contrast was marked—the loose-limbed gait of the Malay in his rubber flip-flops, the compact movements of the Japanese who made his prowl forward into a swift bow of salutation.

Raziah said, "You can play me."

Shimura hesitated and before he replied he looked around in disappointment and resignation, as if he suspected he might be accused of something shameful. Then he said, "Okay, let's go."

"Now watch him run," said Evans, raising his glass of beer.

Raziah went to the baseline and dropped his sarong. He was wearing a pair of tennis shorts. He kicked off his flip-flops and put on white sneakers—new ones that looked large and dazzling in the sunlight. Raziah laughed out loud; he knew he had been transformed.

Squibb said, "Tony, you're a bloody genius."

Raziah won the toss and served. Raziah was seventeen; for seven of those years he had been a ball-boy, and he had learned the game by watching members play. Later, with a cast-off racket, he began playing in the early morning, before anyone was up. Evans had seen him in one of these six o'clock matches and, impressed by Raziah's speed and backhand, taught him to serve and showed him the fine points of the game. He inspired in him the psychic alertness and confidence that makes tennis champions. Evans, unmarried, had used his bachelor's idleness as a charitable pledge and gave this energy and optimism to Raziah, who became his pet and student and finally his partner. And Evans promised that he would, one of these years, put Raziah up for membership if he proved himself; he had so far withheld club membership from the Malay, although the boy had beaten him a number of times.

Raziah played a deceptively awkward game; the length of his arms made him appear to swing wildly; he was fast, but he often stumbled trying to stop. After the first set it was clear that everyone had underestimated Shimura. Raziah smashed serves at him, Shimura returned them force-fully, without apparent effort, and Shimura won the first two sets six-love. Changing ends, Raziah shrugged at the verandah as if to say, "I'm doing the best I can."

Evans said, "Raziah's a slower starter. He needs to win a few games to get his confidence up."

But he lost the first three games of the third set. Then Shimura, eager to finish him off, rushed the net and saw two of Raziah's drop shots land out of reach. When Raziah won that game, and the next—breaking Shimura's serve—there was a triumphant howl from the verandah. Raziah waved, and Shimura, who had been smiling, turned to see four men at the rail, the Chinese waiters on the steps, and crouch-ing just under the verandah, two Tamil gardeners—everyone gazing with the intensity of jurors.

Shimura must have guessed that something was up. He reacted by playing angrily, slicing vicious shots at Raziah, or else lifting slow balls just over the net to drop hardly without a bounce at Raziah's feet. The pretense of the casual match was abandoned; the kitchen staff gathered along the sidelines and others—mostly Malay—stood at the hedge, cheer-ing. There was laughter when Shimura slipped, applause when the towel fell from his neck.

What a good story a victory would have made! But nothing in Ayer Hitam was ever so neat. It would have been perfect revenge, a kind of romantic battle—the lanky local boy with his old racket, making a stand against the intruder; the drama of vindicating not only his own reputa-tion as a potentially great tennis-player, but indeed the dignity of the entire club. The match had its charms: Raziah had a way of chewing and swallowing and working his Adam's apple at Shimura when the Japanese lost a point; Raziah talked as he played, a muttering narra-tion that was meant to unnerve his opponent; and he took his time serv-ing, shrugging his shoulders and bouncing the ball. But it was a very short contest, for as Evans and the others watched with hopeful and judging solemnity, Raziah lost.

The astonishing thing was that none of the club staff, and none of Raziah's friends, seemed to realize that he had lost. They were still laughing and cheering and congratulating themselves long after Shimura had aced his last serve past Raziah's knees; and not for the longest time did the festive mood change.

Evans jumped to the court. Shimura was clamping his press to his racket, mopping his face. Seeing Evans he started to walk away.

"I'd like a word with you," said Evans.

Shimura looked downcast; sweat and effort had plastered his hair close to his head, and his fatigue was curiously like sadness, as if he had been beaten. He had missed the hatred before, hadn't noticed us; but the laughter, the sudden crowd, the charade of the challenge match had showed him how much he was hated and how much trouble we had gone to in order to prove it. He said, "So."

Evans was purple. "You come to the Club quite a bit, I see."

"Yes."

"I think you ought to be acquainted with the rules."

"I have not broken any rules."

Evans said curtly, "You didn't sign in your guest."

Shimura bowed and walked to the clubhouse. Evans glared at Raziah; Raziah shook his head, then went for his sarong, and putting it on he became again a Malay of the town, one of numerous idlers who'd never be members of the Ayer Hitam Club.

The following day Shimura left. We never saw him again. For a month Evans claimed it as a personal victory. But that was short-lived, for the next news was of Raziah's defection. Shimura had invited him to Kuala Lumpur and entered him in the Federation Championship, and the jersey Raziah wore when he won a respectable third prize had the name of Shimura's company on it, an electronics firm. And there was to be more. Shimura put him up for membership in the Selangor Club, and so we knew that it was only a matter of time before Raziah returned to Ayer Hitam to claim reciprocal privileges as a guest member. And even those who hated Shimura and criticized his lob were forced to admire the cleverness of his Oriental revenge.

*Sarah Totton's short story shuttles confidently between present and past, fact and fantasy, here and there—not to mention its hero's left and right hands. It is at once an old-fashioned sports story and the most closely observed and carefully recorded account of a (fictional) tennis match to appear in this book.*

# Match Point

## Sarah Totton

I have just been broken. The beaded numbers on the board blink off then light up with the new score: six points to five in the tiebreak. It's the fourth set of the Wimbledon singles final. I flick a glance at Chip's seat in the stands, but it's empty. I take a deep breath before turning back to the baseline to wait for my opponent to serve for the match.

Craig Skellsy stands at the baseline wearing a shirt so white it's almost blue, wraparound shades, silver dreadlocks bound with a dragon green headband. He thumbs a ball out of his pocket and begins to dribble it. It's match point and the crowd is fizzing like a shaken can of pop.

"Come on, Skellsy! Fire the rocket," someone shouts.

Skellsy grins. His reply is drowned in the crowd's laughter.

Chair umpire Toddhill Crane speaks into the mike, "Ladies and gentlemen, quiet please."

It's funny. I remember, back in '84, this reporter from *Tennis* magazine coming to interview me for an article. "Those Quirky Players" it was called. She'd just been talking to Kent Carlsson, "The Perpetual Motion Machine." Twitched his whole body between points when he played. Looked like he was having a seizure. Developed tendinitis in his knees. Retired at twenty-two.

"According to Bud Collins," she said to me, "you've got one of the lowest serve tosses in the history of tennis."

I shrugged. "It's a little unorthodox, but it gets the job done."

"Has your coach ever tried to get you to change it?"

"If he did, he'd be looking for a new job."

"Mac Spilota's your coach?"

"That's him."

"He used to coach Jay Berger, didn't he? Jay's got a quirky serve, too."

"Jay's service motion is injury-related," I told her. "And Mac's never coached him."

Mac's attitude was "If it ain't broke, don't fix it." And you couldn't argue with the results; my service motion worked, all right. I could place the ball anywhere on the court. My elbow would get sore after long matches and I'd have to ice it. But it never really caused me any problems. Until Gstaad.

The ball taps the court as Skellsy winds up for the serve. His service motion is textbook. I target the ball as he tosses it. When he snaps his wrist, the ball dissolves with speed, heading right for my body. I dodge out of its path as my racquet bucks; it pops up about a hundred feet. The ball floats and the breeze edges it over to Skellsy's side of the net. He steps in to pick it off, tracking it with his hand. I shuffle backwards as he smashes it into the open court. The ball flies in a clean arc toward the stands and Skellsy turns away, throwing his hands up in a victory salute. I crab-step backwards, punch the back stop with my foot and kick off, flicking my racquet. It boosts me an extra six inches; I reach for it, just peg it with the tip of the frame. I follow the ball as I hit the court on my heels and go down. And I see it tap off Skellsy's back and bounce onto the grass.

I have been delivered.

Once I can breathe, I roll over and get up. All the spectators are on their feet as well. I have a sense of falling forward, only I haven't moved.

"Six-all," says Crane.

Skellsy appears preoccupied with adjusting his racquet strings. He pauses to towel off before heading to the sidelines. As we change ends, he looks at me and smiles. It's not the smile that he flashes for the cameras, or in the TV ads he's famous for.

"Nice shot, you fucking smartass," he says casually as we pass each other.

I realize that he didn't see me make the last shot. He thinks I hit him deliberately.

The crowd is still applauding. That shot must have looked spectacular. And that's how I had to play to win a point from him: Craig Skellsy, young upstart, bristling with talent and ego, my nemesis, my jinx. I'd rather face Lendl in the finals than Skellsy. I'd rather be playing anyone but him.

I got a tape of it so I could watch it. So I could see how it happened, why it happened.

Tiebreak. 20-19. Gstaad, Switzerland, 1985. Serving for the fourth set against Craig Skellsy. I looked different then, a few years younger, hair a bit longer. Something else, too; I was scared, but it was only a momentary tightness. I used to tell myself, "The worst thing that can happen is you lose the point." I know now that worse things can happen.

I bounced the ball with my left hand twelve times. Always twelve. My old routine. Service toss. The ball came out of my hand and stayed . . . at the level of my eyes. Right there, just before the racquet whipped around to hit it, I clicked the pause button. Tracking buzzed across the screen at that point. In the middle of the motion that destroyed my career. . . .

Two months of surgery, follow-up exams, physio, constant pain. That year, I watched Wimbledon from a TV in a hospital room. I remember one scene vividly, coming out of the doctor's office after my last follow-up exam. I thought my life was over. I couldn't play tennis anymore. It was somebody's fault, I knew that. Things like this should never happen, not if you do everything right. I took it out on Mac. He was in the waiting room and I walked right past him. He caught up with me in the parking lot, a magazine he'd taken from the waiting room pressed to his chest. It was *Sports Illustrated* and Craig Skellsy was on the cover.

"What happened, Chris?" he said to me. "What did the doctor say?"

"Don't talk to me," I said. "Remember that time I wanted to switch up my serve and you said, 'Things are working fine, Chris. Let's keep it that way.'? If you hadn't said that, I might still be playing. You were supposed to coach me, not stand there and watch me fuck up my arm until it's permanently damaged."

I saw that curl of his mouth, the same look he used to give me after I'd lost an easy match, like he was expecting it.

Then he put his hand on my shoulder. "I'm sorry, Chris."

It was the same thing he always said after I lost. But this wasn't a lost match; it was a hell of a lot more.

"You're sorry? Great. That helps a lot."

I never spoke to Mac again. I hung up on all his calls, unplugged the phone.

Getting used to it was the hardest part. I understood what the doctor said. I just didn't grasp that my life had completely changed. As soon as I got home that first day, I tried picking up my racquet and hitting some balls against the wall, just to see if I could do it. I thought the doctor must be wrong; there was no way I could be doing it one day and then not. But when I tried, a shot I could have hit in my sleep before Gstaad, I couldn't control the ball. My racquet felt unbalanced. I couldn't hold the head up or control the swing. I had hit better when I was five. That's when I realized what it all meant: watching Wimbledon on a TV screen for the rest of my life. I smashed every racquet in my racquet bag. I took a knife and punctured all the balls. I knew I would have to retire some time, but I'd figured on another eight years. But it wasn't just that. It was the fact that I hadn't finished my last match; I'd retired from it. My last moment as a professional was approaching that god-damned chair umpire and telling him I wanted to stop because I couldn't take the pain.

Mac always told me never to push myself if it didn't feel right. I'd been up two sets to one against Skellsy at Gstaad. Sometimes I'd sit up at night, watching that tape and ask myself what would have happened if I'd just hung on until the end of the set. If I'd known it was going to be the last match I'd ever play, I would have played to the end. I would have stuck around to shake hands. To hear the applause.

Skellsy seems to have sobered up. He's up two sets to one, two points from the match. But I just saved a match point. I sense him hitch in mid-motion as he serves, springing toward the net.

"Foot fault!"

"Foot fault my *ass*," Skellsy says without missing a beat.

The serve itself was in and past me before I could move. Would have been an ace. He bears down on the linesman, twirling his racquet. People in the crowd are whistling. He says something to the chair umpire that I can't hear over the noise. Crane shakes his head emphatically. Skellsy isn't going to win the argument and he knows it, but he likes to see how far he can push an umpire, especially this one. Last year, Crane defaulted him from a tournament for verbally abusing a lineswoman. Skellsy apologized publicly for the incident, but I think he still carries a grudge. Skellsy says a few more words just to get his point across before letting it drop. The crowd applauds as he turns back and serves again. This one goes right into the net.

"Seven-six, Picta."

It's my serve now. Chip says that I rush big points, but Skellsy is making me wait; he meticulously reties the green laces on his shoes, then, just as I start into my service motion, he holds up his hand, apparently bothered by some movement in the stands behind me. I straighten up and pace a bit behind the baseline, waiting for people to settle. If I win this point, I take the set. If I lose it, he's two points away from holding the trophy.

For a long time, I didn't know what the hell to do with myself. The only thing I'd ever done was play tennis. It was the only thing I *could* do. It was the only thing I'd ever wanted to do. I could have tried coaching, but I couldn't stomach the thought of working with a guy my age, playing pro. I had too many regrets. Toddhill Crane used to play pro, too. Then he became an umpire. But I didn't want to take the chair. That's got to be the most thankless job there is.

Then one day in 1986, I ran into a guy from ESPN who'd interviewed me a few times, and he offered to try and get me into the commentator's booth. I thought I could handle it. And I did. For a while. But then it started bothering me, watching those guys down there, knowing I should have been playing them, only I couldn't. Around that time, Craig Skellsy was just starting to make it. He was the new face on American tennis. Not just talented, but charismatic, too, he loved the media, basked in front of the camera. But he had a major ego. No one noticed it back then. He was shooting up the rankings, racking up casualties among the top players. He had just left the junior circuit when I'd played him in '85. I retired from that match and he won the final. Gstaad was his first pro title, his big break. No one knew who he was until then.

In 1986, Skellsy made it to the semifinal of the U.S. Open. One of the regulars in the booth was sick and I was asked to interview Skellsy. He was leaning back in his chair when I came into the room. When he saw me, his eyebrow raised a touch, appraisingly, and a half-smile crossed his face like he wasn't too impressed.

I read the questions off the prompter.

"How would you define yourself as a player?" I asked him.

"You want to rephrase that question?"

I paused for a moment, looking at him. Then I thought, *Screw the script.* "Would it be fair to say you're an impulsive player, as opposed to a *thinking man's* player?"

The sarcasm wasn't lost on him. Or on the producer, who I could see from the corner of my eye was making throat-cutting gestures in my direction.

"I'd say I'm a pretty *successful* player, Chris," said Skellsy. "Compared to some."

"You'll be facing either Edberg or Chang in the finals. Do you think you're up to it?"

"No," said Skellsy, deadpan.

"What?"

"Not 'til I've bought a new pair of shades."

"Pardon me?"

The patronizing smile never left Skellsy's face. "It was a joke, *Chris.*"

"No," I corrected him. "A joke is funny."

ESPN never asked me back. My commentating career was over. I took to spending my time looking through the fences at players on the practice courts. And then one day when I was out there, I saw Steffi Graf practicing with her father. She was in a playful mood, hitting trick shots behind her back. And then I saw Peter Graf hit the ball to her backhand side, and Steffi flipped the racquet to her left hand and pummelled it back at him—almost as if she'd known I was out there, waiting for a sign. It was at that moment that I realized I could go back, that my career wasn't over. And that's when I became a lefty.

I wipe the racquet handle on my shirt and glance up at Skellsy. He's standing way over in the doubles alley, thinking I'll swing the serve out wide. It's the only thing I do better now than I did when I played right-handed. I've been using that serve a lot in this match. The grip is hot in my left hand; in my right, the cool fuzz of the ball as it hisses against the strings. I toss it two feet above my head and launch my whole body into it, cracking it straight up the middle. Skellsy has to lunge just to touch it and his return pings it into the net.

"Game and fourth set, Picta. Eight points to six. Two sets all."

We're into a fifth set. I allow myself to celebrate with the shake of a fist.

It was January 1987. I was taking shots against the cannon. Grant Connell and Glen Michibata were hitting balls on the practice court next to mine. Later on, in the locker-room, I noticed Connell staring at the scars on my elbow as I pulled on my warm-up jacket.

"Surgery," I told him.

"How long you been out?" said Grant.

"Since 'eighty-five."

"You got a coach yet?"

"No."

I thought he was going to spout a few platitudes and take off, but he didn't. He fished a pen out of his jacket and wrote a number on a bit of paper.

"If you're looking for one, try this guy: Chip Whitland. He's a lefty. And he's a good coach."

I'd never heard of the guy, and after Mac, I didn't want to deal with another coach. It had been hard coming back to the tour; I was so out of condition. My ranking had dropped right off the ATP chart because I hadn't played a match in two years, so that meant I had to play qualifiers just to get into the first round of a tournament. I checked out my draw for the Australian Open; I was playing guys so far down the list, I'd never even heard of them. And then I realized that these guys were better than I was.

After losing my first qualifier in straight sets, I gave Chip Whitland a call. He sure as hell wasn't Mac Spilota. Called him up, told him who I was. There was a pause and then this quirky Australian accent buzzed back at me, "If you'd stayed on the court, you would have won that match in Switzerland."

The first thing he did when we met—he didn't even shake my hand—was to send me out onto the court and tell me to serve. I was working on a lefty version of what I'd been doing all my life. The ball toss was a little higher, about at my forehead now. Chip exploded.

"What the hell was that?"

"A serve."

"No it wasn't. I want that ball toss in front of you, two feet over your head."

"Look, if I do that, the wind's going to blow it all over the place."

"The wind isn't your problem. You want to try a comeback with two useless arms, find another coach."

That was one thing about Chip. He didn't think twice about telling me when I was wrong. Mac had never done that. There were a lot of things Chip taught me that Mac never even tried, and not just technical stuff, either. Once we got the serve straightened out, he started nailing me on my tactics. When my ranking started to climb, it was really hard dealing with the losses. Mac used to console me. Not Chip.

By a stroke of appalling luck, I had to play Skellsy in the second round of a Florida tournament. I psyched myself out. Just the sight of Skellsy's face made me cringe. Having to play him again was too much to take. The tables were turned from Gstaad. This time, I was the long shot and he was the favorite. And I didn't disappoint the oddsmakers, though I did win a set. Afterwards, I felt awful, tired-out, and I just wanted to get the hell out of there. Chip met me in the locker-room.

"You call that a match?" he said.

"I didn't lose it, Chip. He won it."

"Save that crap for the press. You lost that match in the locker-room, before you even picked up the racquet."

"Look—"

"*You* look. You had one chance to get back into it, and you played a defensive shot."

I knew the point he was talking about. I tried to bluff my way out. It had always worked with Mac.

"I hit a solid volley," I said, "right inside the line. I made the safest play."

"And he picked it off. You should have gone cross-court."

"Nine out of ten I would've missed."

"If you'd missed, it would have been a brilliant miss. But you made the safe shot and you lost like a loser."

Chip had made a tape of Skellsy's mistakes. Big ones, little ones, tactical, technical—but that was the thing about Skellsy: Even when he missed, he made it look like part of the plan. I watched that tape, but when Chip pointed out the mis-hit trick shots, all I saw was that incredible footwork. When he cued Skellsy's tactic of running around the ball to hit a forehand, I didn't see that as a weakness, even though it pulled him outside the lines, out of position. No one could take advantage of a forehand like that. Skellsy puts so much topspin on the ball that it looks like an egg coming over the net. He hits the ball harder than anyone on the pro tour, and his placement is pinpoint accurate. That's something you're born with: power and precision. Chip told me I could beat him, but all I could think of was shaking hands with him at the net and knowing that he'd beaten me.

Fifth set, eighth game. Elapsed time is nearly four hours and I'm running out of steam. My semifinal against Krickstein took nearly everything I had. That match was a warm-up compared with this one. And there'll be no more tiebreaks. The fifth set at Wimbledon is played to the bitter end.

Craig Skellsy is serving at three games to four and thirty-fifteen. I'm waiting to receive, my toes just touching the titanium paste of the baseline. Chip may think I don't play the big points well, but I know how to recognize them. And this is one now. At the edges of my eyes, movement ripples in the stands: hats, programs, paper, fanning a breeze I can't feel. All of it dims as I focus on the ball. I hit the return, a bit high, but deep in the corner, with an angle sharp enough to pull Skellsy out of the court. He has to run it down, but by the time he gets to it, he's whipped that arm back and he blasts the forehand. There's so much angle on it that by the time it lands in my court, it's traveling nearly parallel to the net. It spins off the sideline as I chase it. And it's about to bounce again when I reach it. No time to swing; I tap it back with an all-wrist shot. It goes around the net post, barely a foot off the ground, and drops into his court. My momentum carries me off the court and I realize I'm heading into the side-stop. As I pull up, my foot catches, slips on the rain cover, and I pitch headfirst into the press box. My palm whacks a tripod and it jackknifes, buckling under the TV camera it's supporting. The whole thing collapses and comes down on top of me. The crash is so loud the ground vibrates. I can't hear anything but my ears buzzing. And when that fades, dead silence. There's a broken-glass tingling in my hand. I'm watching this woman, not the one from *Tennis*. She's got her hair tied back.

"My God, are you okay?"

She's lifting the camera up with two hands. It's lying on its side.

I don't know what's happening, only I shout at her to stop.

She's looking down at me as I'm trying to grab her arm so she doesn't move the damned camera any more.

"Oh shit," she says and covers her mouth.

She's pulled away by someone behind her. Takes the camera with her, and most of my hand, it feels like. And this guy says, "Just stand back."

"But look—"

"You can't do anything for him. Stay out of the way."

The tripod slides off my back as I roll away from them, kicking against the ground. My foot tangles in some cables and I curl up, shaking, one hand covering my eyes. It's not just the pain. That was my racquet hand. My playing hand.

I work backward until I bump the side wall, then use my heel to push my back up against it until I'm sitting. The other foot's still looped in a cord and I don't have the strength to shake it free. I cover my face, breathing deeply and try to think of something to distract myself from the pain. After a while, the nausea goes away. It comes back in a rush as soon as I pull myself up, but I clamp my throat closed and swallow hard until it goes again. I take a couple of steps toward the baseline and remember my racquet. It takes a while to find it, what's left of it. The cameras swing around and follow me. I can hear the shutters clicking like a swarm of locusts.

The frame is banana-shaped. Someone high up in the stands laughs, nervously. Now I feel like crying. For the first time, I realize how far it is across the court. The crowd is quiet. Crane is looking at his stopwatch. I pick up a new racquet from my bag. Now comes the worst part. I look down at my hand. At first I'm almost relieved. I was expecting blood. The skin's unbroken, but it's starting to swell up around the knuckles of my first two fingers. It's dead white with a couple of dark red blotches. I look at it for a long time before I press the racquet handle against my palm and try to grip it. My thumb is the only thing keeping it there; I can't move any of my fingers. I turn around then, and look for Chip.

*Where are you? What am I supposed to do now?*

His seat is still empty. I grab some tape from my racquet bag, press the racquet handle against my hand with my knee and wrap it around and around until it's good and tight, so it's not going to slip. I bite down on the end, rip it off and drop the roll.

"Time violation. Warning, Mr. Picta."

If Crane expects a reaction, he's not going to get one. Two ballboys are standing rigid by the net.

"Ice," I say as I walk past them.

I return to baseline and crouch there, waiting for Skellsy. He's got his back turned and he's tying up his shoes. When he finishes that, he holds up his hand for a ball. His motion as he bounces it is almost casual. I'm worried if he hits one of his rockets that it'll rip the racquet right out of my hand, but he misses the service box by about three feet. He stares over at his coach and wipes his mouth on his sleeve. He spends a couple of seconds readjusting his racquet strings before he takes up his service stance again.

This time, the ball flicks over the service line and booms off the backstop.

"Fault!"

Skellsy, coming in behind it, pulls up short. "Oh come on! No way was that out." He turns to the chair, hand on his hip, gesturing with his racquet expectantly. "That was right in front of you."

The crowd starts to whistle. That double fault gives me break point. If I win this game, I'm up five games to three. Small wonder that Skellsy is upset.

Crane moves the mike aside and speaks directly to him. "*He* saw the ball long." He points to the linesman. "And *I* saw the ball long."

"You just don't have the *balls* to overrule it, Todd." Skellsy turns to the linesman. "Yoo-hoo!" Skellsy waves at him with his racquet. "You want to open your eyes now? We're trying to play a match here." The linesman lowers his arm and puts his hands behind his back. He's staring along the service line, away from Skellsy. He doesn't have to acknowledge anyone but the umpire.

Crane adjusts the mike and speaks into it. "Thirty-forty."

Skellsy doesn't move. "I want the referee out here."

Crane has stopped arguing. He addresses the microphone. "Let's play."

Skellsy hacks the court with his racquet, denting the purple frame and chopping a slice in the turf.

"Code violation. Warning, Mr. Skellsy."

"Up yours," says Skellsy. Taking deliberately slow steps, he walks to the sideline for a new racquet. He mutters half-audibly as he pulls off the plastic wrap and tests the tension of the strings, pinging the racquet face against his palm. Then he takes a long drink from the water bottle. Every now and then, he looks at Crane pointedly.

Skellsy has less than thirty seconds to get his act together and serve for the next point.

Crane puts his hand over the mike and speaks to him again. "You're running out of time, Mr. Skellsy."

"You know, I'm getting sick of your voice, Todd," says Skellsy, sharply.

"You've already had one warning for bad conduct."

"That's because you wouldn't overrule that fucking call!"

"Code violation, unsportsmanlike conduct. Point penalty, Mr. Skellsy. Game, Picta. Picta leads five games to three. Final set."

Skellsy stands there, his face hot and his mouth open, staring at Crane like he doesn't believe what he's just heard. It's a few minutes before Skellsy collects himself. He takes his wristband across his eyes, puffs out his cheeks, and heads over to my court.

I desperately wish that I could rest now, but I have to serve. I walk around the opposite side of the net to the other court. I nod at the ballboy twice and he sends me two balls. I pocket one and let the other drop. I bend over with my hand on my knee, and when I can, I scoop the ball onto the strings and pop it to my right hand. Another ballboy brings me some ice in a plastic cup. He's got the wrong idea.

"No," I tell him. "A bag of it."

I crush the top of the cup, folding it down, and hold it against my knuckles. That tape is starting to tighten; if my hand keeps swelling, it's going to cut off the circulation. I toss the cup back to the boy. I can't afford another time violation.

I take a practice swing and wince. I'm in trouble. I can't shift my grip for the serve because the tape is too tight.

The fans, the papers, are still. The air is thick with silence. Even the cameras have stopped clicking. Crane's eyes go from me, to my opponent, to me.

*Any ideas, Chip? Any kind of input would be nice about now.*

It was April 1988, and we were gearing up for the grass-court season and Wimbledon. Chip had me practice against Connell and Michibata.

"You want me to play both of them at the same time?!"

"Go ahead," he said in that don't-argue-with-me tone. So I tried it. And I was right. They blew me off the court. At five games to love, I gave up and went to the side.

"Get back out there," said Chip.

"What's the point? I can't win."

"Exactly."

I looked at him, but he didn't explain himself. He just picked up the racquet and held it out to me.

Back on the court again, I played even worse. Glen even pegged me in the head once. After that, I was ducking whenever he hit the ball. I thought that was playing smart. Chip disagreed.

"You've won two points in the last six games."

"What do you expect? They're using me for target practice."

"I want you to win two more."

"You're nuts!"

"Get back out there."

"No," I said.

"Think *I* can do it?"

I laughed at him.

So Chip went out there. And won the next two points. Stood behind the baseline and hit an underhand serve. A shot that barely made it over the net. Glenn was standing way back, expecting Chip to nail it. He couldn't get to the net in time to return it.

"Hey, wait a second," I said. "That's . . . unorthodox."

"It's legal," said Chip. "Now shut up and watch."

Glenn stood much closer to the net and returned the next serve well. Chip put up a lob about seven feet high and not deep enough. Grant stepped in and tracked it with his raised hand. It should have been an easy pickoff, but he smacked it into the net.

"You were lucky." I told Chip. "That was a bad lob."

"It didn't have to be good," he told me. "He was looking right into the sun."

I didn't have an answer for that, so I kept my mouth shut. After that game, Chip took me aside while Grant and Glenn were packing up their gear.

"Listen, Chris. I'm trying to prove a point here. Some time soon, you're going to find yourself in a match you can't win. If you give up, that's it. But if you make him pay for every point he takes away from you, if you believe you can win, he may start to believe it, too. And once he does that, he's yours. No matter how much better he is on paper."

I don't have the power to nail the serve, and Skellsy is standing about six feet behind the baseline. So I try it. I hit a drop shot, underhand from the baseline. Skellsy is quicker than Glenn, and it's not a good drop shot. He rushes the net. He gets to it before it bounces again, but has no time to do anything with it. He taps it up. It hits the net tape and then dribbles back into his court. The whole point is so quick that it's over before anyone realizes what I just did. Then there's a buzz of surprised murmuring from the audience. I look at Crane, but he just calls the score.

"Fifteen-love."

So, the bastard wasn't lying. It really is a legal shot. Skellsy knows it, too, but he isn't stupid. It won't work again. Now he's standing about two feet inside the baseline. I check the sun, but it's to the side of the court, not behind me. So I'm out of ideas.

Skellsy adjusts his headband before assuming his receiving stance, beating a sharp tattoo on the grass with his feet. If he knows I can't run, he'll try to force me. All he has to do is hit the ball all over the court. Shots I'll have to run for, reach for.

The toss is wild. I let it drop before catching it again. My right hand is shaking so much, I'm not sure I could hand the damned ball to the ballboy without dropping it. My concentration is slipping, too. I can hear the crowd, the jet tearing overhead, the canopy rippling against the backstop, my heart beating. . . .

I take a deep breath and toss again. This one's even worse, but I try to hit it anyway. Stupid. It's a slow floater that sits about five feet over the net, begging to be picked off; it's probably the worst serve I've ever hit. Skellsy pounces and nails the return before I can take a step. There is a deadly eagerness in the way he moves. Like a vulture dropping out of the sky. If it weren't taped to my hand, my racquet would be lying on the ground.

"Fifteen-all. Ladies and gentlemen, quiet please." Crane looks at me as I approach the chair.

"Get the trainer," I tell him.

He nods once. I look at him for a flicker of recognition. That those were the exact words I said to him before. In Gstaad.

Skellsy wins the next two points easily, taking the game to make it four-five. I know I was lucky to grab even one point in that game. It's turning into Gstaad. I'm sure that's what he's thinking, too.

It was the second week at Wimbledon. As grass-court specialist Tim Mayotte once remarked, this is when we really get down to business. I was in the players' Tea Room, waiting to meet Chip when I heard someone's voice, really excited.

"You're not going to believe this," he said, walking past me. "Court Two."

I turned and saw John Fitzgerald leading Mark Woodforde toward the stairs. John had a wild look in his eyes. I went to the window overlooking the scoreboard and I got that tight feeling in my gut. "Court Two: A. Rye vs. C. Skellsy." Andy Rye had won the championship a year earlier. This match was expected to be a blowout. But Rye had just lost the first set six games to love. I headed for the stairs.

People were already packed five-deep along the observation deck on the third floor and there were more pushing in behind me. They could smell an upset. John managed to push through to the guardrail, but I couldn't see a thing.

"What's going on?"

"This is disgusting. It's merciless."

"What's the score?"

"Three games to love in the third set for Skellsy."

"Third? What about the second?" I said.

No one in front seemed to hear me; they were too busy looking down into Court Two.

Someone came out of the Tea Room behind us.

"Shit! He's getting blasted."

I didn't recognize the man: blue suit, silk tie, American accent. Probably press. Then I remembered there was a TV back there.

"What was the score in the second?" I asked him.

"Six games to love," he said.

"For Skellsy or Rye?"

"Skellsy."

"You mean Rye hasn't won a *game* yet?" I said in shock.

"Rye hasn't won a *point* yet."

I realized why everyone looked so stunned. The only time I'd ever heard of someone on the pro circuit playing a "golden set"—winning a set without losing a single point—was back in '83, and that was just one set. This was two sets, and it was Craig Skellsy, twenty-year-old American, annihilating the number-three seed and defending champion.

"Is Rye injured?"

"I don't think so, but he's pretty pissed off."

I finally managed to squeeze in close enough to get a glimpse into Court Two. I couldn't see their faces, but I didn't need to. I spotted Skellsy first by his shirt, blinding white in the sun, and the striking green headband, and by that cocky walk as he stepped over to the side for the break. Rye just folded up into his chair and covered his head with a towel. There wasn't much to see after that. Rye gave up and tanked the last set. He won a couple of games, more from Skellsy's stupid mistakes as he tried to entertain the crowd during the points than from any effort on his part.

Lendl put up a bit more of a fight in the semis, but Skellsy straight-setted him as well and made front-page headlines with the quote "I am untouchable."

There is no doubt in my mind that he believed it.

Greg McDougall, the ATP trainer, is waiting for me when I get to my chair. I drop into it and cover my head with a towel. I can see the black mesh of the net and Skellsy's feet as he walks to his chair.

Greg snips the tape with his scissors and peels it off gently. The feeling starts to come back into my hand. My thumb has cramped up and I can't uncurl it.

"How bad is it?" I ask him.

There's a bit of a pause, then he says, "Better ask for an injury time-out."

He's telling me it's serious. A time-out would give him three minutes instead of the ninety seconds allotted for the changeover. I pull the towel off my head and hold up three fingers to Crane. He nods.

Greg digs out a roll of tape and a handful of tongue depressors. I study the umpire's chair so I don't have to watch. I try to gulp some water down while he's doing it. I start talking to myself, inside my head, over and over: "If it ain't broke, don't fix it . . . don't . . . don't . . . don't ever stop trying."

Last night, I put in that tape of Gstaad again.

Skellsy was holding the trophy. You could count the teeth in his smile. The tape ended and the picture blinked off. I heard Chip step into the room behind me. He took the tape out and put it on the table.

"You know why you do this to yourself, Chris?"

I shook my head.

"Your worst enemy isn't him. It's you. And you can't admit it."

"Time," says Crane.

"Good luck," Greg says.

I look at my hand. Greg has taped the tongue depressors to the front and back of three of my fingers. I couldn't bend them now even if I wanted to, and there's no way in hell I can hold onto the racquet.

Then, bang. I realize.

This isn't Gstaad. I'm standing on grass. I'm older now. Smarter. And I've played pro tennis with two different hands.

I head for the baseline with the racquet gripped in my right hand. The way I was born to hold it. I feel like turning to the stands and waving at everyone, especially Chip. Except he's not watching from his seat.

The fans are shouting again. Some of them for me this time. Crane has to ask them twice for silence before they settle down. Skellsy waits, a little impatiently. He stops dribbling the ball and turns his head, with those reflective shades, towards me. Then he blows on his fingers and bounces the ball again. The balance is shifting; I can feel it.

Skellsy and I trade points. I don't know what's eating him. He seems tired. Or something. But he's not hitting his forehand as hard as he was in the last set. If he did, he'd be beating me right now.

It's thirty-all. My hand tightens on the racquet tape as I wait for

Skellsy's serve. I'm ready for it. I've been ready for it for years. I rip the return right back into his face.

He makes a desperate stab volley and the ball hits the net tape. It's going to land on my side. I watch it die and before I can think, I'm running with everything I've got left just to get to it. I throw myself forward and touch it up. It falls as I do and I hear it strike the ground. Twice.

The crowd is roaring in my ears as I lie there. For a while, I don't move. I see the ball picked up by a figure flashing past me. My left hand has gone numb, but I don't need it now. The trainer is standing by Crane's chair, watching me.

I stand up and look at the score: Thirty-forty. Break point. No. The crowd is rippling and popping with intensity. It's not just break point; it's match point. I don't know how long I stand there before it finally sinks in. I start shaking. As I walk back to the baseline, the applause and the whistling go up in pitch. The championship. It's there; it's bouncing right in front of me. It's glinting like the gold chain around Skellsy's neck. Skellsy clenches his jaw, then lifts the ball like a shining trophy and throws himself into it.

I block the return and move in behind it. It strikes the baseline with a white puff of titanium. He winds up and snaps a sharp cross-court backhand. Two feet from the net, I slice a backhand volley. He comes under it with his racquet and shoots it into the sky. I pivot on my foot and tear back to the baseline. I dive forward and drive into that swing every pain in my body, from here to Gstaad. I hit the grass, and everything is gone with the ball. Everything but a sound, and the crowd takes it up and overwhelms me.

*Martin Amis's satirical novel* The Information *explores the rivalry between the writers Richard Tull, whose once-promising career has been stuck in neutral for years, and Gwen Barry, his university-classmate-turned-literary-superstar. The two men compete (in Richard's mind, at least) for critical acclaim and the spoils that attend it, and somehow Richard always loses; Gwen's agent is the notorious Gal Aplanalp, while Richard is unrepresented, and although Richard's wife, Gina, is beautiful, Gwen is married to Demeter de Rougement, a titled aristocrat. Still, they maintain a façade of friendship, competing regularly at billiards and chess—and tennis, at an all-male and fiercely egalitarian London sports club. Like the billiards table and the chessboard, the court becomes a venue for Richard's snobbish disdain for (read: bitter envy of) Gwen's style—or, as Richard sees it, lack thereof. Meanwhile, the vaguely malevolent Steve "Scozzy" Cousins, who has been lurking just beyond the consciousness of protagonist and antagonist since the start of the novel, continues to observe them both.*

# From *The Information*

## Martin Amis

At the Warlock Sports Center he parked the dusty Maestro next to Gwyn's new Swedish sedan, which was still gulping and chirruping, Richard noticed, as its computer ticked off the final security checks. Then, abruptly without intelligence, the car seemed to settle back into its silent, sullen crouch, and its sullen vigil. Leaving the Maestro unlocked (it contained nothing but banana skins and the fading carbons of dead novels), Richard strode through the car park and its exemplary diversity of stilled traffic, like an illustration of all you might meet on the contemporary road with its contraflow and intercool: hearse, heap, dragster, dump truck, duchess-wagon, cripple-bubble. He duly sighted Gwyn, strolling, with slowly swinging sports bag, along the brink of the bowling green, where sainted figures in white shirts and white hair archaically bent and straightened on the shallow yellow lawn. The protective affection that a nice person is expected to feel when observing another nice person who is innocent of this scrutiny—such affection, Richard found, was not absent in the present case so much as inverted or curdled: his face was all glints and snickers, and he felt briefly godlike, and exhaustingly ever-hostile. Just then, over the black slope of the tudoresque clubhouse, a loose flock of city birds reared up like a join-the-dots puzzle of a human face or fist. . . . The gap between the two men closed. Richard broke into an ankle-lancing trot and was no more than a racket's reach from Gwyn's shoulders when, with a blat of the side door, they exchanged the late-summer air for the dense breath of the clubhouse.

All men are faced with this. But wait. . . . First we have to get past the hatch of the booking office and the sexual indifference of the pretty girl who worked there, then the notice boards with their leagues and ladders (dotted with multicolored drawing-pins and one dying, throbbing wasp), then the aggressive levity of the Warlock manager, John Punt. "Gwyn," said Richard, as they stepped on into the clubhouse proper and the greater bar. And? There it lay: the pub of life. Eighty or ninety souls, in knots and echelons; and here came the familiar moment, a dip in the sound, a gulp, a swallow and a selection of profiles turning full face, as if on a rap sheet. All men are eternally confronted by this: other men, in blocs and sets. Equipped with an act, all men are confronted by an audience which might cheer or jeer or stay silent or yawn rancorously or just walk out—their verdict on your life performance. As Richard remembered, he and Gwyn used to be equally unpopular here at the Warlock, never directly addressed, quietly sneered at. As Gwyn, with his pewtery hair, his body as tall as his sports bag was long, moved past the low tables to the tag board there were cries and croaks of greeting, of "Still scribbling?" and "Sold a million yet?" The acceptance world. As if Gwyn was suddenly visible now, adjudged not to have been wasting his time; TV had democratized him, and made him available for transference to the masses; the life performance was seen to be worthy of sagacious applause. Whereas Richard, as a figure, was still entirely alien. For one thing, nobody could bear his habit, while on court, of shouting *shit* in French.

"I won't be much good to you today," said Gwyn (they had ten minutes to kill). "What with this Profundity thing."

"What with this what?"

"Profundity thing. Haven't you heard about it? It's a literary stipend, awarded every year. Administered out of Boston. Called a Profundity Requital."

"Don't tell me," said Richard cautiously. "Some loo-paper heiress. Looking for a tony way of dodging tax."

"Far from it. They're already calling it the mini-Nobel. The money's ridiculous. And you get it every year. For life."

"And?"

"I'm told I'm on the shortlist."

John Punt, his face scalded and broad-pored from the sun-ray lamp, often referred to the Warlock as a *dinosaur.* By which he meant: no Jacuzzis, no parasols, no quiche counter, no broccoli juice. Instead: unhealthy fare served all day long, smoking allowed and even encouraged, continuous and competitive drinking and strict non-exclusivity. Anyone could join the Warlock, cheaply and right away. Within the outer bar was an inner bar, an antiworld where many men and few women sat in arcs staring at hands of cards or kwik crosswords or architect's drawings or lawyers' briefs or escape routes, where bankruptcies and bereavements were entrained by a twingeing shake or nod of some great ruined head, and where, at this moment, behind a mephitic banquette of cigarette smoke, his back turned, Steve Cousins sat talking the higher shop with three bronzed pocked mug shots: the most exalted villainspeak (no detail, just first principles) about getting back what you put in and this being life and this being *it* . . . Gwyn and Richard stood between the two arenas, in a latticed passage that was also an amusement arcade: golf video, Bingomatic, Poker Draw, and, of course, the Knowledge Machine. Instead of a jukebox there stood a black upright piano on which, after lunch, drowsy criminals would occasionally interpret some tremulous ballad. The clubhouse acoustics had a funny tilt to them; voices sounded warped or one-way, as many mouths nuzzled the necks of cellular telephones; many an ear was plugged with Walkman or hearing aid, nursing its individual tinnitus.

"A Profundity Requital," said Richard pensively. "Well. We know one thing."

"What's that?"

"You're not going to get it."

Gwyn, who was wrong, flexed his forehead and said, "A million people can't be wrong."

Richard, who was also wrong, said, "A million people are *always* wrong. Let's play."

Anyone who shared the common belief that the decline of British tennis was a result of the game's bourgeois, garden-party associations would have felt generally braced and corrected, at the Warlock Sports Center, to hear the ragged snarls and howls, the piercing obscenities and barbaric phonemes which made the wired courts seem like cages housing slaves or articulate animals in permanent mutiny against their confinement, their lash-counts, their lousy food. On the other hand, anyone watching Gwyn and Richard as they prepared to play would at once agree that Richard's clear superiority owed everything to being middle class. Gwyn was encased in a new track suit that looked as though it had been designed and marketed that morning; its salient feature was a steadily contoured bagginess, a spacesuit or wind-bubble effect, reminding Richard of the twins' salopetts and the padded boiler beneath the stairs. Richard himself, more subtly, and more horribly, for once, in a way, was dressed in wrinkly khaki shorts and, crucially, an off-white top—which was old, which wasn't modern, which glowed with its prewar sour-milk light (numb and humble now, against the burnished ease of the T-shirt), the light of longjohn seams, old surgical tape, old field hospitals, old triage. Even his shoes were intolerably antique: beige, canvas, intended to enfold the thoughtless trudge of explorer or humorless imperialist. You expected him to carry a wooden racket in a wooden press and a plastic shagbag full of bald balls pried free from the undergardener's lawnmower.

Through the window of one of the Warlock's games rooms (not in use at present: after six it became a grot of darts) Steve Cousins watched the two novelists begin their game and wondered what they'd be like at *his* sport. In other words he was wondering what they'd be like at fighting—or, even more simply, what they'd be like to beat up. This involved him in pseudo-sexual considerations, because, yes, the truism is true, and fighting *is* like fucking (proximity alone sees to that, plus various texture tests and heft assessments you wouldn't otherwise be making); and, while we're at it, the truism is true, and the criminal *is* like an artist (though not for the reasons usually given, which merely depend on immaturity and the condition of self-employment): the criminal resembles the artist in his pretension, his incompetence, and his self-pity. So, for a moment, Scozzy watched Gwyn and Richard like an animal—an articulate animal. The wild were humans who were animals while still being human. So their minds contained a meteorology of good/bad, warm/cold, tastes fresh/tastes old, and, concerning humans, he is kind/he is cruel, he is familiar/he is new, he is controllable/he is uncontrollable. He is strong/he is weak. Looking at Richard and Gwyn, Steve couldn't honestly stay that either of them would give him any bother.

The match began. He watched. And not with an untutored eye. Like many *faces* he had spent a significant fraction of his life in sports clubs and leisure centers; such people had a lot of leisure, a lot of time to kill, this being the polar opposite, in their universe, to *time,* as served, in an institution. Steve could see the hateful remains of Richard's antique technique, its middle-class severity: the shoveled forehand, the backhand with its heavily lingering slice. Look: you could see his socks had a pink tinge to them. The dull blush of the family wash. Two kids: twins. He could play a bit, Richard. Though the love-handled midriff was well prolapsed, it did turn to shape the shot; though the legs were hairless and meatless, they did bend. As for Twinkletoes on the other side of the net, in his designer rainbow gear: as for Tinkerbell there, flitting around with her wand . . . What you had here was one man playing all the tennis, up against a maneuverable little hacker taking the pace off everything, always obvious, never contrary, with no instinct to second-guess or wrong-foot. Steve was scandalized by Gwyn's lack of guile.

So why all the temper—from Richard's end? No way in the fucking world was he going to lose to this guy. Dear oh dear: the swearing, the racket abuse. The way he wiped visible deposits of tea or nicotine from the corners of his scum-storing mouth. Hang on. Some old bat from the mansion flats was sticking its head out of the window:

"Less of that language, Richard!"

"Sorry!"

Must do it a lot: she even knew his name! He must be famous for it, his language. Round these parts anyway. Round Court 4 anyway. Now here's something interesting. Nice angle on his approach shot (Richard), taking Twinkletoes way out of court—crashing, indeed, into the side wire. Oof. But he managed to get it back somehow: an apologetic plop over the net. And as Gwyn comes haring back for this lost cause, instead of just smacking the ball into the wide-open spaces Richard tries to slide it in behind him, down the line. And puts it out.

What was that Richard said, bent over the net post? "Oh Jesus. Nda! Piece of *shit!*"

What was that Gwyn said, standing in the tram lines? "Richard, you're a gilder of lilies."

Gilda, thought Steve. Lily. Lil: Means tit. But he understood. Like over-egging the pudding. Gilders of lilies. Now. Steve's *intention* . . . In common with all the very worst elements at the club, Steve wasn't a Tennis Member of the Warlock, nor was he a Squash Member or a Bowls Member: he was a *Social* Member of the Warlock. So it was with quiet confidence that he strolled upstairs with his glass of Isotonic, to the darts room, which was empty and stood tensed in its unnatural shadows, the windows all smeared with light-excluding cream paint or paste. This gloom and silence and sudden solitude made him momentarily uncertain about who he was or might be. Low-level unreality attacks didn't necessarily disquiet him—because they didn't *feel* unreal. They felt appropriate. Steve expected them, saying to himself, after all, there's no one quite like me. Yet. And it wasn't a delusion of uniqueness, not quite. He just believed he was the first of many. Many Scozzys were out there waiting to happen. I am a time traveler. I come from the future.

Steve's intention was to be unforgettable. Gwyn, or Richard, or maybe both, would not forget him. And that was a promise. Gilders of lilies. You don't get too many of them, he said to himself as he silently closed the windows: not in my line of work. I'm the only one.

"Played," said Gwyn.

"Thanks," said Richard. "Tough."

They shook hands at the net. Tennis was the only time they ever touched. Games were the only reason they ever met. It had become clear about six months ago that Richard was no longer capable of getting through a dinner in Gwyn's company without disgracing himself. Though Gina and Demi still met up sometimes.

"I'm improving," said Gwyn.

"No you're not."

"I'll get there."

"No you won't."

Using the net as a guide rail or a walking-frame, Richard reached his chair. He sat down suddenly and at once assumed a posture of tranced or drunken meditation. Gwyn remained standing—under the shadow of the mansion flats, from which the detailed noises of DIY scraped and whined against the air: drill, plane, sander.

"I don't know what it was today," said Gwyn. "Couldn't get my head right. Couldn't find the desire. It's this Profundity thing. Ridiculous really," said Gwyn, who still pronounced "really" *reely.* "It's not even announced till the spring."

"Oh I get it. Nothing to do with technique or talent or timing or anything. You just couldn't be fucked."

"Yes, well I was all over the bloody shop today. Couldn't get my backhand working."

Richard was enjoying his breather—and *breather* was definitely the word he wanted. "You haven't got a backhand. It's just a wound in your side. It's just an absence. Like an amputee's memory of a vanished limb. You haven't got a forehand either. Or a volley. Or an overhead. *That's* the trouble with your game. You haven't got any shots. You're a dog on the court. Yeah. A little Welsh retriever."

He put a cigarette in his mouth and, as a matter of silent routine, offered one to Gwyn, who said,

"Just couldn't concentrate. No thanks."

Richard looked at him.

"I packed it in."

"You *what?*"

"I stopped. Three days ago. Cold. That's it. You just make the life choice."

Richard lit up and inhaled needfully. He gazed at his cigarette. He didn't really want to smoke it. He wanted to eat it. This move of Gwyn's was a heavy blow. Almost the only thing he still liked about Gwyn was that Gwyn still smoked. Of course, Gwyn had never smoked seriously. Just a pack a day. Not like Richard with his carton-eons, his suede lungs, his kippered wisteria . . . Richard was reminded of another inexpiable exchange he'd had with Gwyn, on the same court, on the same green chair, under the same gut-colored sky and the same summer moon. A year ago, when *Amelior* was taking off and all the other stuff was coming down, Gwyn turned to him, courtside, and said abruptly: "I'm getting married." Richard replied, at once, "Good. About time." And he meant it. He was as they say "genuinely pleased." Pleasure came to him in the form of voluptuous relief. Yes, good. About time Gwyn shackled himself for ever to that speechless pit-pony, Gilda: his teenhood sweetheart, invisible Gilda. Even now Richard could close his eyes and see her small shape in a dozen different bedsits and flatlets, her averted face damp with steam as she served up yet another bowl of spaghetti, her pale hair and sore and coldly upper lip, her (or maybe his) functional underwear on a curved string above the fibrous white tubes of the gas fire, her phobic humility, her unpoetic sadness, her lumpy, childish emerald-green overcoat that came from another time and another place. "Great. I bet Gilda's thrilled. Is Gilda thrilled?" Gilda was good. Richard didn't fancy her. He didn't even want to fuck her *once*. So we must imagine his moodswing when Gwyn paused and said, "No. Not so's you'd notice. No, I think we can say that Gilda is definitely not overly chuffed. Because I'm not marrying *her*." Gwyn wasn't marrying Gilda Paul. He was marrying Lady Demeter de Rougemount, a celebrated knockout of limitless fortune and imperial blood whom Richard knew and admired and had recently taken to thinking about every time he came. "There it is," said Gwyn. Richard failed to offer his congratulations. He stalked off, ostensibly to locate and solace Gilda. In fact he just drove away in his Maestro and parked it somewhere and sat in it sobbing and swearing and smoking cigarettes.

"You bastard," said Richard. "I thought we were in this together."

"Three days ago. Hark at you gasping away. Couple of years I'll be having you six-love, six-love."

"What's it like?"

Richard had *imagined* giving up smoking; and he naturally assumed that man knew no hotter hell. Nowadays he had long quit thinking about quitting. Before the children were born he sometimes thought that he might very well give up smoking when he became a father. But the boys seemed to have immortalized his bond with cigarettes. This bond with cigarettes—this living relationship with death. Paradoxically, he no longer wanted to give up smoking: what he wanted to do was take up smoking. Not so much to fill the little gaps between cigarettes with cigarettes (there wouldn't be time, anyway) or to smoke two cigarettes at once. It was more that he felt the desire to smoke a cigarette even when he was smoking a cigarette. The need was and wasn't being met.

"Actually it's a funny thing," said Gwyn. "I gave up three days ago, right? And guess what?"

Richard said long-sufferingly, "You haven't wanted one since."

"Exactly. Well, you know. Time. The future."

"You've thought about it, and you'd rather live for ever."

"Isn't that what we scribble away for, Richard? Immortality? Anyway, I think my duty to literature is plain."

One more male ordeal awaited them: the changing room. The changing room had the usual hooks and benches and too few coat hangers, and steamy mirrors for men to lean backwards and comb their hair at, if they had any, and much effortfully evaporating male sweat (stalled in this process, and forming a furtive mist which slowed the air) together with competing colognes and scalp gels and armpit honeyers. There was also a shower stall full of pulsating backsides and soused and swinging Johnsons which of course forbade inspection: you don't look. Gwyn's new affectation of staring at things with childlike wonder remained unexercised in the changing room. You don't look, but as a man you mentally register yourself, with inevitable and ageless regret (it would have been *so* nice, presumably, to have had a big one) . . . Naked, Richard watched Gwyn, naked, and vigorously toweling his humid bush. Richard was excited: Gwyn was *unquestionably* nuts enough for the Sunday *Los Angeles Times*.

They walked back through the bar, which gave them time to start sweating again, and out into the late afternoon. Richard said carefully,

"You were saying? About immortality?"

"Well, I don't want to sound pretentious . . ."

"Speak as your heart tells you."

"Milton called it the last infirmity of noble minds. And—and someone said of Donne when he was dying that immortality, the desire for immortality, was rooted in the very nature of man."

"Walton," said Richard. He was doubly impressed: Gwyn had even been *reading* about immortality.

"So you know. You're bound to have such thoughts. To flesh out the skeleton of time."

"I have been looking again," said Richard, even more carefully, "at *Amelior* . . ."

The unspoken wisdom between them was as follows. The unspoken wisdom was that Richard, while taking a hearty and uncomplicated pleasure in Gwyn's success, reserved the right to keep it clear that he thought Gwyn's stuff was shit (more particularly, *Summertown*, the first novel, was forgivable shit, whereas *Amelior* was unforgivable shit). Oh yeah: and that Gwyn's success was rather amusingly—no, in fact completely hilariously—accidental. And transitory. Above all transitory. If not in real time then, failing that, certainly in literary time. Enthusiasm for Gwyn's work, Richard felt sure, would cool quicker than his corpse. Or else the universe was a joke. And a contemptible joke. So, yes, Gwyn knew that Richard entertained certain doubts about his work.

"First time through," he went on, "as you know, I didn't really think it came off. Something bland and wishful. Even ingratiating. And programmatic. An insufficient density of elements. But . . ." Richard glanced up (they had reached their cars). No question that Gwyn had been patiently waiting for that *but*. "But second time through it all came together. What threw me was its sheer originality. When we started out I think we both hoped to take the novel somewhere new. I thought the way forward was with style. And complexity. But you saw that it was all to do with subject." He glanced up again. Gwyn's expression—briefly interrupted to acknowledge the greeting of a passerby, then stolidly reassumed—was one of dignified unsurprise. Richard felt all his caution disappear with a shriek. "A new world," he went on, "mapped out and reified. Not the city but the garden. Not more neurosis but fresh clarity. That took its own kind of courage," he said, still weirdly capable of meeting Gwyn's eye, "—to forge a new art of the brave."

Slowly Gwyn held out his hand. "Thanks, man."

Jesus, thought Richard. Which of us is going nuts faster? "No," he said. "Thank *you*."

"Before I forget, Gal Aplanalp is off to L.A. any minute, so you'd better give her a call. Tomorrow. Morning."

And then they parted in the car park, under the afternoon moon.

*Like many aficionados of the game, the characters in Philip K. Edwards's short story see the tennis court as sacred ground, any violation of which is bound to trigger a harsh reprisal. Thus a struggle that is both cultural and generational has consequences that are dramatic and, in some sense, permanent.*

# The Petition Parade

## Philip K. Edwards

In my old life back in Maryland, back in the '70s, I used to gather with other guys on Sunday mornings the way I do now at the coffee stools in the Quik!Stop up here in Pennsylvania. Only then it was at the spectator benches inside the fence at the clay courts, and there was a tennis racket instead of a newspaper under my arm.

The other thing about then was that we were there for the exercise. Now the only exercise we get is walking up from the parking area, which at the Quik!Stop is only about thirty feet from the door. Until recently, that is. Since my last dog died I now walk all the way from home, which involves leaving my back door, walking down my quarter-mile driveway to the highway, crossing the highway very carefully (once I just plain didn't see a large black SUV in the far lane and nearly walked into its side, which was at the time moving quite fast), and then walking across the Tonoloway Creek bridge up the equivalent of my driveway again to the front door of the Quik!Stop.

How does that odd mix of people I used to associate with on those summer Sunday mornings compare with this group? Well, we were free enough of such Sunday constraints as demanding young children and mandatory religious attendance, and we had a sense of camaraderie without any particular intimacy. Back then, of course, we still had the stamina and enough functioning limbs to play at tennis. Except for Shillerton's knees, which even so were all right if he stood in one place and swatted at the balls that came his way. (It was Shill who used to growl out, on cue, "We don't play tennis here, we play *at* tennis!")

Another thing we have in common with that old crowd is that nobody at the Quik!Stop much cares what anybody else's labels are. I know there are some Republicans in this group, I'm pretty sure one gent my age is a Jew, and one man is well-known to be gay. But the thing is it doesn't matter because none of us would ever say "gun nut," or "Jew-boy," or "queer" anyway, we're all just too nice for that.

What I'm remembering these days on my Sunday morning walk to the Quik!Stop is what happened one summer at that other gathering place so long ago. It's the dog, or lack of a dog, that reminds me. Since now I walk because I don't have a dog to worry about any more, it's natural that my mind often wanders back to that time.

The way it worked back then was, town players would get there when they could, the earliest at eight or so. (I would bring my little dog, Moses, and tie him up outside.) The first one in would unlatch the chain-link gate to the clay courts (never the asphalt courts). Like now, he might have his paper and a cup of coffee, and he would sit in the front row while he waited for someone else to show. If he didn't have a paper, or if it had rained, or if the clay otherwise needed brushing, his waiting time could be spent walking the eight-foot drag crosswise (never long-wise) in stripes from the near corner of Court One to the far corner of Court Two.

When a second player had arrived the process of lining the courts could start. This involved opening up the shed (the combination was scratched on the side of the building), bringing out the string, and topping off the lime in the rickety liner. One person pushed the liner while another held the string. Sometimes the two would wait for a third person to arrive. That way there was a lot less walking, and more time for play. If a fourth person showed up in time, he could be locating the line markers (wooden pegs, spikes, some marked with a wisp of colored nylon, but others not); as he found each one he would center the ball of his foot on the marker and do a half-pirouette, leaving a distinctive swirl in the clay.

But only with the right shoes, because a pirouette on a clay court with any other than perfectly flat-bottomed tennis sneakers will dig into the clay and leave a ragged concavity. Worse yet, if such wrong shoes have actual treads, as they are walked to the next marker they will leave behind mini-clods of clay that will deflect a hard-hit ball in ways you can hardly imagine. Ditto for bare feet, so nobody in this group would dare show up in anything but smooth-soled shoes.

Jim Q and I were acknowledged as the fastest liners, though Stinky Jones and seventy-five-year-old Carter Hutchinson made straighter lines; we'd hear about it all day if a ball would have been in or out but for our wobbly line. Percy was the all-time pro at lining without benefit of a string—he'd hunker over one marker, eyeball the marker at the far end, and make a beeline for it without diverting his gaze. Klinker was best at doing the pirouette over the markers—his swirls were legendary, and sometimes they could still be made out a week later.

When the lining was done, four players (the first four players—it didn't matter who was pals with whom) would start a match. Usually on Court Number One, acknowledged to be the superior court. Sometimes pairs or triplets (incomplete doubles teams) would warm up on the other court. Once the two courts were full, newcomers would wait until a pair was defeated and then take their place against the winners. Thus winners could stay on the court all day if they kept winning, but courtesy (or the need for a drink of water) usually compelled them to yield to a fresh team before long.

The day would go on pretty much in this manner from early Sunday morning to late Sunday afternoon, though few individuals stayed longer than a couple of hours. By the time the early crowd, of which I was usually a part, had broken up and drifted away, a fresh ten o'clock crowd, which included a few ladies, would have appeared, infiltrated, and taken over. Later, an afternoon crowd, which might include a few visiting out-of-town friends, would pick up the pace. Shillerton was the exception. He played with all these shifting groups; maybe his limited movements during the actual games allowed him these regular six-set Sundays. If, around noon, the number of competitors dwindled to less than a quorum, Shill usually took a break to read his paper for a while. Then, by two in the afternoon some of the early players were back for a second round, sometimes with an extra. Carter's brother from Clear Spring was one regular. Chuck Bean, an expatriate but still a favorite son, was another.

I haven't told the other fellows here about what happened that summer. Not yet and maybe never. What I was doing then with those guys has no relation to what I'm doing now with these guys. No common thread, no shared memories that would serve to introduce the topic. No war. Though I did tell them about wrecking my father's '39 Ford wooden station wagon and about winning the spelling bee in seventh grade. I have told them about falling out of a car, which was much earlier than that summer, and I've told them about hurting my right hand, which was later. And I think I have mentioned that in-between I used to play tennis.

They don't know that I fell out of the car because I was trying to prove to my father that I had locked the door by then unlocking it and opening it at fifty miles per hour—that would be too complicated to explain (as it was then). But they do know about the hand, because I had to explain why I always try to take the stool on the far left. I was in an accident once in which my right hand was pushed through a mass of bent sheet metal as lethal as a razor-blade sculpture. The doctors put the hand back together and I can open and close it all right, but can't feel much of anything. When I'd learned to use the muscles to grasp things, and eventually to hold on to things without crushing them (using the evidence of my eyes to gauge how tight to squeeze) I got to showing off, using the hand as though it were perfectly normal. Then once I grabbed and held tight to a steaming coffee mug that had just come out of the microwave. By the time it got through to my brain that something was wrong, the skin on my hand was burned smooth. I still hold things in my right hand, but never coffee mugs.

Tennis wasn't only for summer. It began after the last frost if there was a dry spell, or by the first of May at the latest. (It also didn't end with the summer. If you think a clay court is a slow court just try a frozen clay court—didn't matter how cold it got, we played until the first snow came and that put the courts to bed for the winter.) The field of players was sparser when we started again in the spring. It wasn't just that some of the players were sensitive to the cold, or that they tended to have more free time in the summer. It was also built into the history of the place—before it was a suburb, it was a summer resort. The clay was native, and practically free; if you dug a basement, you got a free tennis court.

Native clay makes a good, hard court, but unless it is tempered with some aggregated material it becomes too hard when it's dry and too slippery when it's wet. It needs this extra material to keep it flexible. Our courts were not only native clay, meaning from the area, but also natural clay, meaning that the clay was still in the place where it had formed long ago. There was so much near the surface that you wouldn't say it was thick, you would say it was deep.

This clay needed to be rolled and dragged and its aggregate replenished regularly to keep it flexible. Over the winter the aggregate would sink into the clay itself, and in early spring the surface was vulnerable to hardening up as though baked in a kiln. I remember one year in which it had received the sloggy footprints of large boys doing some act of vandalism. It was impossible to roll or drag those footprints out. Dogs were never allowed into the court area because it was fundamental that they would leave near-indelible impressions of pads and claws.

At the Quik!Stop we talk mostly about our environment (not THE environment). If it's wet we talk about the rain, if it's cold we talk about snow. We talk about crops (not that we raise any, but we know people who do), and we talk about fish even though we don't fish (Tonoloway, right out the window, is an endangered trout stream). We talk about roads and traffic, but we only talk about schools (the high school is out the windows on the other side) as they relate to property taxes. We don't talk about religion or politics. Our gossip is spent on the out-of-staters who stop at the Quik!Stop for gas and snacks—there are some strange people in the world, and some Sundays it seems that a significant percentage of them stop at the Quik!Stop.

At the tennis courts we talked about our environment, too, which was tennis. You don't talk religion at a political rally, and you don't talk about politics in church. As Ollie Sirk once said when someone re-marked that he seemed to have left home without his racquet (and then repeated it as often as he was set up), "No, I didn't forget my racket. My racket's tennis."

There's always an old guard. There was an old guard in town and at the courts, too. You could tell the old guard because they were in the government; heck, they *were* the government. Ollie was part of the old guard and I was part of the new guard. Of course Carter was part of the old guard, the oldest of the old. But what that meant for Sunday tennis was only that they were cagier and we were more reckless. We were faster, but they were more efficient. The doubles teams could be an old and an old against a new and a new, or an old and new versus a new and old. Oddly enough, though the odds are even, the combination of three of one and one of the other seldom materialized.

The year was 1973, a watershed year in public opinion about the war—the majority had turned against it, at least in their hearts. People like me thought it was high time we told our government how we felt. Several of us had been on the Mall for the march on Washington and participated in the one-day Strike for Peace, and now we were frustrated with the lack of response by the government. Some of the municipali-ties, and not just the California nutcase type, had gone on record as opposing the war. We thought our little town, with its annual June elec-tion coming, should step up and be counted among them.

The town paper, always eager for items, had published the text of our petition and publicized our "Petition Parade." We intended to get a solid majority of registered voters to sign the petition, which asked only that the town fathers include a referendum on the ballot in June asking whether or not the town would send this statement to the White House: *The Town of Shady Grove hereby calls for the immediate and total withdrawal from Vietnam.*

We made up a banner that read "Give Peace a Chance" in large let-ters and "Vietnam War Petition Parade" underneath. Jim Q had added "TIME TO GET OUT" under that. We wore armbands with a peace sign Magic Markered on. (Years later I found my armband in a drawer. I was ashamed to observe that the tail of the peace symbol had been left out—it looked like a Mercedes star.)

One Sunday, six of us adults started down Grove Avenue, with three of the kids fanned out ahead with petitions on clipboards. We still needed forty names—a tall order—to achieve a majority, but with the names we already had, the Town Council would have to place it on the ballot any-way. Within two blocks we had added six names and two more marchers and we were feeling pretty good about it all. As we passed the last house before the tennis courts I think it was I who came up with the idea to approach the players.

The afternoon session was underway, but it was a small crowd. A doubles game was in progress on Court One. Shill and Doc were waiting on the stands. The players were Carter and Mandy on one side and Stinky and Flatbush on the other. Instead of sending the kids out with the clipboards, I waved the "parade" to a halt and approached the courts, clipboard in hand, by myself. A point was concluding as I clinked through the gate, so I continued onto the court, stride unbroken.

Carter gave me a quizzical little smile as I neared, but it was a warm enough greeting. I strode right out onto the court and asked him would he sign our petition. He took it from me and scanned it quickly, once and then again.

I will never forget how the innocent silence of the few seconds it took him to read the important paragraph and absorb its meaning turned into a different kind of silence, a deadly calm-before-the-storm silence, a silence suddenly loud by the change in his features, transformed from politely mystified to downright menacing. Then how his head nodded up to look me straight in the eyes, a look that said, "I don't know you." Nor how his head nodded back down to stare at the hand—his hand—holding the clipboard, then up at me again, then down to my shoes, not smooth-soled shoes, but a pair of Hushpuppies with hard-edged soles and distinct rubber heels, then over at Moses, innocent but standing just behind me, clearly in the service area of Court One.

Then he acted, thrusting the clipboard directly away from him as if he had suddenly noticed it was burning. It struck the court beyond my feet and dug up a little divot. The pen went spinning away, as eager as Carter to be rid of the thing. Through clenched teeth he seethed the words, "I will not. This is the President's business, not our business. Good day."

At that point I could no more have asked the others to sign than I could have tried to make a joke of Carter's reaction. It was all over. I retrieved the clipboard and pen and tiptoed off the court on the balls of my feet. Moses was close at those heels that did not touch the ground until I was out of the gate. The silence had followed me out—the clink of the gate-latch had the impact of a gun being fired—and we resumed our parade in that silence until we had left it behind.

Everyone knew to keep quiet until we were out of earshot. Then Ellen hissed, urgently, "What did he say?" I didn't let on what I knew, that I had offended a friend and broken some important rules. Instead I tried to laugh it off. "Carter's old guard—he said it was the President's business." That cracked her up and I was grateful not to have to say anything more.

We did two more blocks and picked up four more signatures, but the time between signatures was stretching out. The afternoon was moving along, so we decided to take a shortcut across the park and onto Maple, where the higher density of older cottages would give us a better shot at making our goal. We had turned onto Maple and reached the point where the drainage ditch crossed under, just before the houses started, when we heard a car coming up behind us. This had happened on Grove and the car had been patient enough to wait until we could rearrange the banner and move to one side. But this car, a Cadillac, was bigger and came up faster than those in the rear were comfortable with. The kids were quickly pulled to either side, but the ditch prevented them from getting far enough off the pavement. The car horn blew a frightening warning, but then it did slow way down. We were relieved when we could see that it was Carter behind the wheel.

He maneuvered the car as though to thread the space between the children, but it was too narrow. The apologetic moms redistributed the kids to one side while we got the banner out of the way. The car had never stopped moving, though very slowly, and it now seemed poised to make its move past our group. But just as the way was clear for Carter to drive through, Moses did what no dog should do to a man in a new Cadillac whatever the motive—what he should not do to a policeman who has pulled over to ask why he is on the loose, what he should not do to a tattooed man with a ponytail in a brand-new pickup truck. He jumped up to his full height with his paws extended and his claws full out in front against Carter's car door. He jumped up repeatedly, barking as he was doing it, each time landing his claws on the chrome, then sliding them down off the chrome to the paint, and then along the paint, and in spite of the barking everyone could hear the click and slide as the nails dented chrome and dug into paint.

Carter yelled, "Hey!" and then tried to push the dog away. He accelerated a little to scare the dog off, all the while looking left and right lest any marchers be in the way. His face got redder than usual as he kept pushing at the dog while his head swung wildly left and right and his foot kept tapping the accelerator and the car lurched forward in short gains. Suddenly the road ahead was clear. Carter took the open path and accelerated to get away from the marchers and the dog. But Moses's paw got caught under the door handle so as the car started moving so did Moses. Moses knew there was trouble and tried to pull away, but his paw was caught sideways under the handle. As the car moved forward Moses's back legs were picked up off the ground and swung forward. Carter swerved left then right, and Moses's captured paw gave way and his body started to drop away. His back legs hit first and he tumbled into the ditch just as Carter's Cadillac's left rear wheel slipped into the ditch, off the drain tile and onto Moses. It hit him in the neck and pushed his head into the mud, running right over it.

I heard, or think I heard, the sound of a bone breaking. Carter righted the car and stopped it immediately. It was as though he had heard that awful sound, too. He got out and looked, and looked away, and looked again. Moses was behind the car and half in the ditch now, gasping, I guess you could call it—a sound like an animal without vocal cords.

I was stricken dumb like everyone else. Eventually I was down on my knees, with my hands on Moses's muddied side and chest. His breast was rising and falling in some kind of desperate way, but his eyes weren't open; it was as though he were in a dog dream. I stayed in that position waiting for some change, and eventually there was a diminishment of the gasping, then a new silence. I didn't know what to do with him, but I knew he was dead. After some time passed, in which I thought both about the strangeness of my situation and the loss of my dog, it occurred to me that I had some duty to do. I thought about walking home to get my car, but I realized that wasn't the right thing. So I just picked him up (there was only a little blood by his nose and mouth) and started off toward home. I didn't know what I was doing, and neither did my two close friends, but they let me go. Then all of a sudden Moses and I were home and I told Janet and that was the end of Moses.

We buried Moses in a corner of the yard. I didn't go back to Sunday tennis that summer and two years later I injured my hand. It wasn't long before people connected the accident (with the hand, I mean) with the fact that I didn't play tennis any more. They didn't connect Moses's accident with tennis, just with the parade. But it was all connected somehow. The casualties of war are often unenumerated.

The Royal Tenenbaums *is the story of three child prodigies grown into dysfunctional adults and how they make peace with their sneaky, withholding father (the titular Royal Tenenbaum). Margot Tenenbaum won a prestigious playwriting grant during early adolescence, while Chas Tenenbaum was a teenaged tycoon. Their brother, Richie, was a tennis champion (he won the "U.S. Nationals" three years in a row)—until the love of his life, adopted sister Margot, married the writer Raleigh St. Clair.*

*For the past year, Richie has traveled the world alone on the ocean liner Côte d'Ivoire. Now he has returned, to make his forbidden love known to Margot. In this excerpt from the screenplay of the film, Richie and his father reminisce about the day at "Windswept Fields" (read Forest Hills) when he lost it in front of the Tenenbaum clan and the world.*

# From *The Royal Tenenbaums*

## Wes Anderson and Owen Wilson

CUT TO:

*Richie and Royal looking at an impressive monument in the middle of the cemetery. An inscription says: Veteran of Two Wars. Father of Nine Children. Drowned in the Caspian Sea.*

ROYAL

That's a hell of a damn grave.

*Richie nods. Royal says wistfully:*

ROYAL

I wish it were mine.

CUT TO:

*Royal and Richie walking together among the gravestones.*

ROYAL

It's a shame, isn't it?

RICHIE

What?

ROYAL

You probably had another good two to three years of competitive play in you.

RICHIE
(*shrugs*)

Probably.

ROYAL

I had a lot riding on that match, you know. Financially and personally.

*Richie nods. Silence.*

ROYAL

Why'd you choke out there that day, Baumer?

RICHIE
(*pause*)

I don't know, Dad.

INSERT:

*A television set tuned in to network coverage of a tennis match on grass courts. Richie is playing an Indian player dressed all in white. A title identifies him as Sanjay Gandhi.*

*Gandhi serves. With a bizarre swing, Richie hits his return directly off the court and deep into the stands. He shakes his head and talks to himself. It is briefly revealed that he is wearing no shoes and only one sock.*

ANNOUNCER
(*voice over*)

That's seventy-two unforced errors for Richie Tenenbaum. He's playing the worst tennis of his life. What's the feeling right now, Tex Hayward?

TEX HAYWARD
(*voice over*)

I don't know, Jim. There's obviously something wrong with him. He's taken off his shoes and one of his socks, and—actually, I think he's crying.

*Richie is shown preparing to serve with tears all over his face. He hesitates. He looks into the stands.*

ANNOUNCER
(*voice over*)
Who's he looking at in the friends' box, Tex?

*Margot and Raleigh, holding hands, watch from their seats in a courtside box. They look very concerned.*

TEX HAYWARD
(*voice over*)
That's his sister, Margot, and her new husband, Raleigh St. Clair. They were just married yesterday, Jim.

*Richie stares at Margot and Raleigh. He looks to Chas, with Rachael, Ari and Uzi. He looks to Royal in a lonely seat up in the nosebleed section. Royal stands up and walks towards the exit.*

*Richie serves suddenly, underhand, barely tossing the ball into the air. Gandhi nails his return, and Richie attempts to play it by throwing his racquet at the ball.*

CUT TO:

*Royal and Richie standing together.*

ROYAL
I kind of disappeared after that, didn't I?
π

RICHIE
(*shrugs*)
Yeah, but I understood. I know you're not very good with disappointment.

*Royal nods. He kicks a pebble on the ground.*

# Part IV

## Mixed/Doubles

*"I'll take the right-hand side, if you don't mind," she announced. "Oh, and what about apologizing?" she went on. "Shall we do it after every stroke, or at the end of each game, or when we say good-bye, or never? I get so tired of saying 'sorry.'"*

—A. A. Milne
"Pat-Ball"

*Wealth and class, gender roles and sexual desire: Lee Harrington's long short story dramatizes all of them, against a Riviera landscape worthy of a post-Impressionist painter. Where else could this sweet, sad, distinctly Jamesean tale of American naïveté take place but on a tennis court?*

# The Fourth

### Lee Harrington

"And what is it you do?" the English woman said.

"Technically I'm an athlete. A triathlete." Gayle, an American, was visiting an employment agency run by English people for English-speaking people in the South of France. She handed the woman her resumé and added, as if it would make a difference, "I'm training for the Hawaii Ironman."

"Yes, I see," the woman said, but she regarded Gayle over the tops of her glasses in a way that suggested that no, she didn't see. This woman was dressed far too seductively, in stiletto heels and a shocking pink suit. Her silk blouse was cut so low the lace of the woman's bra showed—a pink bra, clearly expensive and exotic and French. From the moment the two shook hands, Gayle was thrown off by the Bra Factor—shouldn't a career placement administrator be wearing a mannish, corporate suit? In black or navy or grey?

"And what sort of job is it you're looking for?"

Gayle paused. A brass plaque on the English woman's desk said, in cursive, *Specializing in Domestic Service since 1983.* Gayle had a bachelor's degree in sociology, and back in the States she had taught Phys Ed, but none of that mattered in the South of France. All they wanted you to do here, it seemed, was show cleavage and speak French. But finally Gayle cleared her throat. "Well, anything really. If I don't get a job soon I'll have to go back to the States, and, well, I just don't want to do that."

"I see," the woman said. Eyeglasses in France were the equivalent of miniskirts in New York City: flashy, sexy, impossibly expensive, available in a riot of colors, and people over a certain age just shouldn't wear them. But everyone did. "And you're how old?"

"Twenty-three," Gayle said. "I just graduated from college a year ago, and I came to France to train because the cycling over here is so good, and, well, I just never left." The woman stared at her without blinking, so Gayle went on: "I've been trying to get a legitimate job for over a month now because my savings are running out. I'd like to teach English, for example, but I don't have a working permit. So I thought I might do something under the table—like nannying or watering lawns."

"How is your French?"

"Not very good, I'm afraid.",

"What are you skills then, as an . . ." The woman scanned Gayle's resumé, as if looking for something useful to say. "Athlete?"

"Well, I can baby-sit. Or house-sit. I could walk someone's dogs."

"Have you worked as a nanny before?"

"I used to baby-sit for my younger sister."

"Have you cleaned houses?"

"Not technically. But I clean my own apartment all the time."

"I see. And have you waited tables?"

"Oh, yes. Absolutely. In college, during the summers."

There was an intake of breath here that gave Gayle hope, but the woman said: "At a restaurant, I suppose. An American restaurant?"

"Yes."

The woman pursed her lips, and Gayle saw that her lipstick was seeping into the lines around her mouth.

"Well, let's see what we might have." The woman swiveled in her chair to face a file cabinet behind her and pulled out some paper. "House-sitting positions do come up occasionally, though it's a bit too early in the season for that. Now as far as nannying or gardening, I have to be honest with you and say you're going to be difficult to place. Domestic service is a serious profession, Miss Brewster, and most of the applicants we get are trained in their arts."

"I see," Gayle said. She knew that at this very moment she should have defended herself; she should have stressed that she was educated and personable and quick to learn. But those would have been the words of a fighter, someone spirited, and Gayle had left her spirit back in New York City. With a man named Dick.

"She actually said that domestic service was an art?" Gayle's friend Clara asked later that afternoon in their kitchen. Clara laughed so hard that she sent herself into a Gauloise-induced coughing fit, and Gayle had to slap her on the back.

Clara wiped the tears from her eyes. "She's full of bullocks, that one. Was she wearing that fucking pink suit?"

"Oh yes," Gayle said.

"And it's not a bloody fucking art. You just have to be stupid and be able to swallow a lot of bull." Clara worked as a cook on a motor yacht, and it was she who had referred Gayle to this particular employment agency in Antibes.

"And a lot of cum, I suppose," Gayle said. She was trying to be cheerful and witty, like Clara, but she sounded sad.

"If you want to rise up the ladder," Clara said with a wink. "As any proper girl should."

Clara and Gayle were roommates, but not for much longer. Clara's ship was about to set sail, literally, as in less than three weeks the owner of the yacht was flying in from Saudi Arabia and wanted to embark on a three-month summer cruise of the Mediterranean, starting in Corfu.

"I think I botched the interview," Gayle said.

"Why do you say that?"

"She wished me luck when we shook hands to say good-bye," Gayle said. "Wasn't she supposed to say, 'I look forward to speaking with you soon'?"

"Did you lie to her?"

"Of course I didn't."

"Well, Duckie, you were *supposed* to. Don't tell me you went and told her the truth."

"Not all of it. Just some of it. I did tell her I was low on money, but I didn't elaborate on the Hotel California aspect of my predicament— that not only can I not afford to stay in France, I can't afford to leave, either."

"Ah. Fuck her," Clara said.

Clara had lied her way into her current job. When she had moved to Antibes from London two years earlier, she knew she wanted to work on a yacht—that was it. She wanted the travel, the glamour, and the year-round tan, so when a sous chef spot opened up on the *Mohammed*—the largest boat in the Antibes marina, and the third-largest private boat in the world—Clara marched down to the employment agency and said she had been cooking all her life.

"And had you?" Gayle had asked when she first heard the story.

"Fuck no! Never cooked a lick. My mum never cooked either—we grew up on canned Spam sandwiches and takeaway. But that's not the point. The point is I knew I was capable of cooking, and took the necessary steps to get that job. Bullshitting! Now there's an art!" Clara went on to convince the ship's Saudi head steward that she had apprenticed at some of the finest restaurants in Paris, and then in Lyon, and she listed, in perfect unaccented French, all the dishes she herself had created, and the Saudi head steward, all the while hypnotically nodding his head, inevitably made her an offer, because Clara's dishes did sound delicious, and she had big round tits.

"You see, Duckey," Clara now said. She opened the utensil drawer and pulled out a bottle of orange nail polish. "The trick to getting anywhere in life is projecting yourself into the future a little bit. You're stuck in the past."

It was Clara, for the record, who had insisted on calling Gayle's ex-boyfriend "Dick," even though his name was actually Peter.

"And let me remind you, Gayle, that you could get a job anywhere. You've got blond hair and long legs and a nice arse." Clara began to paint her nails. "You should have no problems at all."

"Right," Gayle said. But the thing was, Clara was brash and ballsy. Whereas Gayle was just plain scared.

Clara gestured to a bowl of candy on the counter. "Hand me one of them Hershey's Kisses will you, Duckie? And be a love and peel it for me? My nails are wet."

Gayle peeled the chocolate and placed it in Clara's open mouth.

"Wear a tight T-shirt next time you go on an interview," Clara said. "Show them the goods."

"That just seems wrong to me," Gayle said. "I mean, are people here really that shallow?"

Clara looked thoughtful for a moment. Then she broke into a chocolate-coated grin. "Yesh," she said. "Absho-fucking-lutely."

Gayle had been living and training in France for nine months now, and yet she still could not get used to the blatant sexism. There were breasts on billboards and breasts on the currency and breasts on daytime TV. On Clara's friend Mark's giant, satellite-powered television, she once saw an Italian game show in which a blindfolded man had to feel up a long row of smiling, topless women. The object of the game was to pick out which set belonged to his wife. *Formidable!* All this bothered Gayle, or at best confused her, yet if she tried to talk about it with any of her English friends—the only kind of friends she had made in France—they called her a Puritan or a prude. "It's just tits!" Clara would say with a wave of her cigarette. "Get over it." But it was not, to Gayle, just tits. It was something she could not put her finger on. All her life she had been raised to believe that being female meant, well, just being another person with hopes and dreams and aspirations. No distinction was ever made between her and her brother, Tom, in terms of what they could or could not do. Gayle, finding herself to be a gifted swimmer and runner, went in the athletic direction. Tom, good with numbers, went into finance. Who would they have been had they been raised in France, or in England, where the daily paper featured a topless girl every morning on Page Three?

Oh, but there was no time to ponder this all now. The matter at hand was not the bare-breasted women on Gayle's franc notes, or the giant poster of a teenage girl's ass (otherwise known as an advertisement for cellulite) Gayle had to pass every morning as she set out for her morning run, but her dire financial situation. Peter had given her a certain amount of money when she left New York, as kind of a kiss-off present (which Gayle was too bitter to refuse), but that supply was disappearing quickly. Faster than you could hang up the phone and say *Dick!* She had hoped to make some money placing in some of the triathlons she had entered, but so far Gayle had won nothing.

"Come down to the marina with me," Clara said in the morning. "And try to talk your way onto one of the boats."

"But I keep telling you I can't work on a boat," Gayle said. Clara, with her perma-tan and hard drinking and her sleeping-with-the-new-crew-members on every trip to sea, looked about eighty. And Gayle needed to train. "I have to stay here, on dry land. Where I can ride my bike."

"Most of these yachts don't go anywhere, though. You know that. They're all for show. For a bunch of filthy-rich fucking Arabs. You can work as a deck nigger, cleaning toilets and polishing brass. It's a man's job, really, but once they get a look at you they'll realize they'd rather enjoy having you on your hands and knees scrubbing the decks in your tight, white shorts."

Gayle frowned. "You really say 'Deck nigger'?"

"Ugh. Don't be such an American," Clara said. "Come along, then. And make sure to wear those tight, white shorts."

But before Gayle could even contemplate the horror of showing up for an interview in tennis shorts, the phone rang, and it was the English employment agent.

"You're not going to believe it," the woman said.

"What?" Gayle said.

"I've just been speaking with Lord Rosscommon, the Marquess of Hardcastle for those of us in the know, and he's looking for someone to play tennis!"

Gayle was confused. "Today?"

"Oh, no, no, no, no, no!" the woman said musically. "Let me explain. Lord Rosscommon is very rich. Let me repeat: *Very.* Rich. He has a villa in St. Tropez where he spends his summers, and he keeps quite a large staff, and he's just phoned me to tell me he'll be needing someone to come live on his property and be available to play tennis, should any of his guests require a fourth."

"I don't understand," Gayle said. She suddenly had visions of Page Three, and being made to play topless and bounce around in a skirt.

"Darling. It's a dream job. I haven't seen the estate, but of course I've heard about it. *You* will live there," she said. "*He* will pay you. Generously, I'm sure. You do play tennis, don't you?"

"Well, yes, but—"

"Good. I'll arrange an interview with him. He's in St. Tropez now and is going back to England in three days to tend to some business before the summer season begins. He wants to have this position filled before he departs."

And thus it was that less than twenty-four hours later Gayle found herself rendezvousing with Lord Rosscommon at the train station in St. Tropez. They had arranged to meet underneath a certain clock near the ticket counter, and Gayle recognized him at once. He was a pleasant-looking older man, in his fifties perhaps, with sandy hair and a slight build. His very way of standing, with his hands resting leisurely in his suit pockets, smacked of aristocracy and wealth. He seemed patient and optimistic, yet the way he kept scanning the crowd nervously, and tugging on his perfectly crisp tie suggested he was also a bit distracted and confused. Gayle knew the type: Here was a man so rich and privileged he knew he could afford to buy whatever he wanted, yet he hadn't quite figured out how to acquire the more abstract, more elusive things such as Wisdom and Happiness and Love.

Satisfied that she had pegged him, Gayle approached Lord Rosscommon and introduced herself.

"Ah, Miss Brewster," he said, "How delightful! So good of you to come all this way." Up close he was tan and toned and well-preserved, which suggested time spent at gyms, salons, and cosmetic surgeons. And as he took her hand and shook it, Gayle thought she could feel, in his handshake, a certain decency and gentleness. But then she thought: Maybe his hands are so soft from all those manicures and shea butter treatments. For at this point Lord Rosscommon had begun the not-so-subtle eye crawl, which started with her feet, lingered on her ankles and muscular thighs, followed the hem of her skirt to the outline of her hips, up the waist and then *Arret!* His eyes widened when he got to her breasts.

"So, my dear, you are a player of tennis?" he said. His aristocratic accent somehow made the word *tennis* sound sinister and lascivious, and Gayle instinctively crossed her arms.

"Yes," Gayle said. "These days I'm actually more of a triathlete, but I used to play tennis when I was young." She heard Clara's voice saying *Remember to lie through your pretty teeth and smile while you're doing it.* So Gayle stopped talking and smiled.

"Good," Lord Rosscommon said. "Very good. Have you had lunch?" Gayle shook her head cautiously.

"Very good. I thought we could dine here, in town, at the Vieux Port, and then drive out to my villa so that you can inspect the courts."

He took her elbow and led her outside the station, where a white-gloved driver held open the door of a Mercedes and motioned for Gayle to get in. She sank into a leather seat soft as an atrophied muscle, and marveled at the flat-screen television and the miniature bar. Lord Rosscommon moved in noiselessly beside her, and the car eased off.

"So what is it a triathlete does?" he said as they drove alongside the turquoise Mediterranean. "I must admit I am wholly ignorant on the subject of American sport." So Gayle went into her how-I-became-an-athlete spiel: how she had won state track and swimming titles in high school and got a scholarship to B.U. "For track, but I kept up swimming on my own." There she placed twice in the nationals, once for the five thousand meters, once for the relay, but she didn't start doing triathlons until two years ago, when she entered a small sprint-distance race in Louisiana for the hell of it. "And I won!" she told him. "I was just there for spring break. It was something to do on a Saturday while my friends nursed their hangovers. Winning took me and everyone else totally by surprise. It was the run that did it. They told me later I was about twelve minutes behind the first place female after the bike leg, and I made up that time and more on the run. I beat Lizzie Reilly. The pro!"

"How delightful!" Lord Rosscommon said. "And what happened then?" He had a weird smile on his face—a wry smile, as if Gayle were the subject of some joke unknown to her.

Gayle crossed her legs. The *then* was that she met Peter and found herself consumed with her first real love. And then they lived together for two years, and then he cheated on her—in a callous, blatant way that should have told her something—and then he convinced a mutual friend to tell Gayle that Peter had been cheating on her, using the "logic" that he'd rather see Gayle be mad than sad, and then Gayle, having been flattened by the news, decided the only way she could get over this was to put a large ocean between herself and the culprit, and then she moved to France. And then she embarked on six months of serious athletic training, which left no room for romance or self-pity or thought. And then she began to enter races, but hadn't won any yet, and then she met club-hopping Clara, who taught Gayle how to elevate the habits of eating and drinking into a higher art, and then she ran out of money. And then she had to scalp her return ticket to New York City to a young Algerian man, who was probably a hijacker—but hey, he had fresh francs—and then she found herself sitting in a car with an English nobleman, whose knee was about two inches from hers and gaining, and then she said, "I realized I could really be a contender as a professional triathlete, and you can make more money doing that in Europe than you can in the States. So here I am," she said. "A professional athlete." She turned her body fully toward the window and pretended to be transfixed by the yachts rocking complacently in the water. "It's so beautiful here." Europeans—they had a different sense of personal space than Americans had.

The car turned up a narrow cobblestone street, past boutiques and boulangeries, and into a town square with an old Roman fountain and a magnificent pink church.

"Ah, here we are," Lord Rosscommon said, clapping his hands together. "This restaurant, the Palm D'Or, counts, along with the rose gardens at Hardcastle and Big Sur, as one of my favorite places in the world." He took Gayle's elbow and led her toward an outdoor café with pink tablecloths and advantageous views of the yachts. "The Bellinis here are heavenly. You must try one." He looked at Gayle with raised eyebrows. "Or two."

A fuss was made as the maître d' greeted Lord Rosscommon with a flurry of kisses; then the chef came out, then a woman who appeared to be the chef's mother or wife, then each of the four waiters. Gayle still could not get used to the fact that in France it took large parties at least twenty minutes to greet each other, because each person had to deliver and be delivered of a kiss on each cheek.

The maître d', out of respect to her nationality, simply shook Gayle's hand. "A pleasure, Mademoiselle," he said without smiling, and as he led them to their table and held Gayle's chair, she sensed a touch of disdain in his demeanor, and she realized that he must look down on her. He probably thought she was a prostitute! Gayle had worn, at Clara's insistence, a short, white-cotton dress that showed off her legs and gave, at Clara's insistence, "the suggestion of tennis," but suddenly Gayle felt cheap and tawdry. The other women at the restaurant wore silks and suits of the caliber worn by Gayle's employment agent. They all had deep, even tans and professionally coiffed hair and jewels and gigantic, gold belt buckles and nails that could scratch the skin off their young lovers' backs.

"Lovely, isn't it?" Lord Rosscommon said.

And Gayle had to admit that, yes, it was. She just wasn't sure how she fit into the picture. For she suddenly realized that all of St. Tropez had the improbable good looks of a movie set, with everything matching, everything just right. The pastel-colored buildings matched the boats, which matched the women's handbags—large, elaborate handbags with patterned logos and diamond clasps—which of course matched the women's shoes. Lord Rosscommon's calm, benign eyes matched the color of the water in the marina, which matched the shutters on the pastel-colored bank across the street. The only thing on Gayle that matched this landscape was the peach-colored sports drink stain on her dress, which she had tried to hide with a cheap rhinestone pendant. If the director of this movie saw that pendant, would he yell "Cut!" and chase her off the set?

"Shall I order for you?" Lord Rosscommon said. "I thought we might have something light, like a green salad and a vichyssoise, followed by the roasted sea bass *en croutes*." He snapped open his menu. "How arrogant of them to print this entirely in French."

Gayle nodded and smiled. He was funny, this Ross. She just couldn't tell if he was trying or not.

Soon the food came, along with giant goblets of blush-colored wine, and slowly but surely Gayle was lulled into that curious, hazy state of mind typical of southern France, in which all of life becomes a tribute to the senses. The mushrooms in her crepe tasted richly of earth and forest. The sea beyond them glowed as brightly as a jewel. Sounds rose around Gayle like quadraphonic music: the gilded laughter of the well-coiffed women, the click and tinkle of sails against masts, the honeyed smoothness of Lord Rosscommon's voice as he talked to her about Provence. His words ebbed and flowed into her consciousness, but never quite required a response. *Lavender,* he said. *Chateau Barbeyrolles. Les chevres.* As Gayle lifted her wineglass to her lips (a glass that was always full, with wine that was always cold) she realized that rosé smelled like roses, and she suddenly wanted to see the gardens at Hardcastle, in the summertime, when the flowers were in full bloom.

"What's it like?" she said. "Where you live? In England?"

And Lord Rosscommon went on to describe a house much like the one she had seen on the television series *Brideshead Revisited,* only without Sebastian and Charles. "It's your average English country house. Large, drafty, uninviting, made of stone. We've got a lovely baroque fountain on the south side of the property and some wonderful wooded trails. *I* like it. It's been in the family for years—more years, I'm afraid, than any American can fathom. And I must say there's something to be said for that. All that . . . *continuity.* My son, however, finds it heinous. All of it—the house, the grounds, the seat—all dismissed with one curious word: heinous."

"How old is he?" Gayle said.

"Eighteen."

"Ah."

"He'll probably turn Hardcastle into condominiums when he gets his hands on it. Or one of those tedious conference centers. Now that, my dear, is what I would call heinous."

They smiled at one another, and a certain understanding seemed to pass between them, though Gayle wasn't 100 percent certain what it was. It had something to do with the son, and how little he needed to be tolerated, or perhaps it concerned all teenagers in general, which thereby put Gayle into the category of adult.

Then the desserts came—three tiny pots of crème caramel—each in three different flavors: chocolate, cognac, and vanilla—and Gayle ate hers with a demitasse spoon and let each small bit dissolve on her tongue. They tasted both wholesome and decadent; they tasted of southern France itself, and suddenly Gayle felt, rising within her, one of those realizations that she was having A Moment. As an expat, one can have a lot of these because you are constantly aware of your otherness and thus constantly aware of the sensation of being on a journey. Gayle, in this Moment, felt wise and giddy, for she recognized how large her life was, how adventurous her gestures, how resourceful of the French to drink so much wine. And all at once she saw a life of wealth and luxury rise up before her; she saw two paths diverge in a wood, one of them being a rather sharp, unexpected hairpin turn, but she knew she wanted this tennis job and wanted it badly, with a determination and a focus that she hadn't felt for months.

"And now I think it's time we talked tennis," Lord Rosscommon said, setting his spoon down. "I am fanatical about the game, and many of my friends are, too." He sipped his coffee delicately. "Not that any of us are any good, mind you. But I have spectacular courts. Tell me, do you play on clay?"

"I have played on clay," Gayle said. "But mostly I play on asphalt." *Lie!* Clara's voice said. "I do like playing on clay, though. I like the way it slows your game down. It makes you more conscious of your strokes." Lord Rosscommon seemed to perk up at the mention of *strokes,* so Gayle added quickly: "My whole family plays tennis, so I basically grew up on the courts. And in high school I was on the tennis team."

"Yes, yes," Lord Rosscommon said. "Now, tell me. Would you say you are an A player? Or a B player?" Again he sounded lascivious.

"Honestly," Gayle said. "I'm a B player. But I have . . ."—and here she tried to match his mysterious tone—". . . a lot of stamina." Then, she uncrossed her legs in order to stretch them out and recrossed them the other way. It wasn't quite a Sharon Stone, but it seemed to have the same effect.

"Good, good." Lord Rosscommon signaled to the waiter. "Now, shall we drive out and have a look at the courts?"

Lord Rosscommon's villa, called La Jolie, was situated on a tiny, penis-shaped peninsula lush with palm trees and squat Riviera pines. They passed through an elaborate electronic gate, then up a long white driveway lined with plane trees and flowers. Then the villa itself came into view: peach colored, multileveled, with green shutters and paler green window boxes, each of which was spilling over with bright, yellow flowers. The sun, at that hour, was at such an angle as to light up the whole front of the house with that soft Mediterranean crispness (the same kind of light they try to reproduce in Hollywood with eight-thousand dollar megawattage lamps), and beyond the house was the sea. Trees near the house rocked gently, as if to music, and cast blush-colored shadows on the walls. As they pulled into a circular driveway, Gayle realized she was having another Moment. After all that talk at lunch of lavender and castles, after all that sweet pink wine, she was no longer just the clueless American, but a sexy tennis chick sitting next to a Lord in a Mercedes. He took her hand to help her out of the car, and her face grew flush.

A handsome, tan, blonde man in an apron came to the door with one hand on his hip, as if he were prepared to scold them, and Lord Rosscommon said, with humor, "Ah, here's Whitmore. He is my left hand, and he'll show you round this afternoon. Please do not call him Whitless; he doesn't like it. Now, I must tend to some other business. Thank you, my dear, for a most pleasant luncheon." He said a few words to the driver, who nodded his head, and then handed Gayle over to Whitmore. "Please show Miss Brewster the cottage and the courts."

"*Avec plaisir*," Whitmore said with an exaggerated bow, and his voice was so high and his attitude so camp that Gayle realized, *avec plaisir*, that this man was probably gay. (It was Whitmore who later pointed out to Gayle that the peninsula was shaped like a penis, thus confirming her suspicions.) "Come along, Luv," he now said. "Let's get you out of this sun before you self-combust. Would you prefer to walk or drive down to the courts?"

"Let's walk," she said. She had realized the driveway was made of white shells.

"Oh, good. I can have a cigarette. His *Lord*ship won't let us smoke anywhere near the house. He doesn't like the smell, he says." Whitmore began to lead Gayle down the driveway. "Now, I'm his Lordship's personal assistant," he said, exaggerating both titles camply. "We're very informal here, as you can undoubtedly tell. And no, you may not call me Whitless, but you may call me William, my Christian name. His Lordship is very old-fashioned in many ways, but we tolerate him. He does compensate us rather handsomely. I supervise the housekeeping and the daily staff. Bert serves as chauffeur, as you can see, and inside the house takes on the role of butler. He tends to the door and the drinks and the dining, and supervises any caterers that we bring in for parties and such. We also have a gardener, or so I'm told, who is like a shadow, but grows the most divine roses, and a cook, Madame DuFresne, who is excellent, beyond compare, and she does all the shopping. She's so good that his Lordship hardly dines out when he's here. Make friends with her," Whitmore said, "and she'll pick up anything special you might need at the market. You're vegetarian, I take it?"

"How did you know?"

Whitmore placed his cigarette on the driveway, ground it into the shells with the tip of his shoe, then picked up the butt and placed it in his apron.

"Darling," Whitmore said. "A, you're American. B, the dogs haven't inserted their snouts into your crotch, and C, your skin, if you don't mind my saying, is sallow. You don't get enough iron is what I suspect. Talk to Bert about that. He's an Ayurvedic nutritionist."

"Bert the driver?" Gayle realized she hadn't got a good look at Bert. Like any hired driver, he had slumped in his seat and kept his cap pulled tightly over his head.

"Yes. He's Dutch, but he grew up in India—his father was some kind of diplomat. I should warn you that he *hates* Americans, and women, but fortunately he rarely talks." They were now on a footpath leading through a garden. "His wife was American. Yes, he was married. Sometimes that's what it takes to make a gay man realize he truly is gay. Has two kids as well. Boys. Lovely children. His wife was a real bitch, from what I hear, and now he has simply written the whole lot of them off."

"Where was she from?"

"Miami."

"Well, I'm not from Miami," Gayle said.

And Whitmore said, "Don't I know it! Now, I shall show you your quarters first, and then the tennis courts."

"That sounds fine," Gayle said, but she was thinking, *Quarters?* Her knowledge of what a servant's quarters might look like came from English literature, so she began to expect something dark and dank and cobwebbed, located in a basement or on an upper floor. Something along the lines of the room where Jane Eyre's husband stored his crazy first wife. So when Whitmore led her down a stone walkway, underneath a trellis bowed with purple wisteria, through a small grove of apricot trees, and toward a small stone cottage that overlooked the sea, she did not know what to do with herself. Or what to say.

"This is it?" she said, delighted. "This is where I would live?"

"This is it, honey. We call it the den of sin." Then he must have seen the alarm in Gayle's eyes, because he quickly added: "Oh, it's a darling place. Very peaceful. There's a blue parrot who lives in the plane tree just outside your back window." He led her there to show her. "But he hasn't shown up yet this year. I don't know why. Our cottage is very similar to yours, though a bit larger, and it's on the exact opposite end of the estate. West Testicle, we call it. You are on the East Testicle. We have the better sunsets, I'm afraid to say, but La Jolie is on the best spot—the head."

"We're like bookends," Gayle said.

Whitmore considered her and smiled. "You think books; I think scrota. Therein lies all the difference. Were you a literature major?"

"Sociology."

"Ah. Well, you're very sweet. And I can tell without hesitation that you are a *real* blonde. Bert *hates* peroxide. Come."

Whitmore opened the heavy oak door of the cottage and motioned for Gayle to go through. She was met with the smells of lavender and mimosa and her eyes were drawn to a giant bouquet of the latter in a galvanized bucket next to the hearth. A great stone fireplace with a simple plank mantle was the focus of the ground floor, and its soiled, earthy presence immediately made Gayle feel comforted and somehow safe.

"Lovely isn't it?" Whitmore said. "I decorated it myself. Most of the furniture is local. There are marvelous antiques stores in Cannes. You should have *seen* the place when Lord Rosscommon bought it. Can you say 'Dark Ages'?" Whitmore had done all the rooms in various shades of yellow and purple—pale lemon pinstripes on the upholstery on the fainting couch; a faint lavender print on the wallpaper in the halls. "Yellow is a cheerful color," Whitmore said, as he showed her the kitchen, the bathroom, and the linen closet, filled with embroidered pillowcases and high thread-count sheets. "Purple is pensive. Together they make for a rather balanced atmosphere, don't you think?"

"I hope the bedroom is yellow then," Gayle said, and Whitmore smiled and told her to go have a look.

"But watch out for the second to last step," he called after her. "It always creaks, no matter what we do to fix it." Creak it did as Gayle went up the stairs, in a way that reminded her of sneaking out of the house in her teenage years, and her veins began to fill with that same sort of nervous excitement. As if she were doing something illicit, something that held infinite promise as long as she did not get caught.

Upstairs Gayle found a four-poster bed, with a magnificent eyelet canopy and a coverlet embroidered with tiny yellow flowers. There was also a giant walk-in closet lined in cedar, and another smaller fireplace with a mantle of carved oak. It was the bedroom of a princess and Gayle felt that here, surrounded by its feminine, floral splendor, she would no longer sleep poorly, or have bad dreams. She walked out onto a small balcony, to take in the view, and saw below her the jewel-like Mediterranean, its waves kissing her very own shore. The cottage was perched on a ledge right above the water, and a thin stone path led from her garden down to a private beach. Gayle's heart stirred and the wind whipped her hair and again she felt the beginnings of change, she felt promise. She would live on a ledge on the edge of the world.

"This is more beautiful than any place I've ever lived," Gayle said to Whitmore, downstairs.

"Is it?" Whitmore said proudly. "I am very pleased to be hear you say that. It's always nice to bring a little beauty into another's life. Now, let us go have a look at the grounds, shall we?"

They followed a path through a dense grove of umbrella pines and then, after walking for perhaps fifteen minutes, found themselves in a great clearing, with two tennis courts on one end, a large pool at the other, and a Victorian carriage house in-between. Birds chirped, the sky glowed with an opalescent quality that defied words, and the grass seemed an impossible green.

"We're very well equipped here," Whitmore said, leading her into the equipment rooms. "Everything is top-of-the-line here, state-of-the-art." He showed here where to find the racquets, the practice balls, and the first-aid kit. "This room here," he said, leading her down a long, narrow hallway, "used to be a bowling alley, but too many people injured themselves. I once found a man trying to violate a bowling bowl, and I daresay the poor fellow got stuck."

"I think that's all you need to tell me on that subject," Gayle said.

"Let me show you the changing rooms, then, and the bar." He led her quickly through the men's and women's locker rooms, then into a miniature clubroom, complete with game tables and a carved oak mirror and stained glass. The whole place smelled like unneutered males. "Can you mix drinks?" Whitmore said.

"I've never bartended, if that's what you mean. But I'm sure I could learn."

"Of course it's not an official part of your job," Whitmore said. "And most of Ross's guests would drink straight from the bottle if hard-pressed, but Bert would rather not spend his Saturday nights out here in the toolshed, as he calls it, right through 'til Sunday morning. You'd earn points with him if you performed that service, and sometimes the guests, if they are smitten enough, will give you tips. In fact, they'll always give *you* tips. Now did Lord Rosscommon discuss with you your salary?"

"The woman at the agency did." The pay being offered was so generous that Gayle felt uncomfortable even saying it. Basically, she'd be able to afford to leave France in a matter of weeks. Six weeks.

"And you can stay through the season, 'til September at least?"

"Yes," Gayle said instantly. This was the first lie she had told.

"Good. We'll pay you in francs, or pounds if you prefer, and of course it's all under the table. I usually go into town on Tuesdays, and you're welcome to accompany me should you need to go to the bank. Madame DuFresne goes daily and I suppose you could go with her if you don't mind riding with fish in the backseat on the way home." As Whitmore went on about the details of daily life at La Jolie—when they took their meals, what kind of hours Gayle could expect to keep—Gayle finally realized he was addressing her as if she were hired already.

"Wait. Doesn't anyone want to see me actually play tennis? And aren't you considering anybody else?"

"Darling, come now," Whitmore said. "You must know it's not really about the tennis. We don't want a Lindsay Davenport. We want Anna Kournikova."

"I don't even know who those people are," Gayle said that night to Clara. "That's how un-tennis I am. Should I be doing this?"

"Abso-fucking-lutely!"

"I can't believe anyone could be so rich, or so idle, as to pay someone to hang around and play tennis 'once in a while.' "

"Believe it," Clara said. "And remember, they don't call 'em filthy rich for nothing. What's this bloke's name?"

"Something Rosscommon."

"Hmmm. I'll ask around the marina and see if anyone knows that name. And I'll have my friend Patrick look him up in DeBrett."

"You have to see this place!" Gayle said. "It's this perfect sanctuary. You'll have to come stay with me once you get back."

Clara seemed surprised. "They said you could have guests?"

"I imagine."

"You're hired help, Duckie. I'm not sure you know what that means."

"Well," Gayle said, placing her four pairs of sneakers into a duffel bag. "I guess I'll figure it out."

A few days later a car was sent to retrieve Gayle, driven by the mysterious, Ayur-vedic Bert. Gayle was happy to see Whitmore in the passenger seat, wearing a straw sun visor and carrying a picnic basket in his lap.

"It can be a long drive if the traffic is bad," Whitmore said as Gayle got into the car. "We'll fill you in on all the dirt." Most of Lord Rosscommon's money, he told her as they drove along, was inherited. "And there are gobs of it, let me tell you. But our Lord is one of the few landed gentry to actually make money, not just spend it. Real estate is his business. Selling off family holdings and land. Made a shrewd move in the sixties—sold leases, not the land, makes a killing in rent. His mother was an American. Daughter of the industrialist Henry van der

Luyden. The story goes that she was in love with a fellow American, from a very respectable New York family, but her mother, a veritable bird of prey, wanted her only daughter to marry royalty. Thus the ninth Earl of Rosscommon. Poor Lady Helen fared well in the early years of the marriage, and bore the Earl two sons, but she never quite got over losing her love, the American, and eventually she killed herself. Our Ross was nine at the time. A very vulnerable age, to be sure."

"William feels sorry for him," Bert said. He kept looking at Gayle via his rearview mirror. "Lets 'im get away with murder, all because he lost his mum." There was something about the indirectness of this communication, something about the way his face was reduced to a pair of dark eyes with thick, heightened eyebrows, that made her uncomfortable, so she just nodded her head.

"And that's not the half of it!" Whitmore said. "His wife eventually killed herself, too. Lady Abermarle—Marly, to intimates. Too much inbreeding, is what I say. They were distant cousins, and Marly was never quite right. A tragic beauty, she was. Bore Ross a son, though. And what a son! Now, there's a veritable Frankenstein's monster!" Whitmore went on to describe this son, Rodney, who was pompous and spoiled and, rumor had it, diddled young girls. Ross had spent over a hundred thousand pounds in legal fees trying to keep that one out of prison for violating a minor, but the boy kept getting worse. "When he comes, believe me, I make myself scarce. Faggots, he calls us to our faces."

Gayle felt Bert's eyes on her again, and she sensed for the first time that there might be something dangerous about her position, something to which she had deliberately decided to remain blind. And yet, how else could one cart one's baggage from one place to the next if you didn't put blinders on the horse?

"Poor, Ross," Whitcomb said. "He does his best. Of course he was devastated by the deaths, but Ross has always been very English about it. Never says a word, loses himself in sport. You'll find he's rather religious about tennis. He practices diligently and insists that his guests wear white."

"You're expected to be serious as well," Bert said.

"Of course I will," Gayle said. She looked out the window just in time to see a windsurfer get flattened by a wave. "I have great empathy for anyone who loses himself in sport. At least it's a healthy way to be lost."

"His *Lord*ship is in London at the moment, but will be back in nine days," Whitmore said. "I imagine he'll want you to play a set of tennis with him that Thursday, at one o'clock."

"Of course," Gayle said. "But what do I do until then?"

"Honey, you do whatever you damn well please. Nothing official is required of you when his Lordship is away. That's the beauty of this beast. The whole estate is at our disposal: the beach, the boat, the pools. *We,* that is the hired help, eat breakfast at nine and lunch at one. You are welcome to join us, of course—it's usually just Bert and me, and sometimes Ross even joins us if he's desperate for the company of a couple of old queens."

"Is it okay if I train on the bike in the mornings? And run or swim in the afternoons?"

"Train away. The girl we had last year was a writer, and she holed up in her cottage at all hours typing away. She was a bit too serious, if you ask me, but also, thank God, a bit of a lush, so she perked up once she had some wine in her. *We* dine out most evenings," Whitmore announced, smiling at Bert. "Especially when Ross is away. St. Trop is a glorious meat market at night, and I daresay you wouldn't want to join us. Unless of course," he added, "you have a predilection for hot gay men."

"I'm kind of avoiding the entire male race at the moment. No offense."

"Heartbreak?"

Gayle nodded. She wasn't sure how much she should tell them yet.

"You'll get over it. The good ones always do, and they come out of it better than before. But honey, maybe you should hang around with gay men more often. That way you'll realize that not all of our race is horrid."

"Thank you," she said. "That's very kind."

Eventually they reached La Jolie and Gayle was dropped off at her cottage. "I've put about a week's worth of food in the kitchen," Whitmore said as he helped bring her bags in. "And I've also chilled a nice bottle of Sauternes. A little welcome present from Lord Rosscommon's checkbook, by way of *moi.*" Gayle thanked Whitmore, and he reminded her to call up to the house if she needed anything at any time, and then he and Bert drove off down the white shell driveway.

And Gayle was left alone. Hugely alone. If she stayed still for too long she knew she would think of Peter, so she decided the best thing to do would be to lose herself in sport.

Plus, she had only nine days to brush up on a sport she had abandoned over seven years ago, so she put on shorts and her running shoes and set off for the courts. The air, as she walked, was mild and briny and the pine trees gave off a comforting, hopeful, New England sort of scent. Gayle noticed as she stepped into the clearing that four palm trees stood at the corners of the courts, swaying gently inward like cupped hands. From the equipment room, Gayle chose a new Yonex graphite racquet with a gigantic, almost goofy-looking head. *Can't go wrong with this baby,* she thought with a laugh. Then she carried a bucket of balls to the backboard and looked around to make sure no one was watching because she had no idea how she might perform. Finally, she took out a ball and bounced it a few times on the asphalt to test its spring, all the while feeling like a small, ineffective human being in the midst of a large, insurmountable conflict. *It's just tennis,* she told herself, *it's just hitting a ball,* so she dropped the ball with the aim of hitting some forehand ground strokes against the backboard. Within seconds she realized that her graphite wide-head was unlike any racquet she had ever known. It was as if she were Luke Skywalker playing with a light saber, and she had to step a few more yards away from the board to return her own balls. They went all over the place: over the backboard, beyond the tennis courts. Those that hit the backboard came zooming back past her and got lodged in the links of the barrier fence. Suddenly the sun felt hot and toxic, and Gayle was reminded of the harsh summer sun of her childhood, of hot days on shadeless public courts, of losing *every single time* to her eighteen-foot-tall brother, of her stepmother telling her, rather curtly, at the Dairy Queen afterward not to be such a sore loser, of her stepmother always looking better than Gayle in her little white panty-showing skirts. Perhaps it was then, during all those summers, that Gayle became conditioned to accept placing second. For she was, back then, a very good tennis player. It's just that there were always other people around who were better than she was.

This thought led to other thoughts. Suddenly it seemed that her summers had contained nothing but feelings of longing and loneliness, feelings she somehow channeled from her racquet to the ball, so that loneliness became something she could smack away with all the force of a sixteen-year-old athlete, something she could lob over her brother's head. Until it returned to her and she had to find a new way to smash loneliness back.

Gayle continued to hit the ball against the backboard, and soon she found that she had adjusted to the racquet's otherworldly force. Her forehand came back; her double-fisted backhand, her keen ability to know where the ball was going to go before the ball itself did. And a whole new set of memories opened up to her. Of playing phenomenally; of acing her opponents, of placing shots just inside the far corners of the courts. Gayle remembered with a certain satisfaction the comforting, steady *thwock* of the tennis balls and how that sound remained the same throughout the ages, no matter where the court. She remembered the acute, tinny sound of a fresh can of balls being opened, a sound that gave shape to her loveless teenage summers, a sound that was summer itself. A new day, a new can.

Soon Gayle found herself in a smooth, productive rally with the backboard—forehand, backhand, forehand, backhand—and her skin was filmed with sweat. It was a clean, refined, country-club sweat, and Gayle felt almost French for a moment, and full of courage and strength. She reminded herself that she was an award-winning athlete, and that had to count for something. It *had* to. So Gayle vowed, out there beneath the Mediterranean twilight, not to let this summer crush her. She would do her job and make her money and get back into competitive, Ironman shape.

Over the next few days, Gayle established a routine for herself. First thing in the morning she would swim in the open water, wearing her wetsuit as it was still quite cold. On odd days she would swim for distance and on even days train for speed, and after each session she would shower and change and walk up to the main house to join Bert and Whitmore for a quick French breakfast of croissants, coffee, and fruit. While they ate, Whitmore would fill her in on what was to be expected for the day ahead (and who had got into trouble the night before), while Bert read the *Herald Tribune*. Then, because she still had no tennis obligations, Gayle would spend the rest of the morning on her bicycle, exploring the countryside and mapping out the best forty-kilometer training route. When she returned it was always lunchtime—a matter of great occasion at La Jolie, with three courses and three carafes of wine—and then Gayle, who abstained from the wine in the name of her tennis, would practice on the court for two hours, and then she would have the whole afternoon with everything to think about but nothing left to do.

Sometimes she'd lie at the tiny beach and read triathlon magazines. Sometimes she would write letters or swim. More often than not she would be plagued with visitations by the ghost of Peter, who always seemed to be trying to force his way back into her thoughts, into her tightly closed heart, the way that shark tried to get into the submerged cage of scuba diver Richard Dreyfus in *Jaws*. And so, inevitably, Gayle would find herself at the backboard again, playing against her flat, brick opponent, bashing away her thoughts, wishing all the while that she could practice her interactions with human beings.

On Saturday, Whitmore invited her into town for a shopping excursion, and presented her with her first weekly pay. Because the air outside the shops had such a vital, giddy quality to it; because the colorful bank notes Gayle was given looked so silly as to appear almost fake, she decided to spend this week's installment. She bought herself some tennis dresses and some proper tennis shoes. She bought some new sports

bras, and a tiny bottle of mimosa perfume. And she bought a pale blue
boat-necked dress that, while it looked rather plain on the hanger,
looked dynamite on Gayle.

"Oh, it's perfect," Whitmore said. "You have to buy it. I won't speak
to you again if you don't."

Back at the cottage, she hung the dress alone in the giant walk-in
closet, hoping that she might have an opportunity to wear it some day
soon.

Nights were lonely at La Jolie. The air was always soft, and the palms
swayed gently, and the sea broke against the rocks with a quiet compas-
sion, but within an hour of the sun's setting Gayle would start to panic.
She missed the companionship of Clara; she missed, at times, the re-
lentless cacophony of New York. On such nights, she would often wish
to be back home in the States. Yet, Gayle was starting to realize something essential: that, if truth be told, she would probably be lonely back
there as well. At least here, on an isolated peninsula in southern
France, she had a legitimate excuse for her isolation.

But finally, finally Lord Rosscommon returned—two days earlier
than planned. Gayle had been lying on the beach in a chaise longue,
moving the strap of her bikini every fifteen minutes so that a tan line
wouldn't form; and she had been inwardly gloating because for this she
was getting paid the equivalent of nineteen American dollars an hour,
when suddenly one of the daily housekeepers appeared on the ledge.

"Miss, Miss," the woman shouted in French, waving. "His Lordship
has arrived!" she shouted. "He wants to play tennis right away!"

Gayle waved back and shouted *"Oui, oui, j'arrive!"* and stood to
gather her things. As she hurried up the footpath to her cottage, her
nerve endings shivered with a sense of urgency and purpose as she felt
all at once like a surgeon summoned to perform an emergency proce-
dure. She felt necessary and useful, and then she realized that her heart
was fluttering, and she told herself to calm down. So she showered
slowly, and dried her hair, and braided it à la Anna Kournikova (Clara
had sent her photographs) and stepped into a pair of clean white
panties, a tight, full-length sports top, and a little, white, pleated skirt.
The skirt was so white as to seem bridal, and her tennis shoes glowed.
She looked, in the mirror, like something ready to be sacrificed. But
hey, if her nipples poked through her sports bra and her skirt lifted up
each time she reached up to serve, then her emotional desperation
wouldn't be so apparent. She called up to the main house and was told
to meet Lord Rosscommon on the courts.

When Gayle emerged from the footpath, he was there already—at
the far end of the second court, ready to receive an imaginary serve. He

bounced on the balls of his feet, just as they told you to do in all the textbooks, then mechanically pivoted into the position of a forehand swing. All at once Gayle felt sorry for him. She had expected, somehow, to fear him, and to be vulnerable to such an obvious imbalance in power, but all at once she realized that he was just a rich, awkward, hard-striving man whose wife had died. Much of the imbalance of his position and his title had since been nullified by the fact that she knew some of his secrets. And he did not know hers.

"Ah, Gayle," he said. "Lovely to see you. You've been practicing, I hear."

"I have," she said. "And I'm happy to say it's going well. How was London?"

"Ah. Cold. Rainy. Imposing. But I cleared away a lot of business and am now free to enjoy the summer. I'm very much looking forward to practicing myself. I want to make sure my game is solid before any of my guests arrive."

They began to rally—Ross refused to play any games just yet—and Gayle immediately realized that he was a B player. Maybe a C plus. He was certainly fit, with tight, ropy muscles and a lanky frame, but he thought too much about what he was doing. Gayle could practically see his lips moving as he rehearsed, with each shot, the advice a long-ago pro had given him. *Keep your body facing sideways, Ross. Eyes on the ball. Keep your racket at shoulder level. Aim for the center of the racquet.* Gayle knew that muscles had memory, but she kept quiet, thinking it would be out of line to offer guidance or tips. Plus, Lord Rosscommon seemed to get upset easily, and blasted himself—quite often bashing his poor racquet against the net—when he made mistakes. The more mad at himself he got, the worse he played. Gayle could feel in the ball they lobbed back and forth all his frustrations, and all his sorrows, so she vowed to be gentle with him. To never smash his sorrows back.

"Good heavens I am rusty," Lord Rosscommon told her jovially when they broke for lemonade. "We've got a lot of work cut out for us, my dear, a lot of work. I didn't start playing until I was in my fifties, you know. That, I suppose, is my only excuse. And you, my dear, are a strong player. Technically you are imperfect, but on the scale of power you are like a Williams sister. I think I shall take you on as my doubles partner, and see how we do."

"I'm terrible at the net," Gayle said. The truth was, she was afraid of being hit by the ball there. She had no idea what a Williams sister was.

"Well then, my dear, we shall have to help each other. I am terrible everywhere but."

For the next two days they met on the courts in the mornings, and then again in the afternoons. Gayle found that she liked playing against, or rather with, such a gentle, earnest opponent, and her own game developed a certain finesse. Playing with Ross made her more confident and she had the time, when waiting for his rather weak backhand to come back at her, to set up clever shots. She, too, began to think about her game, but in the manner of chess rather than of bombardment. And it was as if she had entered an entirely new world—one of progress, and excellence, and an output that matched what one put in. There are ways to battle men, she began to learn subconsciously, that didn't involve the use of coercion or brute force.

Gayle grew more confident in other ways as well. There was the praise Lord Rosscommon showered on her, about her intelligence, her daring, her looks, and the fact that it was all delivered with a crisp English accent made the praise settle all the more glowingly on Gayle's skin. She knew she had all the components that stereotypically appealed most to men: the hair, the legs, the powerful breasts and shoulders. But once Peter left her (*Dick!* she could hear Clara say), Gayle began to question the efficacy of these components. Perhaps they didn't fit together correctly; perhaps, as a package, she fell short. In all her nine months in France she had not been able to escape these answerless questions, but somehow, here in the dense, unyielding luxury of St. Tropez, something slowly began to change. Lord Rosscommon's chivalrous handling of her, his tasteful compliments, had begun to buoy Gayle's ego, and in his presence she began to regard herself as something rare and valuable, something to be presented on a silver tray. She found that in the mornings she looked forward to her tennis with an enthusiasm she didn't feel toward her own triathlon training. And that was a glorious, dangerous way to feel.

Quite often after their morning sessions, he would invite her to join him for lunch, and then Bert, with his black raised eyebrows, would deliver the silver trays right to the courts. The lunches were an imaginative combination of French and English: crisp, cold salad greens with a mustard vinaigrette, medallions of monkfish or crabmeat drowned in a decadent, butter-and-herb sauce, and a cheese plate for dessert—an oddity to which Gayle, who always passed on the cheese and opted for the garnish (fresh figs or sliced fruit), could never adjust. Sometimes Madame DuFresne made them curries, or delicate, French versions of the English shepherd's pie and Gayle, as she partook of this food, felt impossibly exotic. She liked dining on the English porcelain with the heavy Spanish silver and the French napkins embroidered with an *R*. She felt like the female half of a couple. Ross often talked of how much he loved America, especially Gayle's hometown of New York City, and she began to suspect that his praises of her country were thinly veiled celebrations of her.

"Could you ever live anywhere else?" he asked her one day at lunch, speaking of New York.

"Well, I do," Gayle said flirtatiously. Her tan by now had darkened and her hair had lightened, and her bank account had gone up into the four digits (in francs, but still . . .).

"I mean permanently. A place where you would have a family and *un chien.*"

"I guess I'm still looking for that one perfect place. But maybe New York is that place, I just don't know. I tend to run away from places, rather than run to."

"I thought so," Lord Rosscommon said, pausing to take a bit of his cold lobster salad. "A victim of wanderlust. Always wanting to be part of something, always wanting to put down roots. But never finding any place good enough. I should show you my country house in England. Now there is a place one runs to."

Gayle felt an immediate rush of blood to her face, throughout her entire system, so she picked at her paella with a fork. And she noticed for the first time that the *langoustines* looked as if they were striving to drag themselves to the edges of the platter, like something recently evolved.

"And *you* seem to be keeping his Lordship happy," Whitmore said on Friday at their morning breakfast. Lord Rosscommon had gone into town to the market, to guide Madame DuFresne in her purchases for the upcoming week. Half a dozen people were expected to arrive that evening and stay for more than a month.

Gayle smiled and poured herself some coffee. "He's a really nice person. And we're both very devoted to our sport."

"And what sport would that be?" Bert said.

"Bert," Whitmore said. "Why don't you stick this croissant in your mouth? And keep chewing and chewing until you find yourself capable of producing something pleasant to say?"

"Who's coming today?" Gayle said.

"Oh, God, don't make me say their names," Whitmore said. "Horrid people. Terribly rich. All couples—three of them, two of whom are Earls. They stick together like fornicating canines, those Earls. And their children! Good God you can't imagine. The Earl of Plowwright has twin boys—almost teenagers—who are the most blatant homophobes. They lisp and prance around whenever I enter the room and no one controls them. Bert, have I ever, in all the time you've known me, lisped?"

"Not once," Bert said. "No children are coming. At least not this weekend."

"Oh, thank God," Whitmore said. And he began to rattle off all that would be expected of them and the other staff over the upcoming weekend, what with the lunches, the dinners, the sailing excursions, and the constant shopping trips to town. "You, darling, are going to be on call while this group is here. They're quite unpredictable. Especially when the children aren't in tow. So I'm afraid you really shouldn't take such long trips on your bicycle."

"What about running?"

"I'm afraid you shouldn't leave the grounds at all. Swimming is fine as long as you don't drown during business hours. And I suppose you could run around the estate. How many acres is it, would you say, Bert darling?"

"Don't know. Thirty maybe, forty. Used to have a friend who exercised his German shepherd by towing her behind his truck with a rope. We could do that, couldn't we, Gayle? Tie you to the Mercedes with a rope?"

Gayle smiled as genuinely as she could. "I'll stick to the trails," she said. But for some reason she felt a bit resentful about not being able to cycle. It was as though she was losing a position she hadn't really quite gained.

By that evening a horde of jolly old Englishmen had arrived. There were the Alton-Merrills—a handsome, elderly couple who called Gayle "Kitten" and chain-smoked French Marlboros. There were the young, dashing Reese-Throckmortons—he a junior member of Parliament; she a startlingly beautiful, very foul-mouthed member of the working class who now promoted dance clubs and wore tight clothes. Then there were the Paynes, and the Cartwrights, and the Plowwrights, so similar in their benign, polite Britishness that Gayle could hardly tell the couples apart. But they all seemed to have known Ross and one another for a very long time, and together they were relaxed, and jovial, and the Reese-Throckmortons liked to tease Lord Rosscommon in witty, cheeky ways. "Crossrommon," they called him, especially on the courts, when he got to smashing his racquet on the net.

Within days a new routine had set in at La Jolie, which consisted for the guests of late risings, leisurely breakfasts, then changing into bathing suits for a swim. Then lunch, sometimes with but mostly without cocktails, and then tennis or sailing or a drive into town. The more ambitious among them would try to squeeze in all three activities, thereby thoroughly exhausting themselves before the real games began: the extravagant dinners, and the drinking that went on until dawn. Gayle remained "on call," but no one went near the courts until well after lunch. So in the mornings she was able to swim as usual, and then worked out on the treadmill and the recumbent bicycle in Lord

Rosscommon's private gym. It was Ross himself who insisted that Gayle use his equipment once he found out she had been "quarantined," as he put it, to within the boundaries of the estate. Gayle was pleased with and touched by his offer. The small, mirrored, climate-controlled room contained stellar machinery, and the treadmill was rigged up with a television set on which Gayle could watch French MTV. Each morning, as she worked out, she hoped Lord Rosscommon might come in and join her, but he never did. In hindsight, that was probably for the best because it slowly dawned on Gayle that this special privilege of hers was causing tension among the staff. She noticed odd looks and hurried whispers, and even Whitmore seemed to hold his chin a bit higher when he handed her each day's schedule.

"Listen," Whitmore said after a few days at breakfast. "Do you think you could wipe down the equipment after you use it? It adds an awful lot of work to the housekeeper's schedule and since you're the only one who uses it . . ." His voice trailed off, and he stirred more sugar into his coffee than he usually took.

"Sure," Gayle said. "That's not a problem."

But Whitmore's comment had made Gayle uneasy. Clara had warned her about the insurmountable divide between masters and servants, and she also told Gayle that she would most likely have to side with the latter. But Gayle, to date, had existed in a nameless, harmless purgatory at La Jolie, in which she was neither a real domestic nor a full-fledged guest. And she actually enjoyed that ambiguous position. It made her feel exceptional and, at best, unaccountable, like a class auditor who doesn't have to take exams. On certain days, when she had trained well in the ocean or played well on the courts, Gayle felt almost untouchable She would return to her cottage at the end of the day giddy with victory and slightly tired from all those hours in the sun, and she would take a glass of wine with her up to the balcony, and behold the careless beauty of the Riviera, and gradually begin to giggle at the preposterous freedom and ease of her "job." Back in the States, her friends all had jobs in cubicles. The only glimpse of the water they got was from the commuter train window on the way back to Queens. So, yes, Gayle enjoyed this purgatory, and during these giddy moments she would even feel proud of her rash, impulsive decision to flee to France. This was the first truly impulsive thing she had ever done in her life, and she was beginning to think that maybe more of such behavior was key. Perhaps Change, Chance, and Impulse would lead her to more exciting adventures, more than she possibly could have envisioned with a rational mind.

But then Whitmore's offhand comment had altered her perspective. Suddenly Gayle realized that all it really boiled down to in the end was: *This is not mine.* And, deep down: *He is not here.* She saw that while she would inhabit this space, and perhaps even leave her mark here, she could not claim it, and she would not set down roots. Gayle had to admit that this was a pattern with her. She always seemed to place herself in situations where she was *in* certain worlds but not *of* them. Where she hovered on the edge of groups she never fully joined. Eventually, restlessness and disillusionment would compel her to seek another place, another promising world she might join.

Then Gayle began to wonder if perhaps she really *should* side with the Lords against the servants. Or the other way around. Perhaps her very tendency to try to be nice to everyone, to deliberately ignore the hierarchies that the English seemed so insistent on assigning, was working against her in ways she could not fully understand. It was a system, after all—a class system. And so, because she felt more of an affinity with Lord Rosscommon than she did with, say, gruff, plump Madame DuFresne, Gayle pledged a secret and subtle allegiance toward the Lords.

As the days went by, Gayle felt more and more certain about her silent decision. For Lord Rosscommon's guests were nothing but pleasant to her. As a race, they seemed to be innately polite and jocular, and this group in particular seemed genuinely happy to have a tennis player among them who could actually play. Plus, everything to them was *jolly* and *brilliant*; every statement required a witty comeback; everyone laughed. They all wanted Gayle as their doubles partner and they all begged her not to "be so serious" when she stood on the opposite side of the net.

"Wilbur," Lady Reese-Throckmorton would say to her husband. "I am simply not going to play against her unless you tie one of her hands behind her back. Hasn't anyone got a blindfold?"

"Give her some gin!" Randy Alton-Merrill shouted from the sidelines. And Bert would hurry over with a bottle, until he realized that Alton-Merrill spoke in jest.

"I'll be gentle," Gayle said. "I promise. Besides, the only way you're going to get better, Julia, is if you play. Now come out here and serve."

It was a glorious way to spend a summer. There was an ebb and flow to their English that Gayle found soothing and inviting, like warm waves, or milky tea. If truth be told, Gayle now had enough money to leave France, but she was starting to think this setting was too good to abandon. On the courts, she was lauded and accepted. Titled Englishmen praised her abilities and sought her advice. Even after the sets, when Bert brought down the lemonade and the gin and the ice buckets, Gayle was welcome to sit with them, and join in their banter about

Sarah Ferguson and Princess Di. "Women with such bad taste in men should not be allowed to keep their titles," they would say to her. "Don't you agree? Have you seen the Dutchess's Weightwatcher's commercials in America?" No, Gayle had not, but that did not make her any less able to participate in the conversations. She sat among them, confident and well-educated, smug with the knowledge that her legs were better than anyone else's, and that Lord Rosscommon preferred her.

"I don't know how I ever lived without her," he would say, raising his glass in her direction. "I feel blessed." She began to wonder how she had ever lived without servants and fresh flowers in her room every morning, without views of the ocean, without such a fabulous tan. But still, when the last of the ice was gone, and Whitmore announced that dinner was served, Gayle and her legs would return alone to her empty cottage, and she would feel as petulant as a junior high school student who couldn't get into The Clique.

Sometimes, on such nights, when Gayle was still up reading triathlete magazines, she would see the lights at the pool blazing to life at four in the morning. And soon, from the direction of the club house, riding atop the thick sound of cicadas, would come the sounds of music and laughter, of the lifting of champagne bottles from ice buckets, the pops of corks. And Gayle would feel a yearning stronger than her resolve, stronger than her leg muscles, and she would fall asleep feeling physically sore. Why did it happen that she found herself so often on the outside? How did it happen that once again she was not living her own life, but rather that life lived itself around her?

Her only consolation would be to remind herself that she was an Athlete—a paid Athlete—whose very nature was to favor one's body over one's mind. Or one's heart. And in the mornings, when she set off for an early run, she'd see hats on all the statues and cigarette butts in the pool, and she'd manage to convince herself that her quest was far nobler than any of theirs.

And sure enough, she and Ross soon began to dominate as a doubles team on the courts. Something between them had clicked, some psychic connection that allowed them to operate on the court in tandem as if they had been choreographed, and Ross himself said he had never played better in his life.

"You two," the others would say. "It's not fair. They've signed a pact with the devil."

"She's not at all like last year's girl," Hugh Cartwright said in mock wistfulness.

"How so?" Gayle would say teasingly.

"Well, you know how to hold a racquet. You know how to muscle the ball. And you've made old Crossrommon serious. Since when has smoking been forbidden on the courts? Since when has Crossrommon not been cross?"

At this point Gayle and Ross would usually look at each other and smile, and someone would insist that the drinking begin, and Ross would call up to the house to have a tray sent down, and one of the groundsmen would come out to sweep up the courts.

"Gayle, do stay and tell us about OJ Simpson," Lady Payne would say, patting a seat next to her. "Oh, you don't know him, you say? I thought surely you would."

Three more weeks passed in this manner, weeks in which Gayle started to feel like a chaste Jane Austen heroine. She'd stand on her balcony late at night and gaze at the sea and rehash all the ways in which her interactions with Ross were like an eighteenth- century courtship. Courtship then was about verbal dalliances and unspoken affections, all of it culminating in one close-mouthed kiss underneath a trellis, and then suddenly the couple was engaged! These were farfetched thoughts, Gayle mostly admitted, but it all made for pleasant daydreaming, which was a whole lot better than obsessing about Dick.

And then, speaking of dicks, Whitmore announced at breakfast that Rodney was coming in a fortnight, and that Gayle had better be prepared.

"Remind me who he is," Gayle said lazily. She knew what a Williams sister was by then, at least, having subscribed, finally, to a British tennis magazine.

"The son!" Whitmore shouted. "Frankenstein! The man who would be king."

"Batten down the hatches," Bert said.

"He can't be that bad," Gayle said. "Can he?" She had started to put butter and jam on her bread in the mornings, something she would have foresworn months ago.

"Oh, he's just—" Whitmore wiped at his sleeves, as if to rid himself of something caustic. "He's like oil-based paint. He calls us both Bertmore, and despite how many times I complain to his Lordship, his Bratship pretends he can't tell us apart. Last year he and his friends smashed wine bottles inside the pool and the summer before that they pulverized his Lordship's car. Lord Rosscommon simply has no control over him."

"But didn't you say he was only, like, nineteen?" Gayle said.

"*Only* nineteen?" Whitmore said. "My dear, a boy at that age is positively pullulating with testosterone."

"Well," Gayle said. "I'll just avoid him as much as I can."

"*Bonne chance*," Bert muttered with crumbs on his lips. But his French wasn't very good.

Gayle wasn't the least bit worried. In fact, she waited with a certain amount of amusement for the arrival of this so-called antagonist. She pictured a larger, sturdier version of Lord Rosscommon, with thick eyebrows and dark hair. So when a car drove up to her cottage one day and out stepped a pale, skinny, *very* short redhead with transparent eyelashes and freckles on his neck, she almost laughed. He had come to La Jolie by way of Cap D'Antibes and already had the sort of sunburn for which the English had earned the French nickname *ros bif*.

"You the bird who plays tennis?" he said as Gayle stepped out to greet him.

"Bird?" she said, biting back a smile.

"I'm Rodney, Earl of Hardcastle. Pleasure to meet you. Fancy some tennis?"

"I'm supposed to play doubles with your father and the Cartwrights at two," Gayle said. "That wouldn't really give us enough time. Perhaps you could join us and we could rotate."

"I hate doubles," he said. "They'll just have to wait."

Gayle stared at him for a second. She saw a glint of something explosive in his eyes, something almost feral, so she decided it might be best to humor him. "Very well," she said. "If you want to meet me at the courts in fifteen minutes or so, I'll go inside and get changed."

"Atta girl," he said, and then followed her into the cottage without invitation and sat on the couch. "I hear you're good," he called upstairs as she put on tennis whites, but Gayle didn't answer. The way he had entered her cottage spoke of propriety and entitlement. He probably knew where the sheets were kept, and at what time the daily came to vaccuum the rug. "What about me?" he asked more loudly. "Did you hear I'm good?"

"I heard you were on the team at Eton," Gayle said, coming downstairs with her racquet. "I heard you like to smash bottles in the pool." She spoke to him in the tone of a mother, or a baby-sitter.

"Fucking Bertmore!" Rodney said. "Can't keep his bloody mouth shut!" He returned the triathlon magazine he'd been thumbing through to the coffee table and looked Gayle up and down. "So most triathletes are babes, I take it?"

"Most triathletes are good at what they do," Gayle said, grabbing a towel. "Times three," she said.

"Papa says you're a tiger. I like that in a woman."

Gayle forced her face into a smile. He sounded like an understudy in some high school drama club, rehearsing his lines on stage for the first time. And she could tell, as they took the path to the tennis courts, that he was staring at her ass.

The real surprise, for Gayle, was that Rodney Rosscommon was a superb tennis player. For such a slight person, he was an absolute firecracker on the courts. He was also a bit of a John McEnroe, cursing and stomping and smashing his racquet every chance he got. Gayle bore it as best she could, but she found, when she played against such an opponent, that something tightened in her. Her fists were always clenched and her face remained set in a frown, and her game faltered as a result. Most of her corner shots went long and even her fail-safe second serve failed to make it over the net. Young Rodney seemed to take delight in this. "I'm frustrating you," he would say between matches. "Ha! I like that. And, by the way, you suck."

"I'm just having an off day."

"Oh, really?" he said, arching his eyebrows, and Gayle saw, in a flash, his resemblance to his father. The moment passed, however, and then he was just a little red squirt again.

"Really," she said.

But two more days went by in which Rodney kept winning. And the more Gayle resolved to crush him, the worse she played. Her job, which had seemed so sublime just the week before, was now the equivalent of putting on a gray suit and commuting to an oppressive office. Rodney belittled her backhand, made juvenile sexual innuendoes each time a ball went long, and cursed Gayle and her mother if she happened to win a point. She began to approach each day with a sense of dread and failure, and for the first time it dawned on her that she might be one of those athletes who simply hates to lose. She had quit tennis years ago because she wasn't winning. And chances are she would quit again very soon. But what of the triathlon, and all of life's other challenges? What if life really was about winning, rather than how you played the game?

It didn't help that Lord Rosscommon seemed to have faded into the background. He played doubles with the others, and said in passing things like: "We'll let you two kids play among yourselves." But Gayle didn't necessarily want to be associated with this "kid"—it was like sitting at the children's table, far away from the adults and the laughter, at holiday meals.

Fortunately some friends of Rodney's (the dreaded Plowwright twins) arrived the following weekend and the three of them left early Saturday morning for an all-day sail. Gayle was delighted to find out at breakfast that Lord Rosscommon had requested her presence on the tennis courts at ten.

"I've missed you, my dear," he said as she approached the courts as scheduled. He finished tightening his shoelaces, then stood to take her hand. "I have not won a match in several days, and I need you to help me warm up for this afternoon's doubles. You and Rodney, I trust, are getting on?"

"I haven't won a match in several days either," Gayle said.

"Is that so?" Lord Rosscommon said. "He's that good?"

"He's superb," Gayle said. "He seems to have found all my weak spots, and he goes for those."

"Ah, *now* it sounds like we're talking about my son," Lord Rosscommon said. "Come along then, shall we?"

For two hours they rallied, and Gayle found herself instantly reconnecting with the player she had been five days ago. It's possible she was even better; she seemed to have tapped into some critical new current that led from her eye to the center of her racquet and compelled her biceps and shoulder muscles to really strong-arm the ball. By the time they broke for lunch, Gayle was in love with her life again, and confident that life was at least a little bit in love with her.

"What an absolutely perfect day this has been," Lord Rosscommon said in the late afternoon, when the drinks tray had been brought down and one of the groundsmen was sweeping the courts. Everyone seemed pleasantly tired. "My ego has suffered tremendously in the past few days from losing so many sets. Now I am restored." That afternoon the two of them had won three straight sets at doubles, twice in a row. And now the sun was setting, and the sweet peas in the garden gave off a heavenly fragrance, and the sky was so blue and translucent it seemed lit from within itself by some other source than the sun. "Ah, it's good to have you to myself again," Lord Rosscommon said.

Gayle smiled at Lord Rosscommon and watched the way the soft clay submitted to the groundsman's broom. "*We* haven't missed you," Wilbur said abruptly. "We have enjoyed the leisure of playing while drunk."

"And I still lost," Ross said jovially.

The group sat and drank until twilight. Then cicadas began to chirp in the distance, and most of the ladies no longer sat so stiffly in their chairs. There was a mood in the air that could be described as lazy, or complacent. Time seemed to have widened, leaving a space between the hours that only Lord Rosscommon and his guests inhabited—a dimensionless, carefree space that the rich alone could afford. Gayle had taken her shoes off and sat with her feet propped up on the edge of a potted plant. Her skirt barely touched her thighs.

"Let's dine in tonight, shall we?" Ross said. "It's such a lovely evening, and Madame DuFresne can manage something simple, I'm sure. I'm afraid if we go into town we might run into the boys, who I am sure have by now sailed into the marina and are disgracing themselves at Le Bar Sube. Gayle, you'll join us, won't you?"

"Thank you," she said. "I will."

Giddily, Gayle went back to her cottage to prepare. After a quick shower she beheld, with unabashed triumph, her lonely blue dress, and once she slipped it on and stepped into the matching high-heeled sandals, she felt otherworldly. She felt transformed. By this point, she had already drunk one and a half glasses of champagne, and that substance bubbled through her like a magic potion: one that made her witty and pretty and unafraid. She'd felt this way when she first met Peter, but she quickly squelched that thought. She put her hair into a messy chignon, dabbed on some perfume, and hurried back to the pool.

There, the tables had been set with apricot-colored linens, music was playing, candles flickered, and all the guests mingled together with champagne glasses and crudités. Whitmore was placing salad forks at the last of the tables, and Bert, looking rather irritated in a tuxedo, served drinks. When Gayle said hi to the former, he brushed some hair away from his face and gave her a pinched smile.

"I see you've made it," he said, but before Gayle could answer, Lord Rosscommon was there, thanking Whitmore profusely for making the tables look so nice. "I do appreciate your changing your plans to accommodate our rather large party," he said. And then he took Gayle's arm and said: "Who have we here? This morning you were Lady of the Backhands, and now you look like Brigitte Bardot!"

"There is a resemblance," one of the women said. "I suppose." And Gayle thought she saw Whitmore smirk. He was the one who had told her she should wear her hair like that.

"Aren't we lucky to have found this girl? I'd never seen her in civilian clothes," Lord Rosscommon said.

Gayle blushed, accepted a wine glass, and looked at the impossible number of stars above her.

For dinner they had a garlicky fish soup called *bourride*, followed by stuffed calamari with fennel, followed by a tomato and goat-cheese salad drizzled with olive oil, then a meat course (veal, Gayle was told) then a cheese plate, then some fresh, sweet melon served with verbena sorbet. As she ate, Gayle experienced the same sort of sensual, sensory Moment she had had when she first dined with Lord Rosscommon, and now that sensation was coupled with the realization that this sort of Moment could be commonplace. Rosscommonplace! She was getting drunk. Some eighteen bottles of wine were served, and with each one the group became more and more animated and less and less reserved. There was talk of country weekends and hunting parties. There was talk of couples found coupling in garden sheds and in the carriage stalls. Julia Reese-Throckmorton announced to the table that the reason the Duke of Windsor gave up the throne for Mrs. Simpson had nothing to do with love. "I happen to know she was the only woman who knew what to do with his tiny cock."

Everyone roared with laughter, and then the Earl of Plowwright started in on the French. How they were abominable drivers and stingy hostesses and the women all smelled like smoke. "And they all seem to think they are such fantastic lovers. Tell me, Gayle, have you ever slept with a French man?" All eyes were on her. She truly felt as if she were riding a wave of happiness that would never crest.

"No," she said jovially. "And I don't think I'd want to either."

"So you see," said Lady Jane Payne. "The English and the Americans have something in common after all."

Everyone laughed, and Ross put his arm on the back of her chair, and Gayle was feeling as if she had died and gone to heaven, and then Rodney returned with his posse of drunks.

"Where's Gayle?" he said, crashing through the pine trees. Four boys followed him by way of the footpath that led from the sea. "I want to show them Gayle. Ah, there she is."

"My dear boy," said Lord Rosscommon. "Don't tell me you *sailed* here."

"I've come to play tennis," Rodney said. He seemed oblivious to the group of drunk, elegantly dressed diners having port.

"It's too late for tennis," Gayle said. "It's dark."

"We'll put the lights on." He actually came up to where Gayle was sitting and grabbed her arm.

"I'm wearing high heels. This is ridiculous. We'll play tomorrow, I promise." Gayle looked at Lord Rosscommon for support, but all she saw was a gleam in his eyes. It could have been the reflection of a candle flame.

"Oh, come on then," Rodney said. "I told my chums they could see you play."

"No," Gayle protested, but then Lord Rosscommon said, "Yes, play with him, that would be amusing to watch."

Then everyone at the table agreed this was a *brilliant* idea, especially if Gayle was not allowed to change. "We've found her Achilles' heel," one of the men shouted. "Heels!"

The entire drunken group followed Gayle to the equipment room, and cheered as she reluctantly chose a racquet and insisted on taking off her shoes.

"Take it all off!" one of the twins shouted, and Gayle shot this boy a look. He was supposed to be twenty, but he looked about twelve. So did his twin brother. Someone giggled. Lord Rosscommon took her gently by the elbow and told her to be a good sport. She realized, then, that Ross was quite drunk. So she decided she would smash the balls so forcefully at Rodney that he would be incapacitated and give up. Then she could get back to her conversation with Lord Rosscommon about French society, and how an expat could fit in.

But even as staggeringly drunk as he was, even with his double vision that forced him to keep one eye closed, young Rodney would not give in so easily. He lunged, swore, returned shots now and then, and shouted at Gayle to "Bring it on!"

"He's good," Gayle heard one of the men say.

"Well of course, darling," a woman answered. "He spent enough time with *last* year's girl."

"Long!" Rodney shouted as Gayle missed a first serve.

"How long?" one of the twins shouted.

"About ten inches. That would be twenty-five centimeters or so, here in France." He swaggered around the court like a young Marat Safin, his attitude bigger than his heart. "Hit the ball harder, you fucking slag," Rodney yelled as Gayle sent a lob back at him. "Fucking stupid bitch."

Gayle, in response, deliberately hit the ball feebly, without effort, and Wilbur Reese-Throckmorton began to boo.

"We paid good money for this," he shouted. "We want to see a show!" His delivery seemed benign enough, and Gayle thought perhaps she could be a bit more good-natured about the situation if she were slightly more drunk. But as the tennis dragged on she realized that everyone was rooting for Rodney.

"Make her answer for the American Revolution!" one of the men shouted. "Make her answer for that MacDonald's in Trafalgar Square!" She had read in one of her tennis magazines about how, in tournaments, you don't just play against your opponent; you play against yourself and the ump and the crowds, and now Gayle fully understood this. At least in a triathlon you could run past the audience; here she was a sitting duck. Finally, she could stand it no longer, and when the game in progress was finished she said "I think I need some champagne," and began to walk off the court toward Bert.

"Where are you going?" Rodney shouted.

She smiled at him as congenially as she could. "I'm taking a break."

"Get back here this instant, you fucking slag. I want to play!"

She approached Lord Rosscommon. "Could you please request that he not talk to me like that? This isn't very fun."

"He's just playing," Lord Rosscommon said. He twirled the ice in his drinks glass. "And this is your job."

The hair rose on Gayle's arms, and it seemed as if all sound had ceased around them. Even the cicadas no longer hummed. "What if I refuse to play with him?"

"Then you don't have a job."

Gayle tried to make eye contact with Julia Reese-Throckmorton, a former fish-and-chips vendor, but Lady Julia pretended to be absorbed with the contents of her purse.

"Ah, lighten up," Rodney said, leaning arrogantly on his racquet. "How about this—we'll call it a draw if you just show us your tits."

"Yeah," one of the twins echoed. "Show us your tits!"

Gayle's jaw dropped. She looked to Lord Rosscommon for comment. But he just lifted his wine glass to his lips and gave a little shrug. She thought she saw, in his eyes, a glint of laughter, a suppressed smirk.

And all at once it dawned on Gayle, as if some sort of golden pollen of wisdom had drifted down from the palm trees, that Peter—Dick— was nothing but an asshole. A good-looking, incredibly charismatic asshole, but an asshole nonetheless. All these months she thought she had been yearning for the heart of him, for some Great Love, but the truth was, Peter had always been fraudulent. He had always been duplicitous and insincere. Gayle had just been too insecure to call him on it. Suddenly she saw that what she yearned for existed not in Peter, but in herself. She also realized, standing on a clay court beneath the stars, that until she renounced the lot of them, and stood strong, sharks such as these would continue to gnaw their way into her protective cage—unless she could somehow shove an oxygen tank into their mouths and blow the fuckers up.

"Fuck you," she said to Rodney. "You little prick." She told Lord Rosscommon sternly that she was going to bed. And as she walked away, she felt something buoy within her—something that had nothing to do with the champagne. She saw that there was a small kernel of logic to Peter's "better mad than sad" theory. Sadness went inward, into her organs and veins. Anger went outward and evaporated sooner or later, like sweat.

Even as she walked away, Gayle knew that tomorrow morning, when hats graced the statues and the pool was filled with butts, Lord Rosscommon would most likely come to apologize and ask that she forgive him. "You must understand," he might begin, and the thing was, she would. Understand. But that in itself was no longer enough for Gayle. In fact, she probably wouldn't even be there in the morning. In fact, she was already gone.

*During the long Boston winter, a Colombian expat longs for home (the set-ting of Dalia Rabonivich's novel* Flora's Suitcase*) and for the passion she associates with her native country. All the while, she's playing tennis.*

# Love

## Dalia Rabinovich

Sari plays tennis with men. She enjoys the challenge of a man's ground stroke, the sheer force of their returns against her racket. Despite her gender and wedding band, men are seldom reluctant to play with her. She's a beautiful woman, a slender brunette with emerald eyes whose game rivals theirs.

Sari lives in Cambridge, and Harvard always provides her with a cadre of international partners. Bruce from Toronto, Alain from Paris, and Massimo from Rome. Charlie, Sari's husband, calls them her "ten-nis lovers." Charlie doesn't care for tennis. He hates to sweat. In the summer he keeps the temperature in their apartment so low that Sari has to wear a sweater whenever she is home.

Even though Charlie teases her, and the men she plays with are so-licitous, Sari doesn't find them attractive. She knows how to step aside from their flirtation as if it were a ball headed out of bounds.

Andres is from Bogotá, the city where Sari grew up. He is an ac-quaintance from home. They run into one another at a market in Cambridge.

"Sarita?"

Sarita. The diminutive always makes her feel small, insignificant. In America she is known as Sari. Only people from home call her Sarita.

"It's me, Andres."

It's been years since Sari set foot in Colombia. She could easily pre-tend she doesn't remember Andres. But Andres is explaining the connection. "I'm Mauricio's brother. We played tennis at the club. Remember?"

Sari can't recall his game. The memory of those two hours spent on the court is all about rage.

"We should play. You were pretty good," Andres says.

"Sure. Give me a call." Andres hands her his paperback and Sari scribbles her telephone number onto the cover page. He uses his book like a notepad. Her name is sandwiched between a shopping list and directions to the airport. Sari says good-bye and leaves the store, aban-doning by the cash register the milk and coffee she has just paid for.

She arrives home feeling breathless. It is a feeling that always accompanies the memory of Mauricio. Mauricio taught her how to play tennis. He also taught her that hate and love are not opposite emotions.

Sari does not want to play tennis with Andres. Playing with Andres will spark a conversation about Mauricio. She does not want to know how he is or what he is doing. She married Charlie to forget about Mauricio. Up until now, she has convinced herself that it worked.

But when Andres calls, she agrees to meet him at the public courts near her apartment building. It is ten o'clock and Boston, a city where winter reigns for almost seven months, is blanketed by heat. The trees surrounding the courts offer little shade. She can't concentrate. She is thinking about Mauricio. The memory of him is as crisp as the pleats of her tennis skirt. He is standing in the driveway of her parents' home in Bogotá, dressed in golf pants and an argyle vest. He is supposed to be wearing tennis shorts.

"Andres will play tennis with you, Sarita," Mauricio is saying.

Sari has been waiting for him for two hours. She taps her racket against the toe of her sneaker. She is not surprised that he's late or that there has been a change in plans. Nothing Mauricio says is concrete. He is easily distracted. His ideas are like brick dust on a clay court, easily kicked aside. Sari is only in Colombia for three weeks before she has to go back to Cambridge. It's her first day back and already Mauricio is ignoring her.

"Get in the car."

Mauricio's golf buddy is in the passenger seat. No one suggests that he get out. Sari climbs into the back of the sedan, next to Andres. She hates coming back to Colombia. The minute she steps off the plane she is treated like a little girl. Her father deems public transportation unsafe; therefore, she is not allowed to take a bus or a taxi. Her mother clucks like a *duenna* if Sari wears a skirt that is too short or arrives home after midnight. Spending the night with Mauricio is strictly forbidden. "Nice girls sleep at home," her mother says.

Sari can't tell her mother that it's too late. She is no longer a nice girl. She's made love to Mauricio in every corner of her parents' house—in the shower, in the kitchen, in their bed. If she sleeps at home, Mauricio will keep her waiting.

Mauricio drops them off in front of the courts at the country club. Andres suggests they rally, but Sari wants to play a game. She draws the serve. She throws the ball into the air. The angle is wrong and the toss too low, but she swings at it anyway. The impulse to hit something is too great. The ball sails into the net.

"You shouldn't have hit that one. You have to abandon the serve if the toss isn't right," Andres calls out to her.

Sari doesn't know how to abandon things that aren't going well. Mauricio is what her mother calls "a playboy." Sari knows that he sleeps with other women. He never writes or calls. He chips away at her heart daily. It's in so many pieces that she wonders how it can continue to hurt, to ache, to beat.

Sari serves again. Andres's return spins back at her, too fast to do anything but shield her face with the racket. The ball hits the sweet spot and sails across the net, deep into the left corner of Andres's court. He lunges for it but misses.

"Great point." Andres taps his palm against the strings of his racket several times.

His praise is meaningless. Sari says nothing. If she attempts to speak, she will start to cry. She does not want Andres to see her tears. She does not want Mauricio to know that she cries over him.

Sari misses an easy ball and then double faults. She loses the game and every one after that.

"What was the score?" Mauricio wants to know. He has spent the entire day on the golf course. He rests his hand on Sari's shoulder. Even though she is mad at him, the distinct shiver of attraction travels Sari's spine.

"Six-love, six-love, six-love."

"But Sari played really well," Andres says emphatically. "She hit some amazing balls."

Mauricio laughs. "How can you play well and lose six-zero, six-zero, six-zero?" Mauricio has never been beaten. He wins every game. Tennis, pool, Ping-Pong, love.

Sari decides that tennis, like love, is a game where one can play well yet lose miserably. Looking back or ahead is detrimental to both. The object is not to keep the ball in play, but to score. She wants to play better. She wants to win. But she will not be able to practice in Boston. It is winter there and the clay courts near her dorm resemble a pair of Olympic-size swimming pools, placid and celestial blue. Occasionally a gust of wind slips underneath their protective tarps, causing them to billow and ripple.

That night, after a party, Mauricio drives Sari out to his parents' country house. His mother and father are back in the city, not due out until the weekend. They make love on a hammock. It's a tricky feat. The hammock keeps rocking and its strings creak with the thrust of their bodies.

"Do you think you'll ever want to marry me?" Sari asks Mauricio.

"What?" He is drowsy from too much drink.

"Do you think you'll ever want to marry me?"

"Aay, Sarita. Why do you ask such questions?" He rolls out of the hammock and picks up his underwear from the pile of their clothes.

"Because someone else wants to marry me."

"Who?"

"Charlie. Charlie wants to marry me." Charlie is a fellow grad student. Charlie is dull and faithful, qualities Sari wishes didn't go hand in hand.

"Let me get back to you."

He doesn't. And Sari never brings it up again. She returns to Harvard and marries Charlie after graduation. Except for her parents, no one from home is invited to the ceremony.

A decade later, Andres's presence on the other side of the court calls her strategy into question. She's been telling herself that she married Charlie to put an end to Mauricio's game. But perhaps all they are is even. She is married to a man she doesn't love and Mauricio—so she's heard—continues to date aimlessly.

"I need to stop," Sari calls out to Andres. She pretends to examine her palm. "I have a blister. It hurts too much to play."

"My brother was an asshole." They are walking off the court. As predicted, Mauricio's name has come up. "He still is. You were too good for him. It was good that you married Charlie. Mauricio would have made you miserable."

Andres's validation drops at Sari's feet like a dead tennis ball. Charlie. Charlie is a forced error. A mistake in her game. He is a surrogate for love.

*No one plays tennis in this story, one of John Updike's finest ever. And yet, without the dilapidated clay court that hovers in the background throughout, "Separating" would be a different tale, one with less poignancy and power.*

# Separating

## John Updike

The day was fair. Brilliant. All that June the weather had mocked the Maples' internal misery with solid sunlight—golden shafts and cascades of green in which their conversations had wormed unseeing, their sad murmuring selves the only stain in Nature. Usually by this time of the year they had acquired tans; but when they met their elder daughter's plane on her return from a year in England they were almost as pale as she, though Judith was too dazzled by the sunny opulent jumble of her native land to notice. They did not spoil her homecoming by telling her immediately. Wait a few days, let her recover from jet lag, had been one of their formulations, in that string of gray dialogues—over coffee, over cocktails, over Cointreau—that had shaped the strategy of their dissolution, while the earth performed its annual stunt of renewal unnoticed beyond their closed windows. Richard had thought to leave at Easter; Joan had insisted they wait until the four children were at last assembled, with all exams passed and ceremonies attended, and the bauble of summer to console them. So he had drudged away, in love, in dread, repairing screens, getting the mowers sharpened, rolling and patching their new tennis court.

The court, clay, had come through its first winter pitted and windswept bare of redcoat. Years ago the Maples had observed how often, among their friends, divorce followed a dramatic home improvement, as if the marriage were making one last effort to live; their own worst crisis had come amid the plaster dust and exposed plumbing of a kitchen renovation. Yet, a summer ago, as canary-yellow bulldozers gaily churned a grassy, daisy-dotted knoll into a muddy plateau, and a crew of pigtailed young men raked and tamped clay into a plane, this transformation did not strike them as ominous, but festive in its impudence; their marriage could rend the earth for fun. The next spring, waking each day at dawn to a sliding sensation as if the bed were being tipped, Richard found the barren tennis court—its net and tapes still rolled in the barn—an environment congruous with his mood of purposeful desolation, and the crumbling of handfuls of clay into cracks and holes (dogs had frolicked on the court in a thaw; rivulets had eroded trenches) an activity suitably elemental and interminable. In his sealed heart he hoped the day would never come.

Now it was here. A Friday. Judith was re-acclimated; all four children were assembled, before jobs and camps and visits again scattered them. Joan thought they should be told one by one. Richard was for making an announcement at the table. She said, "I think just making an announcement is a cop-out. They'll start quarreling and playing to each other instead of focusing. They're each individuals, you know, not just some corporate obstacle to your freedom."

"O.K., O.K. I agree." Joan's plan was exact. That evening, they were giving Judith a belated welcome-home dinner, of lobster and champagne. Then, the party over, they, the two of them, who nineteen years before would push her in a baby carriage along Fifth Avenue to Washington Square, were to walk her out of the house, to the bridge across the salt creek, and tell her, swearing her to secrecy. Then Richard Jr., who was going directly from work to a rock concert in Boston, would be told, either late when he returned on the train or early Saturday morning before he went off to his job; he was seventeen and employed as one of a golf-course maintenance crew. Then the two younger children, John and Margaret, could, as the morning wore on, be informed.

"Mopped up, as it were," Richard said.

"Do you have any better plan? That leaves you the rest of Saturday to answer any questions, pack, and make your wonderful departure."

"No," he said, meaning he had no better plan, and agreed to hers, though to him it showed an edge of false order, a hidden plea for control, like Joan's long chore lists and financial accountings and, in the days when he first knew her, her too-copious lecture notes. Her plan turned one hurdle for him into four—four knife-sharp walls, each with a sheer blind drop on the other side.

All spring he had moved through a world of insides and outsides, of barriers and partitions. He and Joan stood as a thin barrier between the children and the truth. Each moment was a partition, with the past on one side and the future on the other, a future containing this unthinkable *now*. Beyond four knifelike walls a new life for him waited vaguely. His skull cupped a secret, a white face, a face both frightened and soothing, both strange and known, that he wanted to shield from tears, which he felt all about him, solid as the sunlight. So haunted, he had become obsessed with battening down the house against his absence, replacing screens and sash cords, hinges and latches—a Houdini making things snug before his escape.

* * *

The lock. He had still to replace a lock on one of the doors of the screened porch. The task, like most such, proved more difficult than he had imagined. The old lock, aluminum frozen by corrosion, had been deliberately rendered obsolete by manufacturers. Three hardware stores had nothing that even approximately matched the mortised hole its removal (surprisingly easy) left. Another hole had to be gouged, with bits too small and saws too big, and the old hole fitted with a block of wood—the chisels dull, the saw rusty, his fingers thick with lack of sleep. The sun poured down, beyond the porch, on a world of neglect. The bushes already needed pruning, the windward side of the house was shedding flakes of paint, rain would get in when he was gone, insects, rot, death. His family, all those he would lose, filtered through the edges of his awareness as he struggled with screw holes, splinters, opaque instructions, minutiae of metal.

Judith sat on the porch, a princess returned from exile. She regaled them with stories of fuel shortages, of bomb scares in the Underground, of Pakistani workmen loudly lusting after her as she walked past on her way to dance school. Joan came and went, in and out of the house, calmer than she should have been, praising his struggles with the lock as if this were one more and not the last of their long succession of shared chores. The younger of his sons for a few minutes held the rickety screen door while his father clumsily hammered and chiseled, each blow a kind of sob in Richard's ears. His younger daughter, having been at a slumber party, slept on the porch hammock through all the noise— heavy and pink, trusting and forsaken. Time, like the sunlight, continued relentlessly; the sunlight slowly slanted. Today was one of the longest days. The lock clicked, worked. He was through. He had a drink; he drank it on the porch, listening to his daughter. "It was so sweet," she was saying, "during the worst of it, how all the butchers and bakery shops kept open by candlelight. They're all so plucky and cute. From the papers, things sounded so much worse here—people shooting people in gas lines, and everybody freezing."

Richard asked her, "Do you still want to live in England forever?" *Forever:* the concept, now a reality upon him, pressed and scratched at the back of his throat.

"No," Judith confessed, turning her oval face to him, its eyes still childishly far apart, but the lips set as over something succulent and satisfactory. "I was anxious to come home. I'm an American." She was a woman. They had raised her; he and Joan had endured together to raise her, alone of the four. The others had still some raising left in them. Yet it was the thought of telling Judith—the image of her, their first baby, walking between them arm in arm to the bridge—that broke him. The partition between his face and the tears broke. Richard sat down to the celebratory meal with the back of his throat aching; the champagne, the lobster seemed phases of sunshine; he saw them and tasted them through tears. He blinked, swallowed, croakily joked about hay fever. The tears would not stop leaking through; they came not through a hole that could be plugged but through a permeable spot in a membrane, steadily, purely, endlessly, fruitfully. They became, his tears, a shield for himself against these others—their faces, the fact of their assembly, a last time as innocents, at a table where he sat the last time as head. Tears dropped from his nose as he broke the lobster's back; salt flavored his champagne as he sipped it; the raw clench at the back of his throat was delicious. He could not help himself.

His children tried to ignore his tears. Judith, on his right, lit a cigarette, gazed upward in the direction of her too energetic, too sophisticated exhalation; on her other side, John earnestly bent his face to the extraction of the last morsels—legs, tail segments—from the scarlet corpse. Joan, at the opposite end of the table, glanced at him surprised, her reproach displaced by a quick grimace, of forgiveness, or of salute to his superior gift of strategy. Between them, Margaret, no longer called Bean, thirteen and large for her age, gazed from the other side of his pane of tears as if into a shopwindow at something she coveted— at her father, a crystalline heap of splinters and memories. It was not she, however, but John who, in the kitchen, as they cleared the plates and carapaces away, asked Joan the question: *"Why is Daddy crying?"*

Richard heard the question but not the murmured answer. Then he heard Bean cry, "Oh, no-oh!"—the faintly dramatized exclamation of one who had long expected it.

John returned to the table carrying a bowl of salad. He nodded tersely at his father and his lips shaped the conspiratorial words "She told."

"Told what?" Richard asked aloud, insanely.

The boy sat down as if to rebuke his father's distraction with the example of his own good manners. He said quietly, "The separation."

Joan and Margaret returned; the child, in Richard's twisted vision, seemed diminished in size, and relieved, relieved to have had the bogieman at last proved real. He called out to her—the distances at the table had grown immense—"You knew, you always knew," but the clenching at the back of his throat prevented him from making sense of it. From afar he heard Joan talking, levelly, sensibly, reciting what they had prepared: it was a separation for the summer, an experiment. She and Daddy both agreed it would be good for them; they needed space and time to think; they liked each other but did not make each other happy enough, somehow.

Judith, imitating her mother's factual tone, but in her youth off-key, too cool, said, "I think it's silly. You should either live together or get divorced."

Richard's crying, like a wave that has crested and crashed, had become tumultuous; but it was overtopped by another tumult, for John, who had been so reserved, now grew larger and larger at the table. Perhaps his younger sister's being credited with knowing set him off. "Why didn't you *tell* us?" he asked, in a large round voice quite unlike his own. "You should have *told* us you weren't getting along."

Richard was startled into attempting to force words through his tears. "We *do* get along, that's the trouble, so it doesn't show even to us—" *That we do not love each other* was the rest of the sentence; he couldn't finish it.

Joan finished for him, in her style. "And we've always, *especially,* loved our children."

John was not mollified. "What do you care about *us?*" he boomed. "We're just little things you *had.*" His sisters' laughing forced a laugh from him, which he turned hard and parodistic: "Ha ha *ha.*" Richard, and Joan realized simultaneously that the child was drunk, on Judith's homecoming champagne. Feeling bound to keep the center of the stage, John took a cigarette from Judith's pack, poked it into his mouth, let it hang from his lower lip, and squinted like a gangster.

"You're not little things we had," Richard called to him. "You're the whole point. But you're grown. Or almost."

The boy was lighting matches. Instead of holding them to his cigarette (for they had never seen him smoke; being "good" had been his way of setting himself apart), he held them to his mother's face, closer and closer, for her to blow out. Then he lit the whole folder—a hiss and then a torch, held against his mother's face. Prismed by tears, the flame filled Richard's vision; he didn't know how it was extinguished. He heard Margaret say, "Oh stop showing off," and saw John, in response, break the cigarette in two and put the halves entirely into his mouth and chew, sticking out his tongue to display the shreds to his sister.

Joan talked to him, reasoning—a fountain of reason, unintelligible "Talked about it for years . . . our children must help us . . . Daddy and I both want . . ." As the boy listened, he carefully wadded a paper napkin into the leaves of his salad, fashioned a ball of paper and lettuce, and popped it into his mouth, looking around the table for the expected laughter. None came. Judith said, "Be mature," and dismissed a plume of smoke.

Richard got up from this stifling table and led the boy outside. Though the house was in twilight, the outdoors still brimmed with light, the lovely waste light of high summer. Both laughing, he supervised

John's spitting out the lettuce and paper and tobacco into the pachysandra. He took him by the hand—a square gritty hand, but for its softness a man's. Yet, it held on. They ran together up into the field, past the tennis court. The raw banking left by the bulldozers was dotted with daisies. Past the court and a flat stretch where they used to play family baseball stood a soft green rise glorious in the sun, each weed and species of grass distinct as illumination on parchment. "I'm sorry, so sorry," Richard cried. "You were the only one who ever tried to help me with all the goddam jobs around this place."

Sobbing, safe within his tears and the champagne, John explained, "It's not just the separation, it's the whole crummy year, I *hate* that school, you can't make any friends, the history teacher's a scud."

They sat on the crest of the rise, shaking and warm from their tears but easier in their voices, and Richard tried to focus on the child's sad year—the weekdays long with homework, the weekends spent in his room with model airplanes, while his parents murmured down below, nursing their separation. How selfish, how blind, Richard thought; his eyes felt scoured. He told his son, "We'll think about getting you transferred. Life's too short to be miserable."

They had said what they could, but did not want the moment to heal, and talked on, about the school, about the tennis court, whether it would ever again be as good as it had been that first summer. They walked to inspect it and pressed a few more tapes more firmly down. A little stiltedly, perhaps trying now to make too much of the moment, Richard led the boy to the spot in the field where the view was best, of the metallic blue river, the emerald marsh, the scattered islands velvety with shadow in the low light, the white bits of beach far away. "See," he said. "It goes on being beautiful. It'll be here tomorrow."

"I know," John answered, impatiently. The moment had closed.

Back in the house, the others had opened some white wine, the champagne being drunk, and still sat at the table, the three females, gossiping. Where Joan sat had become the head. She turned, showing him a tearless face, and asked, "All right?"

"We're fine," he said, resenting it, though relieved, that the party went on without him.

In bed she explained, "I couldn't cry I guess because I cried so much all spring. It really wasn't fair. It's your idea, and you made it look as though I was kicking you out."

"I'm sorry," he said. "I couldn't stop. I wanted to but couldn't."

"You *didn't* want to. You loved it. You were having your way, making a general announcement."

"I love having it over," he admitted. "God, those kids were great. So brave and funny." John, returned to the house, had settled to a model airplane in his room, and kept shouting down to them, "I'm O.K. No sweat." "And the way," Richard went on, cozy in his relief, "they never questioned the reasons we gave. No thought of a third person. Not even Judith."

"That *was* touching," Joan said.

He gave her a hug. "You were great too. Very reassuring to everybody. Thank you." Guiltily, he realized he did not feel separated.

"You still have Dickie to do," she told him. These words set before him a black mountain in the darkness; its cold breath, its near weight affected his chest. Of the four children, his elder son was most nearly his conscience. Joan did not need to add, "That's one piece of your dirty work I won't do for you."

"I know. I'll do it. You go to sleep."

Within minutes, her breathing slowed, became oblivious and deep. It was quarter to midnight. Dickie's train from the concert would come in at one-fourteen. Richard set the alarm for one. He had slept atrociously for weeks. But whenever he closed his lids some glimpse of the last hours scorched them—Judith exhaling toward the ceiling in a kind of aversion, Bean's mute staring, the sunstruck growth in the field where he and John had rested. The mountain before him moved closer, moved within him; he was huge, momentous. The ache at the back of his throat felt stale. His wife slept as if slain beside him. When, exasperated by his hot lids, his crowded heart, he rose from bed and dressed, she awoke enough to turn over. He told her then, "Joan, if I could undo it all, I would."

"Where would you begin?" she asked. There was no place. Giving him courage, she was always giving him courage. He put on shoes without socks in the dark. The children were breathing in their rooms, the downstairs was hollow. In their confusion they had left lights burning. He turned off all but one, the kitchen overhead. The car started. He had hoped it wouldn't. He met only moonlight on the road; it seemed a diaphanous companion, flickering in the leaves along the roadside, haunting his rearview mirror like a pursuer, melting under his headlights. The center of town, not quite deserted, was eerie at this hour. A young cop in uniform kept company with a gang of T-shirted kids on the steps of the bank. Across from the railroad station, several bars kept open. Customers, mostly young, passed in and out of the warm night, savoring summer's novelty. Voices shouted from cars as they passed; an immense conversation seemed in progress. Richard parked and in his weariness put his head on the passenger seat, out of the commotion and wheeling lights. It was as when, in the movies, an assassin grimly carries his mission through the jostle of a carnival—except the movies cannot show the precipitous, palpable slope you cling to within. You cannot climb back down; you can only fall. The synthetic fabric of the car seat, warmed by his cheek, confided to him an ancient, distant scent of vanilla.

A train whistle caused him to lift his head. It was on time; he had hoped it would be late. The slender draw-gates descended. The bell of approach tingled happily. The great metal body, horizontally fluted, rocked to a stop, and sleepy teen-agers disembarked, his son among them. Dickie did not show surprise that his father was meeting him at this terrible hour. He sauntered to the car with two friends, both taller than he. He said "Hi" to his father and took the passenger's seat with an exhausted promptness that expressed gratitude. The friends got in the back, and Richard was grateful; a few more minutes' postponement would be won by driving them home.

He asked, "How was the concert?"

"Groovy," one boy said from the back seat.

"It bit," the other said.

"It was O.K.," Dickie said, moderate by nature, so reasonable that in his childhood the unreason of the world had given him headaches, stomach aches, nausea. When the second friend had been dropped off at his dark house, the boy blurted, "Dad, my eyes are killing me with hay fever! I'm out there cutting that mothering grass all day!"

"Do we still have those drops?"

"They didn't do any good last summer."

"They might this." Richard swung a U-turn on the empty street. The drive home took a few minutes. The mountain was here, in his throat. "Richard," he said, and felt the boy, slumped and rubbing his eyes, go tense at his tone, "I didn't come to meet you just to make your life easier. I came because your mother and I have some news for you, and you're a hard man to get ahold of these days. It's sad news."

"That's O.K." The reassurance came out soft, but quick, as if released from the tip of a spring.

Richard had feared that his tears would return and choke him, but the boy's manliness set an example, and his voice issued forth steady and dry. "It's sad news, but it needn't be tragic news, at least for you. It should have no practical effect on your life, though it's bound to have an emotional effect. You'll work at your job, and go back to school in September. Your mother and I are really proud of what you're making of your life; we don't want that to change at all."

"Yeah," the boy said lightly, on the intake of his breath, holding himself up. They turned the corner; the church they went to loomed like a gutted fort. The home of the woman Richard hoped to marry stood across the green. Her bedroom light burned.

"Your mother and I," he said, "have decided to separate. For the summer. Nothing legal, no divorce yet. We want to see how it feels. For some years now, we haven't been doing enough for each other, making each other as happy as we should be. Have you sensed that?"

"No," the boy said. It was an honest, unemotional answer: true or false in a quiz.

Glad for the factual basis, Richard pursued, even garrulously, the details. His apartment across town, his utter accessibility, the split vacation arrangements, the advantages to the children, the added mobility and variety of the summer. Dickie listened, absorbing. "Do the others know?"

"Yes."

"How did they take it?"

"The girls pretty calmly. John flipped out; he shouted and ate a cigarette and made a salad out of his napkin and told us how much he hated school."

His brother chuckled. "He did? "

"Yeah. The school issue was more upsetting for him than Mom and me. He seemed to feel better for having exploded."

"He did?" The repetition was the first sign that he was stunned.

"Yes. Dickie, I want to tell you something. This last hour, waiting for your train to get in, has been about the worst of my life. I hate this. *Hate* it. My father would have died before doing it to me." He felt immensely lighter, saying this. He had dumped the mountain on the boy. They were home. Moving swiftly as a shadow, Dickie was out of the car, through the bright kitchen. Richard called after him, "Want a glass of milk or anything?"

''No thanks.''

"Want us to call the course tomorrow and say you're too sick to work?"

"No, that's all right." The answer was faint, delivered at the door to his room; Richard listened for the slam that went with a tantrum. The door closed normally, gently. The sound was sickening.

Joan had sunk into that first deep trough of sleep and was slow to awake. Richard had to repeat, "I told him."

"What did he say?"

"Nothing much. Could you go say goodnight to him? Please."

She left their room, without putting on a bathrobe. He sluggishly changed back into his pajamas and walked down the hall. Dickie was already in bed, Joan was sitting beside him, and the boy's bedside clock radio was murmuring music. When she stood, an inexplicable light—the moon?—outlined her body through the nightie. Richard sat on the warm place she had indented on the child's narrow mattress. He asked him, "Do you want the radio on like that?"

"It always is."

"Doesn't it keep you awake? It would me."

"No."

"Are you sleepy?"

"Yeah."

"Good. Sure you want to get up and go to work? You've had a big night."

"I want to."

Away at school this winter he had learned for the first time that you can go short of sleep and live. As an infant he had slept with an immobile, sweating intensity that had alarmed his babysitters. In adolescence he had often been the first of the four children to go to bed. Even now, he would go slack in the middle of a television show, his sprawled legs hairy and brown. "O.K. Good boy. Dickie, listen. I love you so much, I never knew how much until now. No matter how this works out, I'll always be with you. Really."

Richard bent to kiss an averted face but his son, sinewy, turned and with wet cheeks embraced him and gave him a kiss, on the lips, passionate as a woman's. In his father's ear he moaned one word, the crucial, intelligent word: *"Why?"*

*Why.* It was a whistle of wind in a crack, a knife thrust, a window thrown open on emptiness. The white face was gone, the darkness was featureless. Richard had forgotten why.

*In the tradition of the preceding Updike piece and of Bo Goldman's master-ful screenplay for* Shoot the Moon, *"Courtship" is another story of mar-riage in which tennis, or a tennis court at least, takes pride of place. This one includes not only the touching and unforgettable image of tennis played in bathing suits, but decent instructions on how to hit a one-handed backhand.*

# Courtship

## Rand Richards Cooper

The crew pulled in at nine sharp, a bulldozer and backhoe, two trucks, and six men in dungarees. *Six men,* he said to his wife, *on a mission of paid destruction!*

They came to take the tennis court.

He had wanted it gone for a long time. Their yard was small; the court filled it to the brim, sticking out on both sides of the house and dwarfing it—an embarrassment, a standing joke. Whenever he and his wife invited a new couple over, he'd watch the reaction. *Dinner at Wimbledom?* they'd kid, or just glance at each other, raising an eyebrow.

Neighbors used it as a landmark. He had actually overheard in the Stop 'n' Shop, from the next check-out: *We're the third house after the guy with the tennis court.*

A man, ruled by a single passion.

The court was a relic of his failed first marriage a quarter century earlier. Losing himself in the tennis craze had been his escape: daily partners at dawn in the park, weekend doubles, every crevice of time filled. When finally he tore free from his wife, he'd bought his modest bachelor house, and, despite straitened circumstances, rushed to put in the court. Now, decades later, he marveled to think that paving his entire backyard once presented a thrilling liberation.

At any rate, he no longer played.

His knee after two operations resembled a pie—bulky, doughy, filled with assorted treats. It was a knee for nine holes of golf, for put-tering in the yard. But there was no yard. The two of them wanted space for planting a garden, and then for a deck to sit out on and enjoy the garden. In retirement he had discovered, or coaxed into being, a plea-sure in living, growing things. He did watercolors.

For years his chief use of the court had lain in watching the twirling choreography of leaves across its pink-and-green stage on fall afternoons.

He was laughably, bizarrely, inescapably seventy.

His wife—his second wife—was younger than he by eighteen years. He relished the two-year intervals when their ages lay in contiguous decades: he speculated that if they hadn't managed to meet in one such phase of proximity, he forty-eight, she thirty, he wouldn't have dared it. His two daughters were grown. Their childhoods had been stable, but not happy enough for them to be in touch with him as often or as warmly as he might wish. They had sided, more or less, with their mother. It had been the appropriate thing to do. In his own dealings with his ex-wife, he had agreed to a policy of minimal contact, exchanging tight smiles at graduations, weddings, and funerals. And now the last funeral had turned out to be hers; decades of two packs a day had caught up with her. He sat in the chapel alongside their daughters. *She was a lovely person,* he said to the older. He couldn't help saying it; the only viable sincerity lay in weeping, and he wasn't. And she couldn't help turning on him, tear streaked, accurate: *How would you know?*

One by one the machines rumbled around the side of the house.

*I can't believe it,* he said to his wife, on her way out shopping. *Finally D-day.*

Often they had discussed getting rid of the court, but always came up against a reason not to. His old dog, the Moofer, who basked his dotage away on the warm surface. A son of hers who dropped out of college, and for whom giving tennis lessons was a single, slender thread of ambition. But eventually her son got his act together; the Moofer died and ascended to hound heaven.

The court, they joked, had run out of appeals.

He watched the men standing by their machines, raising coffee cups, pointing out their plan of attack.

*Don't you want to stick around?* he asked his wife.

*I'll let you handle it,* she said, jingling keys.

She had decided to err on the side of his privacy. He appreciated that. That was something he and his first wife had gotten all wrong. They had dug at each other in an impulse of ownership. Squeezed and squeezed until nothing remained but dread familiarity, so that leaving her he had felt chagrin and guilt, but no sorrow.

He looked out at the court. His life had contained passionate enthusiasms: for cars, photography, tennis, one after another, each yielding to the next. This didn't appall him. No element of fickleness, and certainly not his own, could surprise him at this late date. What after all was a mortal human being but a passionate commitment of which God Himself ultimately tired?

No, what disturbed him was not that his love for his first wife had yielded, but that he could no longer recall it at all, no longer summon it except as an idea: a deduction, a fact, but not a feeling.

He could still summon the feeling of tennis: life lived continually in the groove.

Above all, the dream of a good, clean backhand—legs bent, back straight like Lew Hoad, and stay down!

The other strokes came more easily to him, and so he had lived for the backhand. Any improvement in it constituted a hard-won advance against the presence within him of nearly insuperable obstacles to faith. In public places, in elevators, and in line at the bank, he had practiced—the way some men fingered the knot in their neckties or tugged their cuffs—an abbreviated backhand stroke.

Swing through the ball. Shorten your backswing. Get your shoulders turned. His liturgy and catechism.

And that, perhaps, was why he had held onto the court. It reminded him of a time of desperate disarray; of when he had groped wildly for a prop, any prop, trusting his identity, literally, to whatever came to hand; of when he had lived for a game.

*Maybe I'm the kind of guy who needs to have a few of his embarrassments hanging around,* he told his wife.

Yet they needed the court gone. Recent projects—tomato gardens, a grill area and tool shed he built from a how-to book—entirely filled the narrow corridors of lawn on either side: a vast, paved Sahara with a tiny belt of civilization pushed to its edges.

After his ex-wife's funeral, his daughters came to the house. Refusing to feel at home there had been a long-standing gesture of loyalty to their mother, but after the funeral they forgot; grief made them comfortable. His older daughter tried to make up for her remark at the chapel, inquiring of him and his wife about their trips and plans, noticing small things around the house. Toward the end of the visit she stood at the back window smoking—gruesomely, he thought—a cigarette, and looking out.

*Dad,* she said, *do you know what the first thing I would do if I lived here is?*

That very day he made some phone calls.

The men in the crew finished their coffee and climbed up like tank drivers. He took his mug and went out on the back step to watch.

With jackhammers they attacked the near side of the court, delivering jolts of mayhem which broke the surface up like a cracked cookie. The bulldozer lowered itself to a corner. A fence stanchion tilted, then fell, uprooted, a bulb of concrete clinging to its base. It always surprised him, the matter-of-factness of violence, the artlessness of it. He felt a lack of due ceremony. The bulldozer churned ahead, mashing into the loosened pavement.

*Wait!* he wanted to shout. *Not yet!*

He had remembered something. A vision of his wife, his first wife, on a tennis court somewhere, before they were married. A wickedly hot day in summer. She'd had no tennis dress, and played in her bathing suit—it was someone's lake party; they had swum—a red two-piece with white polka dots. She had no idea how to play tennis, but then neither yet had he. They launched balls in hilarious orbit, laughed at complete whiffing misses. She was looking a look he wanted to drink: tanned deep brown, page-boy haircut, red lipstick she must have sneaked off somewhere to reapply after swimming, sweat or suntan oil glistening from the crook of her arm. At last they came together at the net to retrieve a ball, and she turned and walked back to the baseline, sashaying for him shamelessly, knowing full well what a risqué thing it was to be wearing a bathing suit on a tennis court. Such a knowledge thrilled him; it promised a lifetime of unbearable withholding and unbearable, endless granting, which at twenty-two was precisely all he was equipped to know about love.

The bulldozer plowed ahead, pushing up wafers of green and pink that rose and fell away like ice floes. Clutching his coffee cup, he passengered along, breaking chunk by chunk through the sea.

# Part V

## (Sudden) Death

*The request lay unheeded by the gate of heaven.*
—William T. Tilden
"The Phantom Drive"

*Including even "The Man from Mars," with its Canadian setting and allusions to Southeast Asia, no story in this anthology covers more ground than "Baselines": London to Iran to Providence, Rhode Island. Three temporal settings, too. Liana Scalettar makes it work by binding her contrasting strands of place and time with a shimmering ribbon of frustrated longing.*

# Baselines

## Liana Scalettar

*Honor the dead with stories.* Have I heard that? Made it up? I try here. I try to give two stories to my old friend, Leila. It wasn't me who discovered her body full of drugs last month. It wasn't me who hovered at the edge of her funeral, in sunglasses. Those days, both of them, I'd cut out of work and gone dancing.

May in London. We are all still shocked by the green.

*In the brown house, by the green water, a boatman is waiting. He stands at the window and holds the curtains back. He beckons to the girl who plays around the cattails, and she keeps her eyes averted. She's been warned. Running, she makes the dry stalks rattle. Resting, she touches the stalks' furred tops.*

Leila Pahlevi and I met on Thayer. She had just come from the bookstore and was carrying, one in each hand, two plastic sacks full of books.

"Need a hand?" I asked. I was that way then: shy boy who carries books. Shy boy who attaches himself to impossible women. Leila looked at me for a minute and then handed me one of the bags. French literature—those books with the rough cream covers and the line of red along the tops.

"Here," she said, when we came to her house. I knew it: the pink Victorian with the shell-motif roof on a corner near Wickenden. Home to suburban strivers, not chic, and not often visited by *le jet set*.

"Are you sure?" I wondered if she were stopping at a friend's, and so hiding from me her true address.

"This is my house," she said. We had walked for twenty minutes without exchanging names. I knew who she was, though. Everyone did. Even when, as a democratic gesture, she used her full name on class rolls—not for her the "Alexandra, of Greece" call-outs by sweating T.A.s—everyone knew. At once.

"Well see you then," I said. "I guess." She stopped in her ascent to the sinking porch and turned. Two house-pink spots—perfect as a clown's rouge and unmistakably burning—were on her cheeks, where the bones slanted up.

"Are you taking Nineteenth Century?" she said. No reply necessary. I decided, not for the first time, to buy a belt.

*Threading through the water plants' domain, the girl comes to a waving batch of frog's eggs. The larvae cloud the water. Underneath, like stray thoughts, tadpoles dart into and out of her vision. She pokes at her find with a stick and watches it cling to its home, a submerged part of the dock. With both hands the boatman smoothes his hair; with both, he closes the curtains that have let him watch her. It's enough for today. She has chosen, not the right choice for his tastes, but still. The game can go on.*

I was neither a member of *le jets* nor a suburban striver, but that rarest of the rare, a local made good. My parents lived in a frame house on the other side of Providence, close to Federal Hill, where they loved to go out walking. In my mother's favorite café you could pay with lira instead of dollars; my father thought it was pretentious and clucked his tongue against his teeth when he passed by. My grandparents lived in Pawtucket, in a house whose inside walls were plastered with pictures of saints.

"Study," my grandfather said each time we met. He would look over his shoulder after, as if at some looming academic building, to emphasize that I should have been studying right then.

"How's everything?" I said. "How's bocce?" His game happened rain or shine. Disputed rounds were solved by kneeling men holding yardsticks.

Whenever I asked, he waved his hand in front of his face, which meant, *The same, the same, the same.*

I went every week to see them. I sat in a rose-covered chair.

"I met the Shah of Iran's daughter," I said that week. My grandmother was with us, jumping up and sitting down with the alarmed air of a professional hostess.

"Who?" He stayed facing towards me—I'd surprised him.

"Leila Pahlevi, the Shah of Iran's daughter." My grandmother jumped up again and clapped her hands together once. She might have been planning a menu for a visit by a head of state, that was how intent she became, and how flushed.

"The ex-Shah," I said. I wanted to be clear now, and so not punished later. (He said the Shah's daughter and there is no Shah anymore, but that's what he said, he should study more and not eat cheesecake. How do I know. No. No. I don't know what they eat.)

"Is she pretty?" my grandmother asked.

"She's not my girlfriend," I said.

"Your grandmother can ask a question," my grandfather said. "Can't your grandmother ask a question?"

"She's pretty," I said. Grandma sat down and crossed her ankles.

"All the Orientals are," she said. "That hair."

"Technically," I said, "technically speaking, and not to contradict, but I don't think Persians are Asian." My grandparents looked at me, slowly, without any sense of urgency, through almost-closed lids. It was the kind of lizardish disapproval, silent and imperious, that they favored.

"Who said anything about Asia?" My grandfather wanted me to leave. He'd had enough.

"Jakey," my grandmother said. "Take some cookies." She said this every time I visited, and, every time, I smiled big, meaning *No*.

"Thanks for lunch." I jumped up clapping. My grandmother lifted her cheek to be kissed; it was dry and tasted of perfume, and I wanted more than anything not to break her heart. This feat involved not disclosing that I had been lovers with Mike Genovese for two years in high school, and this nondisclosure was easy, since when I thought of him I puked.

A week after classes started, I met Leila again at a party. Her hair was tied back into eight braids threaded with some kind of ribbon; her dress was velvety; her shoes had heels.

"How's French?" I asked. My friend, Toad, was with me. He had supplied us with a steady diet of cranberry-vodka, pot, and chocolate-covered graham crackers for the early part of the evening, and now was looking at Leila as if she were the curvy silhouette in a souped-up shadow play.

"Fine," she said. (The shadow ankle moves to the right.)

"And the pink house?" (Ankle moves left. A cha-cha.)

"Fine," she said.

"And your other classes?" Conversation was not yet my thing.

"Everything," she said, closing her eyes for a second, "is fine."

"Well." I went for the gold, knowing that I would be passed out soon and lying on our host's Chinese deco rug. "You look very nice."

"Thank you," said Leila. I turned away then—Toad was holding out a carrot stick that had been dipped in something expensive. She hadn't noticed the belt.

After that night there began a series of visits of which I remember very little, now. Leila and Toad and me, always. Her room—as bare and as poorly furnished as anyone else's, always. Occasionally some other nonprincess, some other beauty in jeans and a million-dollar T-shirt, with waxed arms, with what we liked to call "real" things. Real Cartier watch. Real silver coke spoon. Real habit of sometimes, for a moment that could barely be said to have existed, seeming very far away.

"But where do they go?" Toad asked me once. "Where? Why can't we go?" In some anguish. He wouldn't want to follow, I thought then. Now, nine years later, I keep thinking it.

One night: Leila propped up on a cushion patterned with sailboats. Leila with gold flecks gathering at the inner rims of her irises. Toad lying on his stomach with his face pressed to the splintered floor.

"It was a childhood," she was saying. "I don't know."

"In the palace?" I asked. I was that way then, too: There is a palace I will reach if I try hard enough, if I look. There is another way to live than this.

"No, no. In Paris. By then we had already left; we were in Paris. Still elegant, but no palace."

"And you went to school?"

"I went," Leila said, looking at me. "To school. Of course I went to school."

"Sorry." I prodded Toad with my foot.

"With nuns," she said. "Very *Madeline*."

"And then you went to high school?"

"And then," she said, as the goldness kept gathering, "I went to high school."

"And then you applied to college?" Toad was sleeping. I nudged him once more, hard, to be sure.

"Goddamn Jake," she said. "Yes."

"And you got in? . . ." Toad made a sleep noise that sounded like another question.

"Everywhere because of my name. I'm deposed royalty and we get in everywhere. We barely have to write essays, we barely have to pass classes. I wrote my name on the forms and that was it, Jake, that was it—"

I apologized again.

"Shut up," she said. I decided, not for the first time, to stop talking, and bit her neck in a chain pattern. The skin on her legs tasted of fake roses. Between her legs was better, salt, jasmine, ground, sweat.

Another night: Toad awake. The three of us eating pizza and garlic knots. Leila and Toad in white T-shirts, looking like twins. Against the window, blue night pressing in. Toad said something funny and Leila, who had been Garboesque, began to laugh. She held her knees to her chest and laughed. She stretched out on the Salvation Army couch and laughed. She caught the end of a string of cheese in her mouth and laughed and laughed.

"What'd I say?" Toad wondered.

I didn't say anything. Only watched and listened, recording almost, thinking (did I think this?): *I'll want this some day.*

When she was done laughing, Leila dried tears from her face with the back of a sleeve. "I laugh like my mother," she said.

"Farah?" Toad said. Wanting to hold that name, once, in himself. He had gone to New York and looked up old copies of *Look* and *Paris Match* and *Hola*, immersing himself in the story of the woman whom Leila's mother had replaced. And thinking of the replacement. He'd felt power, its cold twilight wing.

"Obviously," Leila said. Or she said nothing.

*Salt water now, not fresh. The boatman's boat is painted blue and red. His oars are striped. Beached, the boat seems like a carnival, but when it's on the water the blue becomes that of the sea. He seems then to be sitting on the water's surface, in cracked rings of sunlight. He takes a fishing rod with him for show. He shells pistachios, skins grapes.*

Another night. Night again, night still. Leila sleeping. One forearm over her eyes. Toenails painted the odd changeful shade of a shell. Toad and I reading, a little, and also finishing a game of cards. Our heads very close. My heart.

"Follow suit," I said. He'd forgotten.

"Yeah," he said. Diamond after diamond, club after club. I didn't say *Let me see the inside of your mouth. Let me taste the salt at your collar bone. Let me see.* We had walked out into the fields near my parents' house that day. ("No thanks," Leila'd said. She sighed with pleasure, stretched out and alone on the couch. "I'm—dreaming now.") We had found child things as we went. Onion grass, curlicue scallion shape, to chew. Dandelion ends to taste. Dandelion clocks. Lucky clover. His ankle-bones, I saw, were rounded and thin.

*The girl stands at the watermark, her hands in protective fists. She's got a lot of sea glass in one. In the other, a knot of purple seaweed. Who is this man who waits for me each day? she thinks. She thinks, what a pretty boat.*

These stories aren't stories, Leila. Paltry things with no endings, no morals. They are moments, rather. Let's say they are, for example, blooms, the clematis I see from my window, blossoms opened like pink starfish against a wall.

Branches are insistent at my window. I've seen a red-winged black-bird here, a dun-colored female cardinal.

Let's say, Leila, these unfurling moments, these memory-trembles, are for you. In your honor. Certainly, I have never been good at gifting. Never known how to offer the right thing.

Toad met Farah finally. Last year, eight years after we met Leila in Providence, six years after we graduated, three years after I told Toad I loved him and watched him flush like someone fatally and fully sick. I had invited him to visit me here thinking, still with the thoughts, still with the weight like a stone in my chest, thinking: *My heart.* I had called Leila, who paused before each response, as if she were overseas. Not in the same city at all.

"Tennis?" she said. I'd thought of it as a way out of talking, a way out of *You look exactly*s and *How long has* and all of it.

"The weather," I said, "has been so—"

"Yes," she said. "Let's. My mother's in from Paris."

The day after Toad's arrival. Leila and Toad on one side, Farah Pahlevi and I on the other. They were trouncing us. The grass smelled new and the plane trees that we could see, beyond the green fence, were in full leaf. Beyond that beyond—invisible but pulsing, like a great gray heart (Can two things be my heart? Can three?)—was London.

Farah turned to look at me. Her red mouth moved, but no words came out. I watched her lips—I wanted to understand. It was some time before I realized that the boom surrounding me had come from a jet. That Farah was in fact speaking. That she was telling me not to double-fault again.

"Okay," I said. On the other side of the net, Toad and Leila stood close together talking. He was taller than she was, now. Their dark heads bent together.

"Hey there," I called. They snapped their faces around and stared: two pale discs, two plates full of sun. I couldn't see their features. But I knew them. For each, I knew every line.

"*Allez,*" Farah said.

"Gotcha," I said. And stood there, bouncing the ball.

"*Mais allez,*" Farah said.

"Chill," I said, too softly for her to hear. Then I was embarrassed by my embarrassment—Madame, I realize that you are the widow of the Shah of Iran and still very beautiful, but I remember the taste of your daughter's cunt and how she laughs and I am in love with your daughter's tennis partner and soon will pick up three men in a row, morning, noon, and night, boom.

"Madame," I said. Farah pouted the way young French girls do—with grace, pushing her lower lip way out—and walked over to me.

"He can't poach," I said.

"Pardon?" she said.

I lifted my chin towards Toad. She twisted her head around.

"He," I said, "can't poach."

Farah looked back at me. "I see," she said. "Very well." We proceeded to lose the match in straight sets. Toad and Leila jumped up and down and touched their hands together and kissed each other's faces showily, twice, *à la russe*. (I have learned French, Leila. I offer here a mere sprinkling.) At the net we discussed what to do next and decided nothing, we would do nothing. Next to her mother, Leila was gigantic and crude, some satirical puppet.

"Good-bye," she said, blinking rapidly. And Farah said, "How pleasant this has been."

*The girl waves at the boatman who has waved, theatrically, first.*

And then Toad went home to Boston. And then I wrote him a thank-you note, even though he had been the guest and I the host. And then I learned that my grandmother was sick and went home and sat by her hospital bed and turned the cranks that moved her up, down, up, down. When she couldn't speak any more, she grabbed my hand hard and held it, and I didn't know if she knew or didn't or hated me or pitied me or wasn't thinking of me at all, and the last is what I came to suspect.

And then I read about Leila in the newspaper. How she had been found when a worried friend made phone calls and cared and had the police force open the door, and how that friend wasn't me. How she had left no note nor, as they say, "showed any signs." How it had been June 10, 2001, which was Toad's thirtieth birthday and had necessitated my sending him an expensive shirt and what I hoped were convincing flowers.

*Salt at her face and hair. The oars are slapping. They were wrong, the girl thinks. What a good boat. What a good man. He has given her fruit and nuts and a necklace. He has given her one grainy handle to work. With zeal, body-pleasure, she settles in to the task.*

Let's say they are blooms, Leila. That open for a moment. Let's say that they are all heliotropic, that all turn their faces to the sun.

*An examination of misplaced envy, no less intense for its wrongheadedness, as well as the paradoxical-seeming desire for failure. Though often mislabeled lack of motivation, the latter is something altogether different.*

# Strokes

## Adam Sexton

Cooper turns the second-to-last page of the *Times* Metro section and cries out in shock: "Unh!"

"Rghluh?" His girlfriend, Helga, is brushing her teeth in the kitchen of their Hoboken apartment. The bathroom's too small to hold a sink. You have to rest your feet on the edge of the shower basin when you sit on the toilet.

Cooper slumps in his favorite living-room easy chair. His only living-room easy chair. Actually, it's Helga's. Scanning the Obit page in a sort of daze, he shakes his head. Sobs build in his chest, climb his trachea toward daylight.

"Bill Rampart died." Cancer, the article says. Cooper begins to cry. Bill Rampart was his first tennis coach.

Helga spits into the kitchen sink, aiming with care so as to avoid a ziggurat of dirty dishes.

"Oh, *Coop.*" Without even rinsing, she hurries into the living room to give him a hug.

Cooper met Helga in college out west, though they didn't begin dating until she came to New York to attend med school at Mt. Sinai and looked him up. After moving in with Cooper, Helga failed her second semester outright and is taking a term off "to regroup."

Helga's face is actually heart-shaped, just as her lips form a perfect pink Cupid's bow. Her body dips and swells like . . . well, like an hourglass. And Helga has a trust fund that takes care of her half of the rent plus the insurance on her Toyota, which she bought with cash. Truth be told, Helga's trust fund often covers both halves of the rent. She also pays for all the food. Helga's great-grandfather patented a horseshoe with cleats so horses wouldn't slip on the ice during Midwestern winters.

"Sweetie, let me hold you. Come to the couch." Her breath smells of mint and baking soda. Stepping across the room, Helga clears debris from the fold-up futon. (The couch is also the bed. The living room is also the bedroom.) First she moves aside a pea green duvet. Then knit-

228

ting needles, a ball of yarn, and what looks like a very large potholder-in-progress. Also a book: Helga has clipped her Itty Bitty Book Light to something called *The Collected Novellas of Gabriel Garcia Marquez*. Helga is always studying, even when she's not attending school. Actually, the problem with school is Helga's need to study everything, all the time. Once while reading about scrubbing-up technique during her first semester at Mt. Sinai, she began to wonder about soap—what it was made of, how it worked. She dragged Cooper to an all-night supermarket in Jersey City, where she bought more than a dozen kinds of detergent. Liquids, powders, flakes, you name it. Back home, she experimented at the kitchen sink for a while before falling asleep in her clothes, her schoolwork neglected. If Helga can't find time to study, she buys the books anyway, just to be safe. And not just the required ones, but all the supplementary texts on all her syllabi. Books that Helga has bought but never opened crowd every room in the apartment—even the bathroom, where they teeter atop the perspiring toilet tank.

The paper says that a memorial service has been scheduled for the United Congregational Church in New Haven, Connecticut, on Saturday. Cooper takes his navy blazer to the drycleaners on Washington Street. First, though, he phones Ravi Choudhury to postpone their weekly squash lesson.

Half a year ago, Cooper was wandering Battery Park after a disastrous legal-proofreading exam on Pine Street. (How was he supposed to know that *restaurateur* had no "n"?) Like Constantine, he looked to the heavens for a sign, and found one:

**1-800-RAQCUET**
**CLASSES START NEXT WEEK**

the sign said, in cottony sans-serif letters drifting eastward with the prevailing winds.

Cooper called the number and snagged an interview with the Owner and Founder of Metropolis Racquet Sports, a guy named Josh Przwalski. Well, an audition was more like it. First Cooper had to locate the company's so-called World Headquarters in a driving late-March rain: a warehouse next to a casket factory on the banks of the Gowanus Canal.

Since the building wasn't voluminous enough to hold the real deal, the tennis court inside was somewhat smaller than it should have been. (Precisely ¾ regulation size, he later learned.) While rain played a Keith Moon drum solo on the building's roof of corrugated tin, Cooper straddled a dented folding chair beside the midget court and zipped through a short-answer quiz on tennis arcana.

> *Q: If your first serve lands long but your opponent hits the ball anyway, thereby breaking a string, is he allowed to replace his racquet before your second serve? (Yes.)*

After the written test, he played a set against the Owner and Founder himself. Przwalski's bandylegs were hairless and the blue-white of skim milk. His front teeth looked as though they'd been sharpened against the bars of a cage. Cooper went up 5-4, adjusting his knee brace, adjusting his shots to account for the reduced playing area. Then he subtly tanked the next two games before tying the score at six apiece and letting his potential employer take the tiebreak. His strategy worked. Przwalski smiled (or was he wincing?) and told Cooper he was hired.

All the way home—the N, to the F, to the PATH to Hoboken—Cooper reviewed his Official Metropolis Racquet Sports Training Manual. *Never eat in front of a student*, the Manual said. *Never ask a student what they want to do. Never refer to a professional player if they didn't study with, or don't currently teach for, Metropolis Racquets.* (The students will find out where "they" studied/teach and go there, the Manual explained.)

Never eat in front of a student?

He had to hand it to Przwalski, though, who had briefly competed on the Middle Eastern circuit (he won the qualies in Qatar once) at about the time that Cooper was playing singles for Stanford. The guy saw an opportunity and, bang-zoom, he was on it like a tarp on the grass in a Wimbledon cloudburst. Venus and Serena, Andy Roddick. Anna freaking Kournikova. Przwalski recognized that tennis's profile had never been higher, its appeal broader—or younger. Sure there was the N.Y.A.C., and the Racquet Club on Park Avenue. But what about the thousands of would-be duffers unable to afford a club membership, intimidated by the very idea? It wasn't as if playing in the New York City parks was a realistic option, with malt-liquor bottles by the drooping nets and crushed crack vials behind the baseline. Plus, what if you didn't know *how* to play? How to score? What to wear?

Przwalski recognized something almost no one else did: that big money could be made teaching groups of New Yorkers the fundamentals of the game. He rented courts at prep schools, mainly, in the evenings and before the kids and teachers arrived each day. During summer vacation and at Christmastime and over Spring Break. But how to spread the word?

The Owner and Founder hired an apprentice skywriter—okay, the guy had never actually *written* with a plane before—to publicize his tennis classes. (MRS's Director of Airborne Advertising, a genial slacker named Dov Shneerson, was dyslexic: thus R A Q C U E T.) Soon after Cooper began teaching for the company, Metropolis Racquets' overhead ads became as much a fixture of the airspace above New York, from Van Cortland Park to Far Rockaway, as disoriented migratory birds.

In his first few months as an MRS instructor, Cooper discovered a knack for teaching that had remained camouflaged until then. Never especially patient, he wasn't much more articulate than your average ex-college athlete, either. Cooper guessed he projected as much authority as most club-level pros—maybe a bit more, since Metro's students were ignorant enough to be impressed by the fact that he had been ranked, once. ("Once" was the operative word here.) Plus he was tall. That helped.

But Cooper had something that other teachers didn't, it turned out. He knew how to flirt. He gathered bits and pieces of biographical ephemera the way his blazer, angled with the rest of his clothes in the Hoboken closet that wasn't quite as deep as a hanger, gathered lint. Then he used this knowledge to cheerfully tease his pupils, thereby flattering them.

"Miriam?" he'd say, to a bleached-blond Latina with gorgeous posture and lines around her mouth like parentheses. "Are you sure you're a Rockette? 'Cause I've never seen a serve with less *kick* on it."

Or "Rick, you're a salesman. So shake hands with the racquet, already!"

Or "Eddie, hey. Now, I know you're from Brooklyn, but this ain't Ebbets Field. Bend those knees, guy, and the ball won't always fly over the fence."

*To Sir with Love* it was not. But halfway through the first two-hour clinic, Cooper had established a persona for each member of the class that was broader than the head of a Prince. Thus caricatured, they chummed it up with zeal. Rick announced to the rest that Eddie had hit the Shot Heard 'Round the World during a volley drill: "What am I, Ralph Branca over here?" Everyone laughed, Eddie mugged, and Miriam gave him a collegial pat on the back, careful not to spoil her fresh manicure. Miriam had freely admitted during introductions that she got into tennis for the outfits, and indeed, her Canal Street–counterfeit Louis Vuitton sun visor was a thing to behold.

The vibe grew so cozy so quickly that three weeks into his Metropolis tenure, praise was drenching Cooper like perspiration at the end of a five-setter in Dallas. Not from Przwalski, who was clearly baffled by the phenomenon. (The Owner and Founder didn't believe in praising his employees anyway, or so said the "Forward" to the Official Manual.) It was the students who couldn't say enough about Cooper, *to* him. And when their ten-week sessions ended, they sent him thank-you cards— gave him gifts, even. A dainty shopping bag of men's skin-care products from a woman who worked in the cosmetics industry. An entire sturgeon from a fish buyer at Zabar's. (Helga folded the thing in half like a pair of pants over a hanger so as to cram it inside their fridge.) Sean Lennon's personal assistant FedExed Cooper a cardboard box containing the collected works of Yoko Ono. He was invited to lunch at Smith & Wollensky's, tea at the Algonquin, dinner at the apartments of pupils and their wives or husbands.

And a Mrs. Choudhury, who attended Cooper's class in a series of saris, asked him to teach squash to her fourteen-year-old son Ravi. Before committing, Cooper carefully reviewed paragraph C on page 19 of his Metropolis Racquet Sports Employment Agreement: the Exclusivity Clause.

> *You shall refer to MRS any inquiry for coaching services received by you from: any student for whom you at any time performed services on MRS's behalf, or family member of such student; a referral from such student or such student's family member; a professional contact of MRS's introduced to you by MRS or through your work for MRS; or a referral from such a contact.*

Now, Metropolis Racquet Sports was actually Metropolis Racquet *Sport*; the company didn't offer instruction in squash. It didn't teach racquetball, paddleball, badminton, platform tennis, or royal tennis. Just lawn tennis—"tennis."

For that matter, though Przwalski was in the process of trademarking an approach to instructing high schoolers that he called Teenis (which conspicuously rhymed with "penis," but Przwalski seemed not to care), at present MRS did not accept students under eighteen years of age.

Therefore: If Cooper could help a family of newsstand owners get their son admitted to Dartmouth—that was the plan—and make fifty bucks an hour doing so, what was to stop him?

Of course, they'd have to keep the arrangement discreet. Cooper knew that if he requested company permission, Przwalski would either respond with a flat no or try to get a cut of the profits. Or both.

"I'll do it," he told Mrs. Choudhury after class one morning. The woman tamped sweat from her brow with the hem of her garment, its opalescent sea green fabric flashing in the slanted sunlight. Her bindi twinkled redly, like a taillight at dusk. "I'll help you get Ravi into Dartmouth."

High in the sky, towering white uppercase letters spelled out

## TAKE A TENNIS LESSON TOADY!

On the morning of the memorial service—it is the second Saturday after the U.S. Open finals—the phone on the kitchen table rings while Cooper is tying his necktie. Ten to one it's the Stanford Alumni Society. Normally he'd let the machine pick up, but Helga's asleep on the living-room futon and Cooper doesn't want her disturbed. She was up all night reading Gabriel Garcia Marquez.

It isn't Stanford calling. Somebody who identifies himself as Mister Jacobson says he wants his daughter to learn tennis from "a Metropolis Racquets–type pro—"

"Sure." Why the fuck call me at home, then? "They're at one eight hundred—"

"—but I don't want to go through the company."

The phone receiver balanced on his shoulder, Cooper stands before the bathroom mirror now. He is molding the knot of his tie, or trying to. The mirror hangs over the bathtub—under the showerhead itself. Thank God for cordless phones, Cooper thinks. "Any particular reason?" Maybe this guy's daughter wants to watch a tennis pro eat.

"I—I've heard some things about them that I don't, that I'm not crazy about."

Cooper's train departs from Grand Central in less than an hour, and the PATH runs infrequently on the weekend. He can't be late for Bill Rampart's service. "Could I call you back some other time, Mister? . . ."

"Jacobson. Well, Cooper, that's . . . no. I'm very hard to reach, you see. I travel a lot on business. But would you be free to meet with my daughter once a week, at a time and place of your convenience?"

This guy's got the strangest accent, Cooper thinks—an odd combination of Southern and, like, Brooklyn. "Daughter" sounded like Sheepshead Bay. *Daw*-duh. "A time and place of your convenience" sounded like Tennessee Williams.

From the other end of the apartment, Cooper hears 1010 WINS's telltale xylophone jingle and an announcer trapped in an echo chamber promising listeners the world in exchange for ten minutes. Helga's clockradio—it's eleven. Cooper needs to move, and fast.

"Look," he says. "Sure. Just . . ."

"I need to pee, honey." It's Helga, at the bathroom door.

"May I have the name of a reference, Cooper? A non–Metropolitan Tennis Sports reference?"

Two thoughts occur to Cooper in rapid succession.

The First Thought: *I'm going to get screwed by this, somehow.*

The Second: *Whatever.*

"Call Mrs. Choudhury," he says, reciting her number in Jackson Heights by memory. "I'm teaching her son squash."

That afternoon, Cooper walks to the town green from the New Haven train station—past the abandoned Coliseum where he saw a Grateful Dead show once, past the retail graveyard that calls itself a Mall. He looks for the church and finds three, evenly spaced and facing in the same direction. One was built in the Gothic style, while the others look more . . . colonial. But which is the Congregational church? It's like a New England version of *Let's Make a Deal.* Luckily, the steps of the church on the right are crowded with men in black, men in gray, some of them steering women toward the door with a hand to the small of the back, while others prepare for a phantom penalty kick.

Once inside, Cooper finds an aisle seat, on the pew in front of the pew where Pam Shriver examines her program. Roscoe Tanner sits across the way, looking quintessentially Tennesseean (if not as somber as he might) in a seersucker suit. In the church's dim interior, Cooper doesn't recognize anyone from his own class, but it's been years and—*duh*—no one is wearing tennis clothes. Anyway, he isn't sure he wants to reunite with old friends. People laugh when Cooper says Hoboken. (Is it really that funny sounding? he wonders each time, irritated.) And telling someone he works for Metropolis Racquets elicits a clueless frown or, at best, a "That skywriting thing?"

Wait. Off at ten o'clock slumps Dickie MacOliphant, Quasimodo in a handmade suit. What's he doing here? Cooper wonders. Dickie played for Stanford, but he never attended Whispering Glades, so Cooper can't imagine how he knew Bill Rampart. Maybe the girl sitting next to him did; a headbanded ash-blond bob keeps tilting in the direction of Dickie's bespoke shoulders.

Dickie MacOliphant is the scion of a California media dynasty so decadent that some of its members have married each other, like seventeenth-century kings and queens. The names of various grandparents, aunts, and uncles adorn residence halls and dining commons on the Stanford campus. Which helps explain why Dickie himself was not only admitted to the university after flunking out of three boarding schools, but managed to make the tennis team despite a conspicuous lack of coordination. Before he knew Dickie, Cooper had never seen someone trip on a hard-court baseline.

In two years playing doubles on the Stanford squad, Dickie never won a match. Not one. Yet he kept competing until he was kicked out of school for cooking crystal meth in his dorm room. Why Dickie MacOliphant didn't simply buy the drugs he craved, Cooper didn't know. He bought everything else—including friends, it seemed. The most unlikely circle of jocks and dweebs, bohos and sorority girls gathered around him, like flies about the shriveled core of a Granny Smith apple. From what Cooper understands, this continues to be the case. Dickie owns a loft in SoHo that is the scene of parties written up in *W* and *Vanity Fair*, someone told him. ("*W?*" Cooper asked.) P. Diddy is a personal friend.

A string quartet from the Yale School of Music plays Rampart's favorite Baroque melodies. His wife, Jean, who owns an art gallery near Rittenhouse Square in Philadelphia, speaks from the pulpit about how much Bill loved Yale. (He was on the team that won the EITA's in '46 and '47, she reminds everyone.) Tony Trabert tells an anecdote about Newport in the early fifties: On the Cliff Walk before their matches at the Casino one morning, he and Bill had to step aside to allow a man dressed as Santa Claus to hurry past.

"It was July," Trabert deadpans. Laughter fills the church.

When things quiet down, Trabert introduces the next speaker: Timothy Zahnburstehalter.

*What. The. Fuck.*

It's true. It can't be. Cooper looks past the shoulders and heads of the dozens of friends and family and students and colleagues who have made the trip to Connecticut this weekend to honor the memory of Bill Rampart. Yup. Having crossed the ill-lit altar and threaded his way behind the communion table shrouded in flocked green fabric, Tim Zahnburstehalter is ascending to the pulpit of United Church.

Zahnburstehalter wears neither jacket nor tie. He wears a chartreuse Fred Perry polo, the shirt's white crown-of-laurels insignia just visible to Cooper at this distance thanks to his remarkable eyesight. A polo shirt! To a funeral! Okay, a memorial service, but still. Zahnburstehalter appears unshaven as well. Leaning on the podium before him like a drunk propped against his local bar, he begins to speak.

"Bill Rampart used to tell me . . ." The word "used" sounds like "youthed." Zahnburstehalter spoke with a slight lisp at Whispering Glades. Now he seems almost to be communicating in Castilian Spanish.

". . . that I would be somebody someday." *Thumb buddy thumb day.* "In fact, he said I would exceed my own wildest expectations. Was he right?" One side of Zahnburste-halter's mouth creeps toward a ridiculous Peter Fonda–in-*Easy Rider* sideburn. "Only time will tell."

The crowd chuckles in what sounds like appreciation. Who *invited* this pompous bozo to speak? Cooper wonders, all but tearing at his own hair. He knows the answer: Zahnburstehalter himself. At the Glades, Zahnburstehalter was a schmoozer, a wheeler-dealer, a notorious politicker who managed to snag the most time with the ball machine, the most games at the chessboard in the lounge. He hid in the bathroom during calisthenics! (It rankles Cooper still.) Even his spot on the academy ladder seemed inflated; opponents regularly defaulted to him under suspicious circumstances, so he had to play fewer matches overall and was better rested when he did compete. A few months ago, Cooper learned from a fellow instructor at Metro-polis Racquets that Pat McEnroe was considering Zahnburstehalter for a men's doubles slot on the Davis Cup squad, despite the fact that he was unranked as such. Fearful of developing a peptic ulcer, Cooper banished the information from his consciousness. Now a dime-size dot at the base of his ribcage smolders again, hot as a black can of Penn balls forgotten in the sun.

Cooper heard from the same Metro teacher that Zahnburstehalter was preparing to open "Strokes," a Times Square "gentlemen's club" with a tennis theme. (Huh?) His only investor: Dickie MacOliphant. This explains why Dickie is chortling at Zahnburstehalter's every pronouncement, six rows away from Cooper. They're business partners.

Stroking his chin like a mime doing "Thoughtful," Zahnburstehalter continues. "Was it a risky prediction to make? Perhaps. But Bill was not a cautious man."

Bill? Cooper thinks. *Bill?* Who among his pupils presumed to call Rampart by his first name? The man was born in the 1920s, for Christ's sake! Cooper holds his head in his hands.

"As all of you know, I've been around the world on the pro tour." This is true, sort of. Zahnburstehalter was Lindsay Davenport's mixed-doubles partner for like six months, while her usual partner was recovering from a torn rotator cuff. "Do they know Bill Rampart's name on the hard courts of Melbourne? They do not. Unlike me, Bill never had the chance to play there—to *win* there."

*Of course* they don't know his name on "the hard courts of Melbourne," Cooper all but bellows to the congregation. When Rampart competed, the tournament was played on grass!

Unconsciously, Cooper has scooted to the edge of his pew. In something very much like desperation, he looks to his right, his left. He turns and looks behind him, to confirm that the other mourners are as peeved at this textbook display of narcissism as is Cooper. To his sickened astonishment, no one he sees is grimacing. Nobody snickers. Not a single eye is on the roll. Instead, all appear to be focused on Zahnburstehalter's self-serving eulogy, rapt by it almost.

What the fuck!

Cooper wants to vault the back of the bench on which he sits and shake Pam Shriver, bring her to her senses. He wants to slap Roscoe Tanner. *Don't you guys get it?* he wants to cry out. This prick isn't honoring Bill Rampart, he's honoring himself. We're watching somebody . . . *masturbate* here!

*Pam.*

Roscoe!

The audience listens, laughs. Sighs. Murmurs pensively as one. Laughs again.

Cooper twitches. Gags. Vibrates with rage.

Walks out.

Before he stands and leaves the church, nearly losing his balance and falling to the marble floor in the process, he looks again at the printed program he was handed at the door, now damp and creased in his racquet hand. But Cooper's anger has grown so massive that he is quite literally unable to read the words there. He can make out the font: Courier, as in Jim. He can't force the letters themselves to cohere, however, much less form legible words. He's not seeing red, quite. But his vision is seriously compromised. Hurrying down the center aisle, he finds himself whacking the program-holding hand against one thigh, having lost all but a tingle in his fingers and palm, his wrist. His forearm.

The worst headache of Cooper's life builds throb by throb. Someone somewhere hammers his hairline with a platform-tennis paddle. On his way across the New Haven green, beneath a now-stormy sky the color of snot, Cooper hears applause tendriling forth from the front doors of United Church, through its open windows; like a Venus flytrap on illegal steroids, the laughter snaps at his heels as he rushes to flee the Injustice Of It All.

The Injustice: Cooper cannot remember a time when he wasn't praised for his easy athletic ability, rewarded for it. He learned to run and jump, to throw and catch, to punt pass and kick, earlier—years earlier—than his peers. To hit a softball, then a baseball. To hit a tennis ball. Watching home movies, he can see that not only did these skills arrive ahead of schedule; they came fully formed, as if he'd been taught the fundamentals of sports and games in some earlier life. In a way, he'd already known how to sink a foul shot before ever touching the stippled rubber hide of a basketball.

A devil-may-care naturalness imbued every move Cooper made, an amazing grace that caused people to gasp when they saw it. To want to be near him. Clearly he had been blessed, and witnesses to his athletic predestination, whatever their ages, crowded close in the hope that some of his careless glory would shine their way. Kids loved him. Adults loved him—*loved* him, and not just parents and grandparents and coaches and phys-ed teachers, but total strangers who happened upon Cooper heading a J.V. soccer ball or shooting an arrow at day camp. Bystanders laughed with joy to see him play bumper pool: "Jesus, would you look at this kid?" He even swam beautifully.

Of course he was made captain of every team. But the number of teams was finite, and so Cooper's schoolmates spent the balance of their attraction to him by electing him president of this and that—insisting that he star in the school play, even. And oh yeah: Cooper got laid. His high school girlfriend from freshman year onward was a cheerleader with a blond flag of hair down her back and a compulsion to dynamite the taboos of her Baptist family. She fucked him with a vengeance, literally, and Cooper felt used, but he wasn't about to complain.

All of it was instinctual. Effortless.

Cooper wanted to join the pro tour upon graduation from high school. At seventeen he was ranked sixth in the East among Junior Boys, having won tournaments in the Catskills and Princeton, New Jersey; he'd even reached the semifinals of the Miami Orange Bowl, and the round of sixteen at the National Juniors in Kalamazoo. College would still be around in a few years, he told his mother and father. And he would never be in better physical condition than he was right then. He would never be hungrier, more full of fire.

His parents wouldn't hear of it.

"This isn't girl's gymnastics," Cooper's father told him, "where it's all over by age eighteen. It isn't baseball, either. College tennis isn't the only route to the top, but it's an accepted path to success in the sport. Look at John McEnroe."

"McEnroe went for two semesters," Cooper pointed out, though he knew by this time that it was a lost cause. "He dropped out after a year, Dad, to join the ATP tour."

"*I* like Patrick," his mother said. "The brother? The nice one."

"We don't want our son busted for crack possession in a Florida motel room. You're going to college."

He went to Stanford. The climate rocked, but the sheer difficulty of his classes stunned Cooper. Worse yet, the school's culture of academic

achievement and social excess didn't value athletics or athletes dispro-
portionately. Cooper's fellow students were too busy cramming for calculus midterms or nursing weekend hangovers or both to notice his
native grace—much less appreciate his triumphs on the court, rele-
gated to a box on the second-to-last page of the campus newspaper.

Still, Cooper signed up for a tutor to help him with his homework
(she didn't *do* his homework, as his tutors had done in high school),
and he prospered at tennis. He won his first two singles matches,
against Hawaii and UCLA. Then, in a tournament versus Arizona State
at the Taube Center, he blew out his knee.

It wasn't while competing that Cooper wrecked his career. Nor was
it during the pre-match warmup, when most tennis injuries occur. He
ruined his right leg, and torpedoed his chances for fame and fortune as
a professional tennis player, when the match that would be his last was
through, with Cooper the victor in a fifth-set tiebreaker. He vaulted the
net to shake his opponent's hand, a definitely corny gesture but one he
had found irresistible, suddenly. The bulbous toe of his right New
Balance sneaker snagged the tape at the top of the net. He went down.
The arthroscopic surgery, the months of physical therapy, only wasted
Cooper's time and his parents' money. It was over.

A Student Health psychologist suggested that Cooper had wrecked
his blossoming career on purpose.

"Sorry?" In place of a couch, the shrink had equipped her narrow
campus office with a foamrubber easy chair that unfolded into a twin-
size bed. Sitting on the chair, it occurred to Cooper that she must sometimes spend the night in the room; the closet near the window probably
hid blankets and a pillow. The blue nylon that covered the chair was
slippery, and Cooper needed to concentrate in order to avoid ending
up on the carpet.

The psychologist shrugged. Her name was Lourdes. Everything
about Lourdes evinced good taste, from her low-key, low-heeled shoes
to her earrings, studs that looked to Cooper like tiny golden tennis
balls. Lourdes spoke in beautifully made sentences founded upon con-
structions like "Neither she nor I." She said "begs the question" and
"notwithstanding." The meticulously matted and framed diplomas on
her wall told a little story: Chico State, UCLA, Stanford. Lourdes had
never heard of Steffi Graf or Pat Rafter.

"You obviously have mixed feelings about tennis, inasmuch as your
parents expected you to succeed at it, yet didn't notice unless you
failed. You've told me repeatedly that when you lost, it was more often
than not toward the end of a . . . game?"

"Match."

"A match that you'd all but won already. Yes?"

"True, but." Mixed feelings about tennis? Cooper'd never heard anything so absurd. Mixed feelings didn't get a person ranked sixth in the East—didn't win that person a scholarship to Stanford University!

Admittedly, there was another angle on Cooper's athletic gifts: the resentment it sometimes sparked in those less sheerly talented. Envy had always walked hand-in-hand with the admiration of others, a dynamic Cooper recognized at a very early age and even attempted to address briefly by playing down his prowess at sports and games. (This lasted for all of one week during the fourth grade, until Cooper unintentionally lofted a kickball over the playground fence and remembered what being a hero felt like.) Later, not just his ease on fields and courts, but his social success and his girlfriends, made him a kind of magnet for ire—the simmering rage of those who succeeded, too, but only by working to exhaustion. By studying at sports, popularity, dating. (The altogether unathletic, unliked, and unlaid tended to worship him, as it was all pretty much an abstraction to them.) How come it came so easy to Cooper? It wasn't fair, they thought—they said—and they were right. It wasn't.

"You don't like me, do you?" Cooper asked Lourdes, pouting, flirting. "You think I'm just some . . . jock."

She called his bluff. "Whether I like you or not," the psychologist said, looking him straight in the eye as she did so, "is immaterial to our discussion."

The week before Thanksgiving, Metropolis Racquets sues Cooper for breach of contract. At least, they threaten to sue.

The Exclusivity Clause.

Based on nothing more than an advanced case of clinical paranoia, Przwalski hired an out-of-work character actor in September to pose as a prospective client. That's right: "Mister Jacobson," who phoned every instructor on the Metro staff in search of unwitting confessions of non-exclusivity. Six of them fell for it, Cooper learns through the grapevine afterwards. Seven, if you include Cooper himself.

The mailman has delivered something called a "draft complaint" (he thinks of his grandmother, shivering in a wing chair) claiming that Cooper

*wrongfully solicited Metropolis Racquets' customers, wrongfully competed with Metropolis Racquets, and misappropriated, improperly disclosed and misused its trade secrets.*

The document accuses Cooper of causing the company "substantial actual and consequential damages in excess of $400,000."

"*Trade* secrets!" Cooper cries, laughing. Or laughs, crying—he's lost track. Cooper and Helga sit at the kitchen table. He blows his nose into a wad of toilet paper pulled from the roll atop the kitchen sink; there is no room for a dispenser in the bathroom itself. "*What* secrets?"

Helga shrugs. " 'Side to the net,' maybe?"

"There's no net in squash."

"Aha! A trade secret!"

"Am I going to debtors' prison, like in some . . . Dickens novel?" Remarkably, Cooper managed to learn a thing or two in college. Would that have happened, he wonders right now, if he hadn't tripped on the net in Palo Alto?

"This is some sort of joke, honey. Let me make your favorite dish tonight. The salmon."

It's no joke. Helga faxes the document to her family's lawyer, in the old Standard Oil Building on Bowling Green. (Their New York lawyer, that is; they have others in Chicago and Minneapolis.) In a phone conversation with Cooper the next day, he explains that plaintiffs never win these cases because—in Layman's Terms—you can't prevent someone from making a living, okay? That doesn't mean the threat of a suit isn't real. Cooper needs to hire an attorney, pronto. Someone who can either settle out of court or—worst case scenario?—represent him before a judge. You don't want to mess around with something like this, the lawyer counsels him.

"Mother *fuck*," Cooper says afterwards. He stands by the stove. It is a sort of 1950s Buick of stoves, gargantuan, a few slim vents in the side of which will provide all the heat for the apartment during the coming winter. So promises the landlord, at least. Outside, the first snowflakes of the season cover the Hoboken backyards like a discarded pair of women's tennis panties, the lacy kind.

$400,000. An attorney. As of the day he receives the draft complaint, Cooper is unemployed. Przwalski has taken over Cooper's Advanced Masters class, only two weeks of which remain anyway.

Cooper spends the winter traveling to and from the Unemployment Office in Jersey City while he continues to tutor Ravi once weekly. He also coaches a stockbroker early Tuesday mornings, at the bubble near Wall Street, where the tennis scenes in *Annie Hall* were shot. Other than that, he mainly watches TV. Helga is preoccupied by not doing her med-school homework.

Money isn't a problem, really, at least until the lawyer's bill comes due; Helga's grandfather's horseshoe cleats continue to pay for food, shelter, transportation. Now that his teaching job is history, though, Cooper misses the love. For a few of Cooper's students did indeed fall in love with him, and some of them even told him so. ShawnTelle, a former Temple track star who rippled when she walked and smiled the white of a freshly laundered courtside towel, once phoned him at home with questions about service return, as if that couldn't wait until class. ("I'm not opposed to *hit* the ball, right? I'm just opposed to *block* it back. Right?") When Cooper, flirtatious as ever, asked to feel her braids sometime—"I've never touched Black hair"—ShawnTelle laughed and laughed. Catching her breath finally, she blurted "I love you, Cooper!"

"Aww. I think you're great, too, ShawnTelle."

"No," she insisted. "I really *love* you."

During his second term at Metropolis Racquet Sports, Cooper taught Advanced Intermediates, many of whom were returnees from his Novice Intermediates class. (Just as Starbucks sells no Regular beverages, McDonald's no Small fries, MRS offers no classes for Beginners.) On the first evening of instruction last summer, on the floodlit courts atop Trinity Prep, he asked all of the assembled students to say what they hoped to gain by taking the course. The session before, an editorial assistant named Kate had returned Cooper's teasing advances with innuendo and "accidental" physical encounters on the court. Now she proclaimed, "I'm back because I want to have Cooper's baby."

Scattered across the backcourt, stretching and bouncing and otherwise warming their muscles, the other thirteen students erupted in cheers, cries of "Go for it, Coop!" and that annoying *Wooooo!* noise that visitors to Rockefeller Center make when the *Today Show* cameras are trained on them. Kate blushed the red of the clay at Roland Garros even as she batted her lashes and smiled. Corkscrews of burnt blond boinged about her face when she walked. Kate's suntanned legs were so long that she seemed unsure about what, exactly, to do with them while sitting. The overall effect was pretty powerful.

Now all Cooper's got is Helga. He feels cheated by this, ripped-off.

Did he lose the job on purpose? Cooper wonders now and again. Lourdes would have said he did. She would have said he'd feared Przwalski's all-too-real resentment and perhaps sought additional attention from Helga—attention that has grown relatively scarce now that she's back in school. That's why he wasn't firm with "Mister Jacobson," didn't insist the motherfucker call Metro. On the other hand, Cooper *was* in a hurry on the morning of Rampart's service, was distracted and sad as he stood in the bathtub, tying his tie while the clock ticked. Sometimes, Cooper thinks, a tennis racquet is just a tennis racquet. Or is it?

Cooper searches his wallet for the therapist's card and locates little besides folded, faded ATM receipts. He ransacks a metal Port-a-File the color of a martini olive that he finds under Helga's desk: nothing. Finally, Cooper looks where he should have looked in the first place, in the chaotic list of mostly crossed-out names and numbers at the back of a pocket diary from the bookstore at school, his poor-man's File-O-Fax. Bingo.

Cooper dials the Student Health Services number in California. After four rings a taped message plays, announcing the hours of the counseling unit and suggesting he call back sometime in the future. Cooper does so, seconds later, and—surprise!—again he hears the recording.

"What the fuck!" Cooper turns off the phone with a punch of his thumb that, had it been a volley, almost certainly would have knocked the ball out of bounds.

Later, he realizes it's Sunday.

It is an afternoon early in December. Cooper settles in for some channel surfing. (Okay, channel Boogie Boarding: Cooper and Helga don't have cable.) Prior to Metro's sting operation, he would have been at work, unloading a bucket of balls somewhere. Instead he's home, in a T-shirt and boxers (tiny crossed racquets on a field of forest green, a Valentine from Helga). His hairy belly stretches the pants' waistband. So far, the threatened lawsuit has manifested itself mainly in the form of junk-food calories. He's on the Häagen-Dazs diet, *à la* McEnroe.

Soap opera—*flip*. "Family Feud"—*flip*. Another soap. Nice implants, Cooper thinks—*flip*. A sitcom (UPN) about a black teenage girl, a sitcom (WB) about a white teenage girl. *Flip, flip*.

PBS.

"Whhhut, would you say, if you had to put it into words. Whhhut is. Dickie. MacOliphant's. Legacy."

Dickie MacOliphant's Legacy?

"—In other words, whhhut does he not so much leave be*hind* Ah mean Ah know he was an athlete and ayyy socialite forlackofabetterword but if you had to. Is it a matter of symbolizing something about the best that each of us has to offer? Hep me here because. He Dickie MacOliphant did whhhut he loved to do and all the great ones, thee *path*finders and the Bill Gateses of the world, a Henry *Kiss*inger, is it about feeding that thing within you that. Whhhut."

The Bill Gateses of the world! Henry *Kiss*inger!

It gets worse. Finally the director of the program cuts to the inter-viewer's guest. Framed in inky blackness, asquint beneath the unforgiv-ing glare of the studio lights, nodding his long, Abraham Lincolnish head is Tim Zahnburstehalter.

"Well, Richard was a champion, like me. He wasn't a champion in the sense of having won titles. No. But I've won titles . . ."

"Title!" Cooper yells at the TV. "Half a title!"

"And that's not what it's about, anyway." Zahnburstehalter is wear-ing the puke green polo from Rampart's memorial service, which he has embellished with a red-and-white check tie that is moiré-ing like mad, shimmying and flickering and all but bursting into video-effect flames on his chest. "What *we're* about. The champions."

"Ack!" Cooper cries, as if reading a comic-strip dialogue balloon. He shuts off the TV and stalks to the kitchen. The daily *Times* lies on the table, exquisitely reassembled by Helga before she departed for Manhattan early this morning. In a frenzy, Cooper seeks the "B" section—"A" sec-tion, Business. *Shit.* World Business, Sports. *It's not even Sunday.* Weekend I, Weekend II (Fine Arts, Leisure), Escapes (*Escapes?*).

METRO.

On the right side of the front page of the section, below the fold, the headline blurts (and yet it does so with gentility, somehow, this being the *Times*), *Tennis Pro Dies of Apparent Overdose.* Beneath that: "Richard MacOliphant Was Poised to Inherit Billions."

Cooper scans five paragraphs: ". . . bathroom floor . . . drug para-phernalia . . ." Hmm. ". . . journalism dynasty . . . 'Strokes' . . . Times Square renaissance . . ." Uh- huh. ". . . 'hero' . . . Zahnburstehalter . . . 'not unlike myself.'"

He reads and seethes, and as he reads, as he seethes, Cooper grows vaguely aware of an odd phenomenon: like a Christmastime display from the 1960s, blue-and-silver lights seem to twinkle in his peripheral vision. First on the right side. Both sides, now. When he smacks into *Continued on Page B9* like a botched half-volley against the net tape, Cooper drops Metro onto the linoleum and scoops up (World Business, *no*, Weekend II . . . ) SPORTS. There a George Vecsey–penned elegy called "To an Athlete Dying Young" spools down the left side of the front page. The piece is broken in two by Dickie's black-and-white year-book portrait from some school for fuck ups Cooper's never heard of. True to form, Dickie's lower lip pendulates wetly. His eyes are vacant as a tennis-club court on the morning of the All-England finals.

Then Cooper comes upon the phrase "golden boy."

"*Golden* boy?" he yells, at the stove, the kitchen sink. "GOLDEN boy?" Dickie fucking MacOliphant was an idiot, a mongoloid—or whatever it's politically correct to call those people now. A doofus with deep pockets, a spaz in a Mazerati. A . . . a . . . *tin* boy, is what he was. Sure, the guy had bales of cash. A name everyone knew. And he'd parlayed those things into a semiglamorous life, if P. Diddy was your idea of semiglamour. But that didn't make him a natural athlete. It didn't make him a golden boy.

"*I'm* a golden boy *I'm* a golden boy," Cooper spits. "Was. I was a golden boy! Not him, not Dickie MacOliphant. I mean, Dickie for God's sake, *Dickie*!" He bends to retrieve the B section and the room twirls. Cooper falls to the floor, taking a kitchen chair down with him.

Sitting on the linoleum now, he reduces Metro to its component parts in the search for page nine. Matters aren't helped by the fact that his right arm has fallen asleep; once Cooper's pride and joy, his bread and butter, the best-coordinated of all his well-coordinated parts, it's now a very long pincushion. What the fuck. He remembers Bill Rampart's obit. He turns with his left hand to the inside of the last page of the section.

Where the hell's the article? It's there, as he will establish later, among obituaries for a Teamsters Vice President; a writer, 55, Who Laced Science Fiction With Dark Humor; and an 86-year-old inventor. But Cooper can't read the words, any of them. They're too blurry, too blobby, too amorphous and motile to make out.

"Bolden goy!" he says. "Gray bee dick car." Vision in Cooper's right eye drops away altogether—as in the ophthalmologist's office when the doctor shifts an opaque slide into position before asking you to read the third line of the chart through that mask of green metal on a long, jointed arm.

The last thing he's aware of as he lies on his back on the dirty kitchen linoleum, gazing like some cyclops through the dirty kitchen window, is the purpling winter sky above New Jersey, visible from this angle but temporarily defaced—by a message literally written on the wind. Oddly, in contrast to the letters and words, the phrases, clauses, and sentences in the *Times*, the announcement above is legible to him, coherent to Cooper:

# HAPPY HOLIDAYS FROM MORTE RACQUETS!

it says.

They really ought to replace that Dov Shneerson, Cooper thinks.

Clouds—real clouds, not the plane-made kind—sprint across the sky from Cooper's right, the south.

* * *

Do you want to know a secret? In the most exclusive of neighbor-hoods on the island of Manhattan, crashing a private party's a cinch, a breeze. A double-bagel match in which you own all the sixes. Just glom onto a group of invited guests and smile, smile. The guests assume you've been invited, too. (That's why you're smiling.) Even the door-man, if there is one, assumes you've been invited. (*But ma'am, I thought he was with THEM!* he'll protest later, epaulettes drooping, Christmas envelope losing weight before his mind's eyes.) Or maybe you live in the host's building and stepped out for a bunch of bananas and a quart of milk and now you're back. In any case, the same code of silence that forbids as much as eye contact aboard the rush-hour I.R.T. rules out any kind of confrontation on stoops or inside New York lobbies, in elevators or foyers.

Right now smiling's a bit of a challenge for Cooper. (So was get-ting dressed: Cardinal-red Stanford sweatpants protrude from the dripping hem of his snow-covered overcoat.) But he fakes it well enough to gain entry to Dickie MacOliphant's downtown loft, with the couple buzzed in just ahead of him. To gain entry to Dickie's wake.

When Cooper regained consciousness, he still lay among the dust bunnies that populate the floor of his and Helga's Hoboken home. Though someone seemed to be using the inside of his face as a back-board (*THOK, shoopa THOK* it went in there, behind his eyes), reading was once more fundamental. Before he stood upright, Cooper learned that Dickie's father had been impaled through the chest by a hang glider twenty years earlier. (How California was that?) More to the point, the last paragraph of Dickie's obit mentioned a private ceremony to be held at the home of the deceased that evening. Gotta love that *Times*! Cooper thought. Without even leaving a note for Helga, Cooper headed into the falling snow, headed for SoHo.

From the PATH station at Christopher Street he hiked downtown through the gauze-wrapped city, then east along Spring, sore head pivoting like a periscope as he squinted north and south along the cast-iron district's cobblestone arteries. *Shhh,* went cabs through the unsalted streets, as if trying to soothe him. *Shhh. Shhh.* But Cooper was oblivious to Balthazar-goers, snowball-throwers, homeward-bounders. New Yorkers helped other New Yorkers start their cars, helped them surmount street-corner sugardrifts that the tumbling flakes had created in a matter of hours. "Whoa! Need some help there?" The neighbor-hood was a dream about the City on this night, a fairytale of New York—like Cooper gave a shit. He was looking for something, on Sullivan and

Thompson streets, on Wooster, and Mercer. On Greene. Up, down; up, down: nothing.

Crosby. *Yesssss.*

P. Diddy's limo. (A wild guess. It's a white stretch SUV, the rear license plate of which reads P 2 THA D.)

Now Cooper yanks on the canvas belt that pulls closed the teeth of the freight elevator. He stands beside the couple on whose snowy coattails he entered. There is a collective stamping of feet and lots of dripping on the elevator's wooden floor.

"Are you going to thee ah MacOliphant thing?" Cooper asks the woman, rhetorically. ("WE'RE HERE FOR THE WAKE," she told the intercom outside.) She's wearing one of those Peruvian hats with the earflaps, its neo-Inca pattern mainly concealed beneath wet whiteness for now. Her eyes are enormous. They are green and glistening, aggie eyes.

"Hmm? Oh. Uh-huh." She sucks some snot back.

"Kermit Perry. How ya doin'?" The guy with the green-eyed girl pulls off a soaking glove and offers his hand to Cooper. The cage they all share—it's the size of Cooper's living room—whirs and clanks toward Dickie's apartment on the top floor.

"He's not a Golden Boy," Cooper says, ignoring the hand. In the distance, drawing closer: a hubub, a babel—but diminished, like the sound of trucks in the snow on Broome Street tonight.

"Sorry?" Kermit's arm still reaches out for Cooper.

*Shake hands with the racquet,* Cooper remembers from so long ago that he can't identify the recollection.

"That stuff in the *Times* today. And on 'Charlie Rose'?" Cooper snorts. "Please! Look, I'm sure Dickie MacOliphant was a very nice person. Well, actually . . . Anyway. It just isn't *true* that he was this . . . natural athlete or whatever." They need to understand this. It is vitally important to Cooper that they understand. He has come to New York from another state to explain things this way, to set things right.

"Right."

They've arrived at the top of the echoing shaft. Now the noise from beyond the elevator door is lithic, so huge and heavy that it perches on the verge of obliterating their conversation, such as it is, if not Cooper and Kermit and the green-eyed girl themselves. A party noise—replete with music and laughter, the shrieking of women. And boy is it loud. Kermit unhooks the latch that binds the elevator door's top and bottom halves together and jerks on the strap and the party noise is five times as loud as it was, ten times. It is the rolling-boulder-behind–Indiana Jones of party noises. Inside, there's a party to match.

Dozens of revelers drink and dance (they are dancing to P. Diddy or Puff Daddy or Sean "Puffy" Combs or whatever the fuck his name is—not that it matters, since the song is actually an old Police song that P 2 THA D just sort of raps over if you call that rapping) and make out in corners and shoot up in bathrooms. (Cooper walks in on someone doing just this who looks an awful lot like David Bowie, though clearly it is not David Bowie. Is it?) There must be a bed beneath the dozens and dozens of winter coats and scarves and hats and purses and briefcases and knapsacks and messenger pouches that form a sort of designer Fresh Kills in what appears to be Dickie's bedroom. If so, it isn't visible, even to the careful observer, which would be Cooper. Atop a loft-within-the-loft, a balcony, a tall girl in a black suit, her mouth a slash, a gash, of red lipstick, actually dances with an actual lampshade on her head to the song that has replaced the P. Diddy song, one fading into the other as if mixed by a DJ. Wait—there *is* a DJ, Cooper realizes, spotting a Moby-wannabe in a corner behind two turntables, one muff of a head-set held to his ovoid, preternaturally white noggin. A DJ at a wake! Cooper thinks. Then Cooper spots that actress, the Eurasian one, who plays the foxy archeologist in the TV show clearly based on *Lara Croft, Tomb Raider* but called something different. What's her name again? Something Carrere. Thanks to the long walk here from Christopher, and the dampness too maybe, Cooper's knee throbs. The music throbs, and above the throb of the music and Cooper's knee a singer whines

*Is this iiiiiiiiit?*
*Is this iiiiiiiiit?*

"DICKIE MACOLIPHANT WASN'T LIKE THAT," Cooper tells a tuxedoed waiter who holds a silver tray sprouting champagne flutes.

"HERE YOU GO." The waiter hands him a glass.

Cooper shakes his head. "I SAID, DICKIE MACOLIPHANT WASN'T A GOLDEN BOY."

The waiter smiles and shakes his own head. Shrugs. Walks away.

Cooper keeps shouting—at waiters and guests, at Tia (TIA!) Carrere and Would-Be Moby and Pseudo-Bowie and P. Diddy (wherever he may be). He shouts because the din of the party grows louder and louder with the arrival of more guests, until the volume of the party-din seems physically impossible to Cooper. Party lights appear, royal blue and twinkly, and Cooper needs to transfer his champagne flute from his racquet hand to his left hand because of the pins and needles, and the pain in his right knee dissolves into numbness, fades toward oblivion, and then the room gets really quiet. No—silent. Cooper's shouting about the Golden Boy business but he hears nothing, and the girl with the green eyes offers him a glass of water but he can't swallow. He's forgotten how to swallow.

The last thing Cooper sees, as they lay him on the coatbed, is the girl's green eyes—a friend of Dickie's, she must have been, or a friend of a friend, at least, and that too seems unfair to Cooper, wrong.

The last thing he feels, forever, is envy.

Envy for a dead guy.

*Finally, a short story that is by turns hilarious and heartstring-tugging. Though the title is not inaccurate per se, a truer label for Jennifer Belle's story might read "Life and Tennis."*

# Death and Tennis

## Jennifer Belle

I went to Damian Neguib's funeral someplace in Queens, sort of shocked that he was dead, although more shocked that he had made it to thirty-five. He looked the way he would have liked to look, good, but dead enough so that people would feel bad. He wore one of his Princess Cruise suits. He was what he would call tan, although he was half Egyptian so you couldn't really tell. I made a mental note of the way he looked in case we met up again some day. He would want to know. Only Damian could be so close to death as to look up its nostrils, not once, but twice, and come out unchanged, spending hours in the whirlpool at Chelsea Piers, taking creatine to puff up his muscles, and spending all day in search of the perfect sandwich. Tuna Fish. No. Egg salad. No. Tuna fish. No. Egg salad. No. Tuna fish. No. Egg salad. No. Chicken potpie. No. Tuna fish. That could be his whole day.

I had the tennis racquet in its case with the strap over my shoulder.

I felt sick looking down at him. My stomach churned.

Once I went to a funeral and the Rabbi said, "She loved her wheel." He said it a few times. "And, of course, most of all, she loved her wheel." I couldn't imagine what her wheel was, but someone later told me it was the game show, *Wheel of Fortune.*

I wondered what the priest would say that Damian loved.

He loved to steal, especially from Bloomingdales. He loved to come up with credit card scams. He loved breaking up happy couples. He loved to rob the homes of his friends and then go to their apartments later to comfort them and help them call the police. He loved fine dining. He loved practicing other people's handwriting, especially women's. He loved Wonder Woman, *South Park, Hedwig and the Angry Inch,* the films of Merryl Streep.

He hated his father, his mother, his brother, Achmed. He hated taking his meds, except the opium.

I couldn't help but notice that I was the only one there, besides his parents.

"You are early," his mother told me, in her Egyptian accent. Egyptian people always sound upbeat even if they're crying. "It does not start for one hour." Then she asked if I would talk to the priest and tell him about Damian.

I followed the funeral director to an office where the priest was sitting behind a desk.

"I'm so sorry for your loss," he said.

For a moment I wondered if he meant the silverware Damian had stolen from me. Exactly one half of the whole set of stainless steel silverware an old boyfriend who owned a restaurant had given me. But then I realized he meant Damian himself. I suddenly remembered the time he had spent the weekend in the Tombs and we'd bailed him out Monday evening and brought him, filthy and giddy, back to the restaurant for shrimp cocktail and veal picatta with broccoli rabe. No. Lasagna. No. Veal picatta. No. Lasagna. No. Veal picatta.

Being with the priest made me feel self-conscious about the tennis racquet. I felt an explanation was necessary, but I wasn't sure what to say.

"Can you tell me some of the things that Damian enjoyed while he was with us?" the priest said.

He enjoyed answering ads in the real estate section for ten-million dollar penthouse apartments and then going to look at them, taking up hours of the agents' time, I thought. He enjoyed getting his friends to come over to clean his apartment. He enjoyed stealing a wallet out of a purse and finding a Tiffany's credit card belonging to a Lisa M. Grosbach and buying a three thousand dollar gold choker with it. (I actually enjoyed that with him, but I made us return the choker when I spotted the video cameras everywhere.) But I didn't have to tell the priest that.

"I understand if you're too upset to speak," the priest said.

The racquet was strapped to my back, like a cross, making it hard for me to sit comfortably. It suddenly seemed wildly inappropriate. It must have looked like I had got a quick game in before the funeral.

"This was Damian's," I lied, laying the encased racket on the desk between us. The word "Head" on the case also seemed all wrong.

"Oh yes, Head, they make the best rackets," the priest said. "I'm from Florida, Gainesville, I just moved up here to New York. I played a lot of tennis down there."

I always thought Florida was filled with Jews. He actually sounded quite Jewish. He said "*Flah*-rida." He looked slightly like Bea Arthur. I knew Damian would not have wanted to be buried by one of the Golden Girls.

"So, your friend, uh, Damian, was generous?" the priest asked. "He lent you his tennis racket?"

The kind word toward Damian made me feel like crying. Actually, he *was* quite generous. That was true about Damian.

We both stared at the racquet until the priest picked it up, unzipped the case, and started twirling it expertly in his left hand. "I'm left handed," he said.

"So was Damian." So was my father.

I had come to associate tennis with death. The only time I had played was with my brother in Atlanta, Georgia. He had moved to Atlanta and I had stupidly gone to help him drive around and look for an apartment there. He liked a horrible place in a gated community with a certain kind of carpeting called Berber that really knocked him out, a pool, and a tennis court. He loved the tennis court even though he had never played tennis in his life. He was so enthusiastic about it, the realtor went to her big car and brought out two tennis racquets and a can of balls and told my brother that we should play a set while she went back to the office to type the lease.

I was angry at him because we had gone to a diner that morning and I had ordered an egg-white omelet and when the waitress left my brother said in a snide voice, "Doesn't that sort of defeat the purpose? Doesn't ordering an egg-white omelet with cheese sort of negate the whole egg-white thing? Isn't an egg-white omelet with cheese sort of an oxymoron?"

I hadn't even ordered it with cheese! He had heard the word cheese in his own mind. He had such a low opinion of me that he was sure I had asked for cheese, which was his idea of the enemy—at my brother's funeral I would tell the rabbi that he definitely did not enjoy cheese. Actually, being older, I would die first. And he hated me for that cheese. Even though I was falsely accused of the cheese, and proved it by digging into the belly of the omelet with my fork that there was no cheese, and told him that I would never order a cheese omelet after one time when I went on some kind of terrible camping trip with our father and we stopped at a roadside diner and my father forced me to have a cheese omelet and "eat like a man," and he got into a fistfight with the cook because it took twenty-five minutes and then I threw up on my sleeping bag, I knew my brother would always remember this breakfast incorrectly. The cheese was on my permanent record. It could not be voided from the great check in his mind.

My brother walked onto the court and surveyed his new kingdom.

"Let me teach you how to serve," he said.

"I know how," I said. I threw the ball up in the air, and then couldn't figure how to rotate my arm the right way.

My brother sent a ball flying toward me, like the angry one-eyed yellow parakeet my mother had brought home from a pet store once. The only other time I had something flying at me like this was once when my father had forced me to play badminton on the beach before I knew I needed glasses when I was nine one summer and missed every single birdie, wildly swinging at the air with my racket while my father screamed, "What are you, blind, girl?" I could not see the shuttle-cock! It was invisible.

A car pulled up right outside the gate of the court and I pretended to be absorbed in watching the woman get out of the driver's seat.

"Come on, serve," my brother said.

The woman was six feet tall and looked like she had never tasted a cheese omelet in her life and had certainly never been told to eat like a man. She had long blond hair.

My brother leered at her. "Now I *know* I want to take this place," he said. Then he swung his racket like a baseball bat and said the words "I'll take it" and "sold" a few times.

That's when the woman took a gun out of her small white Le Sportsac and shot herself in the head. She fell to the cement and all the blood spilled out of her.

My brother called 911 on his cell phone. The police came and we answered questions. Then the realtor showed up and my brother signed the lease.

"Isn't someone getting out of a car and shooting themselves in the head sort of an omen to you?" I asked. "You know, like a sign? Doesn't it make you kind of consider going back to New York?"

"No way," my brother said, writing a check for first month's rent and two months' deposit. "I'm not going to let anything stand in the way of getting a great apartment."

"That's a very good attitude," the realtor told him.

"Can I ask you a very difficult question?" the priest said. "Do you think your friend Damian committed suicide?"

"No!" I said.

"So you believe he died of natural causes?"

Why hadn't his parents told the priest that he had died of AIDS? I wondered.

"Well, we talked about suicide," I said.

"Oh?" the priest said. "Is that something you often discussed?"

"Well, not often," I said. "The usual amount."

"And what did you say?"

"Well, I would never commit suicide as long as Woody Allen was alive. Because I couldn't stand to miss one of his movies. And that's how Damian felt about lunch."

At our last lunch I had a Chinese chicken salad. Oh, God, I couldn't remember what he had. How could I have forgotten what he had? It was my birthday lunch. We fought after because I had encouraged him to go back to college, and he "didn't need the whole restaurant knowing that."

The priest smiled to himself. "Did you see *Hollywood Ending?*" he asked. "I think it was one of his best."

Suddenly, I really wanted to be with Damian and ask him what the hell he had for lunch on my birthday. I had to know what he had for lunch. That was the worst part about someone dying or breaking up with me. I couldn't ask him questions like that. Damian had an incredible memory.

I remembered the lunch we had at the Sporting Club in Tribeca after we had bought the tennis racquets at Paragon with the Visa card we had stolen from my father. We had bought the tennis rackets as props for the Tiffany's heist. We thought they would make us look more like authentic rich people so we wore them as we looked down at the jewelry like tourists on a glass-bottom boat. A school of diamonds, one of sapphires, ocean-proud pearls.

I signed the name Lisa M. Grosbach while Damian made glib comments about not wearing my new necklace on the courts.

We never used the rackets again, but I thought Damian might want one to take with him wherever he was going. He would feel more confident with his graphite Head racquet strapped to his back.

"Oh, God," I said to the priest, looking down at the pool of vomit on the desk. How had I done that? I had stood up, taken the racquet, put it back in its case, and then somehow vomited on the desk.

"It's okay," the priest said. "Please don't worry."

I thought of my brother's white Berber carpet. And the blood from the girl's head spilling onto her white Le Sportsac. And egg-white omelets with cheese and the glistening white teeth of the woman who had sold us the choker at Tiffany's, and knowing there was a white shuttlecock coming at me but being unable to see it, and Damian's giant white plastic pill case that said Vitamin Shoppe on it that held his meds, and Damian lying in a casket lined with white satin. No more tuna fish. No more egg salad. No more opium.

I threw up again on the desk.

Then I ran out of the room and back to Damian. Someone, his six-year-old niece, had put a Pokémon toy in a clear pink plastic purse in Damian's casket near his hand.

I placed the racquet at his feet, the handle sort of resting between his legs. I kissed him on the forehead. I had only kissed him once before, in the ninth grade, during the movie *The Right Stuff*, before he told me he was gay.

The priest was about to begin so I took a seat all the way in the back.

In his eulogy, the priest said that Damian was generous. And that he loved tennis. I think Damian would really have liked that.

# CONTRIBUTORS

**JONATHAN AMES** is the author of *I Pass Like Night*, *The Extra Man*, *What's Not to Love?*, and *My Less Than Secret Life*. He is the winner of a Guggenheim Fellowship and his one-man show of storytelling, "Oedipussy," debuted off-off-Broadway.

**MARTIN AMIS** is the author of several books, including *The War Against Cliché*, *The Information*, *London Fields*, *Money*, and, most recently, *Koba the Dread*.

**WES ANDERSON AND OWEN WILSON** are the screenwriters of *The Royal Tenenbaums* and *Rushmore*.

**MARGARET ATWOOD** is the author of over twenty-five books, including fiction, poetry, and essays. Among her most recent works are the best-selling novels *The Blind Assassin* and *Alias Grace*, as well as *Negotiating with the Dead: A Writer on Writing*.

**JENNIFER BELLE**'s first novel, *Going Down*, was translated into many languages and was named best debut novel by *Entertainment Weekly*. Her essays and short stories have appeared in *The New York Times Magazine*, *Ms.*, *The Independent Magazine* (London), *Harper's Bazaar*, *Mudfish*, and several anthologies. Her most recent novel is *High Maintenance*.

**EMMELINE CHANG** is a freelance writer and editor in New York City. She teaches writing at Gotham Writers' Workshop and in several bookstores throughout the city. She studied anthropology at Princeton and has an MFA in writing from Columbia University. Her recent writing has appeared in *Big City Lit*, *EXPAT: Women's True Tales of Life Abroad*, and the *Re-Generation* anthology. Currently she is at work on a collection of stories about tea *(The Agony of the Leaves)* and a nonfiction book about quirky people and places in New York *(Tango Junkies and Taxidermists)*.

**RAND RICHARDS COOPER** is the author of *The Last to Go* and *Big as Life*. He has taught at Amherst and Emerson colleges; his fiction has appeared in *Harper's*, the *Atlantic Monthly*, and *Esquire*, and on National Public Radio's "Selected Shorts." Cooper is a contributing editor at *Bon Appétit*, a movie reviewer for *Commonweal*, and a frequent contributor to *The New York Times Book Review*. He practices his classic Lew Hoad backhand on the courts of Hartford, Connecticut.

**MARCY DERMANSKY**'s stories have appeared in numerous journals including *McSweeney's*, the *Alaska Quarterly Review*, and the *Indiana Review*. She is a MacDowell fellow and winner of *Story* magazine's Carson McCullers prize as well as the Andre Dubus Novella Award. She lives in New York City, where she is working on a novel.

**PHILLIP K. EDWARDS** was born in Riverdale, Maryland in 1943. He graduated with a B.S. in engineering from the University of Maryland. He is the author of a two-volume history of the town of Washington Grove, Maryland, of which he is a former mayor. He and his wife now reside on their farm in rural Pennsylvania.

**ELLEN GILCHRIST** is the author of seventeen books, including most recently *I, Rhoda Manning, Go Hunting with My Daddy and Other Stories*. She lives in Fayetteville, Arizona; New Orleans; and Ocean Springs, Michigan.

**LEE HARRINGTON** lives and writes in New York City.

**ANNE LAMOTT** is the author of the national best-sellers *Traveling Mercies, Bird by Bird*, and *Operating Instructions*, as well as five novels, including *Crooked Little Heart* and *Rosie*. Her column in *Salon* magazine was voted the Best of the Web by *Newsweek* magazine, and she is a past recipient of a Guggenheim Fellowship.

**TARA McCARTHY** is the author of *Been There, Haven't Done That: A Virgin's Memoir*, and coauthor of *Big Night Out: An Interactive Novel*. A graduate of Harvard University, she has written articles and essays for *Seventeen*, *Mademoiselle*, and killingthebuddha. com, and worked as a music journalist at *Hot Press* magazine in Dublin, Ireland. She lives in Brooklyn.

**VLADIMIR NABOKOV** was born in St. Petersburg in 1899. He studied French and Russian literature at Trinity College, Cambridge, then lived in Berlin and Paris, where he launched a brilliant literary career. In 1940 he moved to the United States and achieved renown as a novelist, poet, critic, and translator. He taught literature at Wellesley, Stanford,

Cornell, and Harvard. In 1961 he moved to Montreaux, Switzerland, where he died in 1977.

**DALIA RABINOVICH** is the author of the novel *Flora's Suitcase*. She holds an MFA in Fiction from Brooklyn College and has taught creative writing at Brooklyn College and Gotham Writers' Workshop. She is currently working on a second novel, *Imaginary Lines*.

**CAROLINE RABINOVITCH** was born in New York in 1970. She has studied painting, attended film school, and played guitar in Brooklyn art-rock bands. She is currently writing short stories and collaborating on a magazine about art and design.

**LIANA SCALETTAR**'s work has appeared in *Arts & Letters* and *Nidus*. Her fiction has won awards from *Glimmer Train* and the MacDowell Colony. She teaches literature and writing in Boston and in New York City, where she lives.

**ADAM SEXTON** has written for the *New York Times*, the *Village Voice*, the *Boston Phoenix*, and other periodicals. His books include *Rap on Rap* and *Desperately Seeking Madonna*, which was translated into Japanese and remains in print after a decade. He teaches creative writing at New York University and writing and literature at Parsons School of Design. He lives in Brooklyn, New York.

**PAUL THEROUX** is the author of numerous books of fiction, memoir, and travel writing, including most recently *Hotel Honolulu*, *Fresh Air Fiend*, and *Sir Vidia's Shadow*.

**SARAH TOTTON** has worked as a rabies researcher for the federal government of Canada, and as a zookeeper in Great Britain, where she fell in love with tennis. She is a graduate of the Ontario Veterinary College and the Clarion Writers' Workshop at Michigan State University.

**JOHN UPDIKE** was born in 1932, in Shillington, Pennsylvania. He graduated from Harvard College in 1954, and spent a year in Oxford, England, at the Ruskin School of Drawing and Fine Art. From 1955 to 1957 he was a member of the staff of *The New Yorker*. He is the author of more than fifty books, including collections of short stories, poems, essays, and criticism. His novels have won the Pulitzer Prize (twice), the National Book Award, the National Book Critics Circle Award, and the Howells Medal.

**DAVID FOSTER WALLACE** is the author of the novels *Infinite Jest* and *The Broom of the System*, as well as the story collections *Brief Interviews with Hideous Men* and *Girl with Curious Hair*. His writings have appeared in *Esquire, Harper's, The New Yorker, The Paris Review, Playboy, Premiere, Tennis*, and other magazines. He is the recipient of a MacArthur Fellowship, a Whiting Award, the Lannan Award for Fiction, the Paris Review Prize for humor, and an O. Henry Award.